Knox County, Tenneessee

MINUTES of the COUNTY COURT

1792-1795

Compiled By:
The Tennessee Historical Records Survey
Division of Community Service Programs
Work Projects Administration

This volume was reproduced from
an 1976 edition located in the
Publisher's private library
Greenville, South Carolina

Please direct ALL correspondence and book orders to:
Southern Historical Press, Inc.
PO Box 1267
375 West Broad Street
Greenville, S.C. 29602-1267

Originally printed & ©: Nashville, TN. 1941
New Material Copyrighted © 2010: Southern Historical Press, Inc.
Reprinted 2010 by: Southern Historical Press, Inc.
Greenville, S.C. 2007
ISBN #0-89308-642-8
Printed in the United States of America

PREFACE

Although the Historical Records Survey in Tennessee has as its
chief purpose the preparation of guides to archival and other historical
materials, a part of the project's program has been the transcription of
selected county records as a method of preservation and as a means of
placing typewritten copies of source materials in libraries and research
centers.

This undertaking on the part of the Survey represents a continuation
of a program instituted under another project, sponsored by the Tennessee
State Library, whose program and personnel were absorbed by the Survey in
October 1938. Records have been selected for transcription with a view
to their administrative importance, their significance as research
materials, and their physical condition. A poorly preserved record is,
of course, selected over a well preserved record of similar content. In
more recent months primary emphasis has been placed on the transcription
of the minutes of the county courts, the governing bodies of Tennessee
counties. The ribbon copies of the transcriptions are deposited in the
Tennessee State Library, at Nashville, with carbon copies being deposited
in the Library of the University of Tennessee, at Knoxville, and, in many
instances, in the courthouses of the concerned counties where they are
used for administrative purposes. The two libraries and the counties
receiving copies act as cosponsors of this operating unit of the project.
For the last year, carbon copies have also been placed in the Library of
Congress.

In the belief that certain transcriptions are of sufficient significance as historical research materials to justify wider distribution, the
Tennessee Survey is mimeographing, for distribution to the institutions
and agencies receiving other project publications, a limited number of such
records. This volume is the first transcription of a Knox County Minute
Book to be mimeographed.

Knox County lies near the center of the Great Valley of East Tennessee.
It was erected as a county of the Territory of the United States of
America South of the River Ohio on June 11, 1792, by Governor William
Blount and Judges of the Territory and was organized on June 16. Knox-
ville, the present seat of government had been located by Governor Blount,
and laid out by General James White the year previous to the creation of
the county. The early history of Knox County and Knoxville is commingled
with the deeds and vision of a small group of men, including General
White, Charles McClung, Thomas Chapman, Robert Houston, and Archibald Roane.
Governor Blount made Knoxville the capital of the Territory in 1792.
Tennessee was admitted to the Union in 1796 and Knoxville remained the
State capital until 1813. The legislature met there for the last time in
1817 when the capital was shifted permanently to Middle Tennessee.

Preface

The census of 1800 showed a population of 12,446, in Knox County, the largest in the State at that time; it has increased in nearly every decade, until in 1940 it reached 178,929, although the ranking of the county has dropped to fourth place. Knoxville has long been a center of one of the leading industrial sections in East Tennessee and is the fourth most populous city in the State.

This volume covers a part of the long period in Tennessee history when the county court, composed of the justices of the peace, was known as the court of pleas and quarter sessions, and before successive legislative acts stripped the court of its common law jurisdiction leaving in its place two almost distinct administrative agencies - one legislative and the other judicial, with jurisdiction centering largely in matters of probate. The Knox County court of pleas and quarter sessions, in the year 1792, designated all of the county officials who were not appointed by the Governor of the Territory, appointed administrators, marked public roads, granted licenses to "ordinaries," levied taxes, heard civil actions of great variety, and tried all persons committing offenses against the peace and dignity of the State. It represented a decentralized government; it was, with its inclusive functions and jurisdiction, an administrative agency in which were found most of the functions and authority which concerned a citizen with business to transact with the government

This volume is intended to be a verbatim transcription. There are numerous apparent errors, but the book was transcribed as it appears. The copyists did not attempt, for example, to correct the clerk's spelling, nor were other apparent inconsistencies investigated. It was inevitable that certain errors would result from the copyists' inability to read the clerk's scrawl; patient research and comparison would, perhaps, have justified considerable revisions in the finished draft. The transcription is not, however, an editorial task. The bars drawn through sections of the text indicate that the words, in the original, are similarly marked or scratched out. The numbers, enclosed in parentheses, throughout the text, indicate the beginning of numbered pages in the original minutes. The index numbers are to the pages of the original volume.

The Survey Project gratefully acknowledges the help and cooperation of County Judge S. O. Houston, who has encouraged the Survey Project in many ways, County Court Clerk W. H. Hall, and Miss Mamie Winstead, Records Custodian.

The original book is in the custody of the county court clerk in the Knox County courthouse at Knoxville. The transcription was made and typed in 1940 by employees of the Transcription Unit of The Tennessee Historical Records Survey. The typewritten transcription was made under the general supervision of Penelope J. Allen and the immediate supervision of Edith L. Pierce. Publication of this book was under the supervision of Mary Alice Burke. Stencils were cut by Patsy R. Floyd, Bessie E. Binkley

Preface

Arthur D. Knox, and Mabel LeCornu. A list of publications of the Tennessee
Historical Records Survey follows the index to this volume.

Madison Bratton, State Supervisor
The Tennessee Historical Records Survey

Nashville
March 28, 1941

ORDINANCE LAYING OUT KNOX AND JEFFERSON COUNTIES

By William Blount Governor in and over the Territory of the United States of America, South of the River Ohio.

An Ordinance for Circumscribing the Counties of Greene and Hawkins, and laying out two new Counties.

Be it ordained that from and after the fifteenth day of the present month of June, the Counties of Greene, and Hawkins, shall be circumscribed by a line, Beginning on Nolichuckey River, at the place where the Ridge which divides the waters of Bent and Lick Creek strikes it, thence with that Ridge to Bull's Gap of Bays Mountain; thence a direct line to the place where the road that leads from Dodson's ford to Perkin's Iron Works crosses the watry fork of Bent Creek, thence down that road to the head of Panther Creek, down the Meanders of that Creek, to the River Holston; thence a North West course to the River Clinch. Again from Nolichuckey River where the Ridge that divides the Waters of Bent and Lick Creek strikes it; a direct course to Peter Fines Ferry on French Broad, then South to the Ridge that divides the Waters of French Broad and Big Pigeon; and with that Ridge to the Eastern Boundary of the Territory.

And be it ordained that two New Counties be laid out and established below the aforesaid line, that is to the Southward and Westward of it, to be distinguished from and after the said fifteenth day of June Instant, by the name of Jefferson County, and Knox County. The County of Jefferson to be butted and bounded by the above described line from the Eastern boundary of the Territory to the River Holston, and down the River Holston to the mouth of Creswells Mill Creek, thence a direct line to the mouth of Dumplin Creek on French Broad, thence up the Meanders of French Broad to the mouth of Boyd's Creek, thence South twenty five degrees East to the Ridge which divides the waters of Little Pigeon and Boyd's Creek, and with the said Ridge to the Indian Boundary, or the Eastern Boundary of the Territory as the Case may be, and by the Eastern Boundary. And Knox County to be butted and bounded by the line of Jefferson County from the mouth of Creswell's Mill Creek to the Indian Boundary, or Eastern Boundary of the Territory, as the case may be. Again from the mouth of the said Creek up the meanders of the River Holston to the Mouth of Panther Creek, thence North West to the River Clinch, thence by the River Clinch to the place   (Pg. 2)   the line that shall cross Holston at the Ridge that divides the waters of Tennessee and Little River, according to the Treaty of Holston shall strike it, and by that line.

And be it Ordained that Charles McClung and James Mabry be appointed Commissioners to run and mark the North West line, from the mouth of Panther Creek to the River Clinch, and the line from the mouth of Creswells Mill Creek, to the mouth of Dumplin, and Alexander Outlaw and Joseph Hamilton, that from Bull's Gap to the Watry fork of Bent Creek, and from Nolichuckey River to Fines Ferry on French Broad, and the South line to the dividing Ridge between French Broad and Big Pigeon.

And be it Ordained that Courts of Pleas and Quarter Sessions shall be held in and for the said Counties, for the due Administration of Justice, for the County of Knox on the third Monday of January, April, July, and October, and for the County of Jefferson on the fourth Mondays in the same Months, and may be continued by adjournments from day to day, not exceeding Six days.

And be it ordained that the Courts of Pleas and Quarter Sessions shall be held for the County of Knox at Knoxville, and for the County of Jefferson at the House of Jeremiah Matthews.

Done at Knoxville, the 11th day of June in the year of our Lord 1792.

Wm. Blount

JULY 16th 1792

Territory of the United States of America South of the River Ohio.   Knox County.

Be it remembered that at the house of John Stone in Knoxville and on the third Monday of July, being the Sixteenth day, in the Year of our Lord one Thousand Seven hundred and Ninety two A Commission from the Governor of the Territory aforesaid, with his Seal thereto annexed, bearing date the Sixteenth day of June in the year aforesaid was produced, by which it appears that James White, John Sawyers, Hugh Beard, John Adair, George McNutt, Jeremiah Jack, John Kearns, James Cozby, John Evans, Samuel Newell, William Wallace, Thomas McCullough, William Hamilton, David Craig and William Lowry are appointed Justices of the Peace in and for said County, And by the Certificate   (Pg. 3)   of David Campbell esquire one of the Judges of the Superior Courts of Law and Courts of Equity for the Territory aforesaid, bearing date the Sixteenth day of June One Thousand Seven Hundred and Ninety two it appears that the before names Justices of the Peace have been duly qualified to support the Constitution of the United States, and have also taken the Oath prescribed by Law for Justices of the Peace within this Territory.

Whereupon James White, Samuel Newell, David Craig and Jeremiah Jack esquires, Justices of the Peace named in the before mentioned Commission appeared and took their Seats.

COURT PROCLAIMED

Charles McClung appeared and produced a Commission from the Governor of the Territory aforesaid, with his Seal thereto annexed bearing the date the Sixteenth day of June 1792 by which it appears that he is appointed Clerk of the County Court of Pleas and Quarter Sessions for the County of Knox, And by the Certificate of David Campbell esquire one of the Judges of the Superior Court of Law and Equity for the Territory aforesaid, bearing date the 16th day of June 1792, it appears that the said Charles McClung hath been duly qualified to support the Constitution of the United States, and had also taken the Oath of Office, Who entered into bond in the sum of Two thousand five hundred Dollars to William Blount Governor, together with James Cozby, John Adair and James White, his Securities, with condition for the faithful discharge of the duties of his Office.

Robert Houston produced a Commission from the Governor of the Territory aforesaid, with his Seal thereto annexed, appointing him Sheriff of the County of Knox, And by the Certificate of David Campbell esquire, one of the Judges of the Superior Courts of Law and Equity for the Territory aforesaid bearing date the twenty fifth day of June 1792 it appears that the said Robert Houston hath been duly qualified to Support the Constitution of the United States and had also taken the Oath of Office, Who entered into Bond in the Sum of Twelve thousand five hundred dollars, to William Blount Governor, together with John Chisolm, James White, Jeremiah Jack, James Cozby and Robert Armstrong his Securities, with condition for the faithful discharge of the duties of his Office.

(Pg. 4)

William Meek, James Anderson, Benjamin Pride, James Gealy, James Neely, John Liddey, Joseph Hart, George Caldwell, William Gray and James Blair, appeared in Court and severally produced Commissions from the Governor of the Territory aforesaid by which it appears that they are severally appointed Constable for Knox County, and severally entered into and acknowledged their bond, William Meek with Jeremiah Jack and James White his Securities, James Anderson, with Jeremiah Jack and Thomas Wray his Securities, Benjamin Pride with David Cowan and John Burk his Securities, James Gealey with John Adair and George McNutt his Securities, James Neely with John Evans and James Mitchell his Securities, John Liddey with John Hart and Alexander Cunningham his securities, Joseph Hart with William Hamilton and Micajah Carter his Securities, George Caldwell with William Wallace and William Lowry his Securities, William Gray with William Wallace and William Lowry his Securities and James Blair with Alexander Bogle and Joseph Bogle his Securities, to William Blount Governor, in the Sum of Six hundred and twenty five dollars, with condition for the faithful discharge of the duties of their Office.

Luke Bowyer, Alexander Outlaw, Joseph Hamilton, Archibald Roane, Hopkins Lacey, John Rhea and James Reece esquires appeared in Court, and severally took the Oath prescribed by Law for Attorneys, they are therefore admitted.

Alexander Caveatt appeared in Court and made Oath that Susannah Caveatt departed this life the 29th day of April 1792

Court adjourned until tomorrow morning 9 O'clock

TUESDAY 17th JULY 1792

Tuesday morning 17th July 1792 Court met according to adjournment present James White, Samuel Newell and David Craig esquires Justices & C

Thomas Chapman appeared, and produced a Commission from the Governor of the Territory aforesaid, by which it appears that he is appointed Register of Knox County, And by the Certificate of David Campbell esquire, one of the Judges of the Superior Court of Law and Equity for the Territory aforesaid, it appears that the (Pg. 5) said Thomas Chapman has taken an Oath to support the Constitution of the United States, and also an Oath of Office who together with George McNutt and Jeremiah Jack his Securities entered into and acknowledged their bond to William Blount Governor, in the sum of Twelve Thousand five hundred Dollars with condition for the faithful discharge of the duties of his Office.

John Rhea esquire appeared and produced a Commission from the Governor of the Territory aforesaid, by which it appears that he is appointed Solicitor for Knox County, he is therefore admitted.

Rhea	'	WILLIAM BURDEN .... Plaintiff	)	
7	'		)	
J. H.	'	vs	)	Appeal
1	'		)	
		WILLIAM CAVENAUH ...... Defendant	)	

This day came the parties by their Attorneys, and thereupon came a Jury, to wit, John Coulter, William Rhea, Joseph Black, William Trimble, Samuel Doak, Moses Justice, Andrew Bogle, Samuel Bogle, Robert Gamble, Joseph Weldon, John McIntire and Pearson Brock who being elected tryed and Sworn, well and truly to try the matter of controversy between the parties, upon their Oath do say the fine for the Defendant, It is therefore considered by the Court that the Plaintiff take nothing by his plaint aforesaid, but for his false clamour be in mercy, and the said Defendant go thereof without day, and recover against the said Plaintiff his costs by him about his defence in this behalf expended.

COURT ADJOURNED UNTIL TOMORROW 9 O'CLOCK.

WEDNESDAY 18th JULY 1792

Wednesday morning 18th July 1792. Court met according to adjournment, Present James White, Samuel Newell and David Craig esquires Justices & C.

Daniel McDonald produced a Commission from the Governor by which it appears he is appointed a Constable for the County of Knox, who entered into bond together with William Roberts and James Gealey his Securities, to William Blount, Governor, in the sum of Six hundred and twenty five dollars with condition for the faithful discharge of the duties of his Office, who hath been sworn as the Law directs.

(Pg. 6)

```
J. H.  '   JAMES W. LACKEY  Asse.    ..... Plaintiff  )
  1    '                                              )    In
  ─    '        vs                                    )    Debt
  4    '                                              )
           WILLIAM COLLECTOR         )                )
                                     )                )
                 and                 ) .... Defendants )
                                     )
           MICHAEL NEINAN            )
```

This day came the Plaintiff by his Attorney and filed his Declaration, and Michael Neinan one of the Defendants having been arrested and not appearing though Solemnly called, on motion of the Plaintiff by his Attorney, it is ordered that Judgment by default be entered against him. And the Sheriff having returned that William Collector is not to be found within his County, on motion of the Plaintiff by his Attorney an Alias Capias is awarded him to Jefferson County against the said William Collector, returnable here at next Court.

```
Rhea   '   ANNANIAS McCOY  .......... Plaintiff  )
  2    '                                         )
A. R.  '        vs                               )  in Case
 48    '                                         )
       '   JOHN COWAN      .......... Defendant  )
```

This day came the Plaintiff by John Rhea esquire his Attorney and the Sheriff having returned that the Defendant is not to be found in his County, on motion of the Plaintiff by his Attorney an Alias Capias is awarded him against the Defendant, returnable here at the next Court.

```
           SOLOMON McCAMPBELL  .......... Plaintiff  )
                                                     )
  3            vs                                     )  In Case
  ─                                                  )
  2        RUSSELL BEAN      .......... Defendant     )
```

This day came the Plaintiff in his proper person, and dismissed his suit.

```
A. R.    '    SAMUEL THOMPSON ......... Plaintiff   )
   4     '                                          )
L. B.    '              vs                          )    In Case
J. H.    '                                          )
  26     '    DAVID LINSEY    ......... Defendant    )
```

This day came the parties by their Attorneys, and filed the Declaration, Plea & Replication, and Issue being Joined, the trial thereof is referred until next Court.

```
A. R.    '    SAMUEL THOMPSON ......... Plaintiff   )
   5     '                                          )
L. B.    '              vs                          )    In Case
J. H.    '                                          )
  27     '    DAVID LINSEY    ......... Defendant    )
```

This day came the parties by their Attorneys, and filed the Declaration and Plea and Issue being Joined, the trial thereof is referred until next Court.

```
(Pg. 7)  '    SOLOMON MARKS   ......... Plaintiff   )
         '                                          )
D. A.    '              vs                          )    In Case
   6     '                                          )
Rhea     '    WILLIAM ROSEBERRY ........ Defendant   )
A. O.    '
  28     '
```

This day came the Plaintiff by David Allison his Attorney and filed his Declaration, and the cause is continued until next Court.

```
         JAMES WHITE   ......... Plaintiff   )
7 ___                                        )
3              vs                            )    In Covenant
                                             )
         JOHN CARTER   ......... Defendant   )
```

The Plaintiff not farther prosecuting, on motion of the Defendant, it is ordered that this Suit be discontinued, and that the Defendant do recover against the Plaintiff his costs by him about his defence in this behalf expended.

```
Rhea     '    JONATHAN CUNNINGHAM ....... Plaintiff   )
   7     '                                            )
J. H.    '              vs                            )    Appeal.
   5     '                                            )
         '    DAVID LINSEY    ....... Defendant        )
```

This day came the parties by their Attorneys, and the tryal of the cause is continued until next Court.

Court adjourned untill Court in Course.

At a Court of pleas and Quarter Sessions Began and held for the County of Knox at Knoxville on the third Monday of October, 1792.

        present   Jeremiah Jack, John Kearnes, William Lowry, John Adair, George McNutt, James Cozby and James White esquires, Justices of the Peace & C.

Ephraim Dunlap appeared in open Court, and took the Oath prescribed by Law for Attorneys   he is therefore admitted.

The following persons were elected a Grand inquest for the Body of this County to Wit;   James Houston foreman, John Hackett, William Lea, George Preston, James Robertson, Alexander Caldwell, John McKean, Samuel Doak, Moses Brooks, William Walker, Alexander Campbell, Charles Diveny, Thomas Reardan, William Gillespie, and William Stockton, who have been Sworn, received their charge, and withdrew to enquire of their present-ments.

Ordered that Thomas Brown be fined five Shillings, for contempt to this Court, which is paid into Office.____

Court adjourned until tomorrow 10 O'clock.

(Pg. 8)

TUESDAY 23rd OCTOBER 1792

Tuesday Morning 23rd October 1792 Court met according to ad-journment   Present Jeremiah Jack, William Lowry, and John Adair esquires, Justices of the Peace & C.

Samuel Acklin who is charged by Rebecca Cusick of this County, Single Woman, with being the Father of her Bastard Child, and Stands bound to appear here and abide by and perform the orderof this Court, concerning the Same, appeared; and thereupon it is adjudged that the Said Samuel Acklin, find Security to discharge and Save harmless the Overseers of the Poor, and Inhabitants of this County from all costs charges and trouble whatsoever by reason of the birth, maintenance of, and bringing up of the Said child, and of and from all Suits charges and demands what-soever. Whereupon the Said Samuel Acklin with Samuel Newell his Security came into Court and acknowledged themselves to be jointly and Severally indebted to the Justices of this County and their Successors in Office in the Sum of Three hundred dollars; Yet upon this condition that if the Said Samuel Acklin, Shall observe and perform the above order of this Court against him, the Same Shall be void.

The Obligation of Elizabeth Hauk, Adam Hauk, and Samuel McGaughey, in the Penalty of One hundred Pounds; conditioned that the Said Eliza-beth Hauk, Supports, and maintains a Bastard Child, which She has been charged with being the Mother of, free from any expence or charge to this County, was produced to Court and ordered to be filed.

Rhea   :   JONATHAN CUNNINGHAM .... Plaintiff)
7   :   )
J. $\overline{\text{H}}$. :   vs   )   Appeal
5   :   )
           DAVID LINDSEY   .... Defendant)

    This day came the parties by their Attorneys, and thereupon
came a Jury, to Wit, James Brock, Samuel Henderson, Paul Cunningham,
Samuel Bowman, Joseph Nance, Jonathan Douglass, James Anderson,
Henry Sterling, Daniel Carmichael, Samuel Sterling, John Walker,
John Wallace, and Major Lea; who being elected, tryed, and Sworn,
well and truly, to try the matter of controversy between the parties,
upon their oath to Say, they find for the Plaintiff his Debt of
two Pounds, eight Shillings and Costs, Therefore it is considered
by the Court, that the Plaintiff do recover against the Defendant
his Debt aforesaid together with his costs by him about his Suit
in this behalf expended & the Said Defendant in Mercy & C.

(Pg. 9)

    William Roberts appeared, produced a Commission by which
it appears, he is appointed a Ranger for this County, who took the
Oath of Office.

               COURT ADJOURNED UNTIL TOMORROW 8 O'CLOCK.

                 WEDNESDAY OCTOBER 24th 1792

    Wednesday Morning 24th October 1792. Court met according
to adjournment, present James White, George McNutt, and James
Cozby esquires Justices of the Peace & C.

J. H. $\frac{1}{4}$:   JAMES W. LACKEY ASSEE ..... Plaintiff   )
         :   )
         :   vs   )   Debt.
         :   )
         :   WILLIAM COLLECTOR &
            MICHAEL NEINAN   ..... Defendants)

    This day came the Plaintiff by his attorney; and the Sheriff
having returned that William Collector is not to be found within
his County on motion of the Plaintiff by his attorney a Pluries
Capias is awarded him returnable here next Court. Whereupon
the Defendant {Michael Noinan in his proper person comes into
Court, and agrees to pay the costs of this suit and upon this the
Said Plaintiff prays Judgment for his costs and charges about his
Suit by him in this behalf expended to be adjudged to him. Therefore it is considered by the court that the Plaintiff do recover
against the Said Michael Neinan his costs by him about his Suit in
this behalf expended; and the Said Defendant in Mercy & C. And tho
Said Plaintiff not farther prosecuting; it is Ordered that this
Suit be Dismissed.

Rhea 2.   :   ANNANIAS McCOY ....·Plaintiff   )
A. R.   :   )
    48   :   vs   )   In Case
           :   )
           :   JOHN COWAN   .... Defendant   )

    This day came the Plaintiff by his Attorney, and the Sheriff
having returned that the Defendant is not to be found in his County,
a Judicial attachment is awarded him, returnable here at the next
Court.

A. R. 4   :   SAMUEL THOMPSON .... Plaintiff   )
L. B.   :   )
J. H.   :   vs   )   In Case.
    26   :   )
           :   DAVID LINDSEY   .... Defendant ·)

    This day came the parties by their attorneys, and by their
Mutual consent, and with the assent of the Court the tryal of the
Issue is referred until next Court.

A. R. 5   :   SAMUEL THOMPSON .... Plaintiff   )
L. B.   :   )
J. H.   :   vs   )   In Case.
    27   :   )
           :   DAVID LINSEY   .... Defendant   )

    This day came the parties by their Attornies and on Affidavit
of the Plaintiff the tryal of the issue is referred until next Court.

(Pg. 10)

D. A. 6   )   SOLOMON MARKS   .... Plaintiff   )
  28   )   )
Rhea   )   VS   )   In Case. ·
A. O.   )   )
)   WILLIAM ROSEBERRY ...... Defendant   )

    This day came the parties by their Attornies and the Defendant ·
filed his plea and on Motion, liberty is given the parties to amend
the declaration and plea.

A. R. 8   :   JOHN WALLACE .... Plaintiff   )
  29   :   )
           :   vs   )   In Case.
           :   )
           :   DAVID SCOTT .... Defendant   )

    This day came the Plaintiff by his Attorney and filed his
declaration, and the Defendant having been arrested, and not appearing,
though Solemnly called on motion of the Plaintiff by his attorney.
It is ordered that Judgment be entered for the Plaintiff against
the Said Defendant, for what Damages the Plaintiff hath Sustained,

by occasion of the Defendants breach of the Promise in the declaration
mentioned. Which damages are to be enquired of by a Jury at the
next Court.

9/6	:	FRANCIS ROWAN .... Plaintiff	)	
	:		)	
	:	vs	)	In Case.
	:		)	
	:	WILLIAM OVERSTREET .... Defendant	)	

The Plaintiff not farther prosecuting, on motion of the
Defendant it is ordered that this Suit be discontinued, and that the
Defendant do recover against the Plaintiff his costs by him about
his defence in this behalf expended.

Rhea 10	:	JAMES ANDERSON .... Plaintiff	)	
J. H.	:		)	
49	:	vs	)	In Case
	:		)	
	:	ALEXANDER OUTLAW .... Defendant	)	

This day came the parties by their Attornies and filed the
Declaration & plea, and Issue being joined the tryal thereof is
referred until next Court.

Rhea 11/7	:	ALEXANDER CARMICHAEL........ Plaintiff	)	
	:		)	
	:	vs	)	In Case.
	:		)	
	:	JOHN SHERRELL .... Defendant	)	

The Plaintiff not farther prosecuting, on motion of the Defendant, it is ordered that this Suit be discontinued, and that the
Defendant do recover against the Plaintiff his costs by him
about his defence in this behalf expended.

(Pg. 11)

Rhea 12/8	:	JOHN LOWRY .... Plaintiff	)	
J. H.	:		)	
	:	vs	)	In Covn't.
	:		)	
	:	ROBERT BLACKBURN .... Defendant	)	

This day came the Defendant by his Attorney, and the Plaintiff
though Solemnly called, came not but made default, nor is his Suit
further prosecuted, Therefore on the prayer of the Said Defendant,
It is considered by the Court, that he recover against the Plaintiff
his costs by him about his defence in this behalf expended.____

```
A. O.  :  SAMUEL STERLING  .......  Plaintiff   )
 13    :                                         )
 ‾87‾  :            vs                           )   In Case
L. B.  :                                         )   Words
J. H.  :  HUGH JOHNSTON &  )                     )
E. D.  :  WILLIAM JOHNSTON )...... Defendants    )
       :
```

This day came the parties by their attornies and the Plaintiff having filed his declaration, the Defendant filed his Pleas and the issues being joined the Tryal thereof is referred until next Court.

```
14   :  HUGH PEARCE  .......  Plaintiff   )
 ‾9‾ :                                    )
     :            vs                      )   T. V. A.
     :                                    )
     :  JOHN GAMBLE  .......  Defendant   )
```

The Plaintiff not farther prosecuting, on motion of the Defendant, it is ordered, that this Suit be discontinued, and that the Defendant do recover against the Plaintiff his costs by him about his defence in this behalf expended.

```
15   :  HUGH PEARCE .......  Plaintiff  )   In Case
‾10‾ :                                  )
     :            vs                    )
     :                                  )
     :  JOHN GAMBLE .......  Defendant  )
```

The Plaintiff not farther prosecuting, on motion of the Defendant, it is ordered, that this Suit be discontinued, and that the Defendant do recover against the Plaintiff his costs by him about his defence in this behalf expended.

```
16   :  PRUDENCE CHISUM .......  Plaintiff  )
‾11‾ :                                      )
     :            vs                        )   A B
     :                                      )
     :  DAVID WALKER  .......  Defendant    )
```

The Plaintiff not farther prosecuting, on motion of the Defendant, it is ordered, that this Suit be discontinued and that the Defendant do recover against the Plaintiff his costs by him about his defence in this behalf expended.____

(Pg. 12)

```
17   :  JOHN WALKER       .......Plaintiff   )
‾12‾ :                                       )
     :            vs                         )   In Case.
     :                                       )
     :  NICHOLAS MANSFIELD.......Defendant    )
```

The Plaintiff not farther prosecuting, on motion of the Defendant, it is ordered, that this Suit be discontinued and that the Defendant do recover against the Plaintiff his costs by him about his defence in this behalf expended.

A. O. 18/50 : JAMES McELWEE   .... Plaintiff)
Rhea   : ·   vs   ) In Covn't.
L. B. :   )
       : HENRY STERLING &)
          JAMES STERLING) .... Defendants)

This day came the parties by their Attornies and the Plaintiff having filed his declaration, the Defendants filed their Plea, and issue being joined the Tryal thereof is referred untill next Court.

A. O. : ABRAHAM RIFE .... Plaintiff)
19   :   )
51   :   vs   ) In Case.
Rhea. :   )
      : JAMES ANDERSON....... Defendant)

This day came the parties by their Attornios and the Plaintiff having filed his declaration, the Defendant filed his Plea; and issue being joined the Tryal thereof is referred until next Court.

J. H. 20 : WILLIAM KERR .... Plaintiff)
A. R.   :   )
   30   :   vs   ) In Case
         :   )
         : JOHN CUSICK .... Defendant   )

This day came the parties by their Attornies and the Plaintiff having filed his declaration, & the Defendant his plea, and issue being joined the Tryal is referred untill next Court.

Rhea 21/31 : JOHN CHISOLM .... Plaintiff)
J. H.   :   )
          :   vs   ) In Case
          :   )
          : MAJOR LEA   .... Defendant)

This day came the Parties by their Attornies, and the Plaintiff having filed his Declaration, & the Defendant his Plea, and Issue being joined the Tryal is referred until next Court.

(Pg. 13)

J. H. 22 : ALEXANDER OUTLAW .... Plaintiff)
A. R. Rhea :   )
   52   :   vs   ) In Case
          :   )
          : WILLIAM LOWRY   .... Defendant   )

This day came the parties by their Attornies, and the Plaintiff having filed his declaration, & the Defendant his Plea, and issue being joined the Tryal is referred untill next Court._____ .

J. H. 23	:	ALEXANDER WILSON .... Plaintiff	)	
A. R. Rhea	:		)	
32	:	vs	)	In Case
	:		)	
	:	WILLIAM LOWRY .... Defendant	)	

This day came the parties by their Attornies and the Plaintiff having filed his declaration the Defendant filed his Pleas, and issues being joined the Tryal is referred untill next Court.__ And on motion of the Plaintiff a Commission is awarded him, to examine & take the Deposition of James Johnston, and others, giving the Defendant legal notice and the time and place of executing the Same.

J. H. 24	:	JOSEPH SEVEIR .... Plaintiff	)	
53	:		)	
Rhea	:	vs	)	In Case.
	:		)	
	:	HUGH DUNLAP .... Defendant	)	

This day came the Plaintiff by his Attorney, and the Sheriff having returned that the Defendant is not to be found in his County, On motion of the Plaintiff by his attorney an Alias Capias is awarded him against the Defendant returnable here at the next Court.___

25	:	JAMES ANDERSON .... Plaintiff	)	
33	:		)	
A. O.	:	vs	)	In Case
Rhea	:		)	
	:	JOSEPH GREER .... Defendant	)	

This day came the parties by their attornies, and the Plaintiff having filed his declaration, the Defendant prayed Oyer of the writing obligatory declared on.

A. R. 26	:	DAVID FRAME .... Plaintiff	)	
A. O.	:		)	
54	:	vs	)	In Case
	:		)	
	:	THOMAS BROWN .... Defendant	)	

This day came the parties by their attornies and the Plaintiff having filed his Declaration, the Defendant filed his Pleas, and the Issues being joined the Tryal thereof is referred until next Court.____

Robert Rhea, and John Liddy of this County comes into Court, and undertakes for the Defendant that in case he Shall be cast in this Suit they Shall Satisfy and pay the condemnation, or render

his body to prison in Execution for the Same or that they the Said
Robert Rhea and John Liddy will do it for him._____

(Pg. 14)

```
Rhea 27   :   PATRICK SLATERY  ....... Plaintiff   )
Rhea 28   :                                        )
    13.   :            vs                           )   In Case.
    14.   :                                         )   A B
          :   JOHN HERRING     ....... Defendant    )
```

        The Defendant John Herring in his proper person comes into
Court, and agrees to pay the Costs of these Suits & upon this the
Plaintiff prays Judgement for his Costs and charges 6 by him about
his Suits in this behalf expended to be adjudged to him. Therefore
it is considered by the Court that the Plaintiff do recover against
the Said John Herring his costs by him about his Suits in this behalf expended, and the said Defendant in Mercy & C. And the Said
Plaintiff not farther prosecuting; it is Ordered that these Suits
be dismissed.

```
A. O.   :   WILLIAM COOPER    ....... Plaintiff   )
  29    :                                          )
  15    :            vs             ·              )
Rhea    :                                          )   In Case
        :   THOMAS KEARNES    )                    )
A. R.   :   MARGARET KEARNES  )                    )
        :   JAMES SMITH       )  ....... Defendants )   Words
        :   SARAH SMITH &     )                    )
        :   JAMES KEARNES     )                    )
```

        The Plaintiff not farther prosecuting on motion of the
Defendants, it is ordered, that this Suit be discontinued and that
the Defendants do recover against the Plaintiff their Costs by them
about their defence in this behalf expended.

```
A. O. 30  :   WILLIAM  COOPER  ....... Plaintiff   )
    55    :                                         )
Rhea      :            vs                           )   In Case
A. R.     :                                         )
          :   JOHN PIPER and                        )   Words
          :   SARAH PIPER     ....... Defendants    )
```

        This day came the parties by their attornies and the Plaintiff
having filed his declaration, the Defendants filed their plea,
and Issue being joined the Tryal thereof is referred until next
Court.

```
A. O. 31.  :   AQUILLA JOHNSTON  ....... Plaintiff   )
Rhea       :                                          )
    16     :            vs                            )   In Case.
           :                                          )
           :   JOHN CHISOLM     ....... Defendant     )
```

The Plaintiff not farther prosecuting, on motion of the
Defendant, it is ordered that this Suit be discontinued and that
the Defendant do recover against the Plaintiff his costs by him
about his Defence in this behalf expended.

(Pg. 15)

32	:	JOHN HICKLAN .... Plaintiff	)	
A. O.	:		)	
34	:	vs	)	In Case
Rhea	:		)	
	:	DANIEL CARMICHAEL ...... Defendant	)	

This day came the parties by their attornies, and the
Plaintiff having filed his Declaration, the Defendant filed his
Plea, and Issue being joined the Tryal thereof is referred until
next Court.

33	:	WILLIAM HOUSTON .... Plaintiff	)	
88	:		)	
J. H.	:	vs	)	In Covn't.
	:		)	
	:	JAMES CRESWELL .... Defendant	)	

This day came the Plaintiff by his Attorney and the
Sheriff having returned that the Defendant is not to be found in his
County a Judicial attachment is awarded him, returnable here at the
next Court._____

	:	JAMES KING .... Plaintiff	)	
34	:		)	
	:	vs	)	In Case
17	:		)	
	:	SAMUEL HENRY .... Defendant	)	

The Plaintiff not farther prosecuting, on motion of the
Defendant it is ordered that this Suit be discontinued, and that the
Defendant do recover against the Plaintiff his costs by him about
his defence in this behalf expended.

A. O.	:	SOLOMON MARKS .... Plaintiff	)	
34	:		)	
A. R.	:	vs	)	Origl. Atta.
J. H.	:		)	
18	:	JOSEPH SEVIER .... Defendant	)	

The Plaintiff not farther prosecuting, on motion of the
Defendant, it is ordered that this Suit be discontinued, and that
the Defendant do recover against the Plaintiff his costs by him
about his defence in this behalf expended.

```
A. R.  :    GUIEN BLACK           ........  Plaintiff )
34     :                                              )
       :              vs                              )   Appeal
19     :                                              )
       :    ALEXANDER CUNNINGHAM   ........  Defendant )
```

The Plaintiff not farther prosecuting, on motion of the Defendant, it is ordered that this Suit be discontinued, and that the Defendant, do recover against the Plaintiff his costs by him about his defence in this behalf expended.

(Pg. 16)

```
A. O.  :    WILLIAM DAVIDSON'S  LESSEE ..... Plaintiff )
Reece  :                                              )
       :              vs                              )   In
 34    :                                              ) Ejectm't.
       :    RICHARD FEN              ..... Defendant  )
D. G.  :
H. L.  :
56     :
```

Lanty Armstrong, on his motion is admitted 6 Defendant in the room of Richard Fen, and thereupon by his attorney filed his Plea and issue being joined the Tryal thereof is referred until next Court.

The following Instrument of writing was proven by the Oath of James Mitchell a Subscribing Witness thereto and admitted to Record to Wit.

I John Herron do publicly acknowledge and Say that I do believe Patrick Slatery was wronged in what is Set forth in an Advertisement Signed with my name, and that the matters in the Said Advertisement against him Set forth are untrue.

Given under my hand this 15th day of October 1792.___

TESTUS   JOHN HERON.
James Mitchell

John Hackett and Luke Lea appeared and produced a Commission from Governor Blount by which it appears that they are appointed Justices of the Peace for this County, who severally took an Oath to Support the Constitution of the United States and also the Oath of Office, and took their Seats accordingly.

Court adjourned until Court in course.

(Pg. 17)

At a Court of Pleas and Quarter Sessions began and held
for the County of Knox at the Court House in Knoxville on the third
Monday of January 1793, __ present James Cozby, David Craig,
James White, Samuel Newell, John Kearnes, Luke Lea; William Lowry,
Thomas McCullough, John Adair, William Hamilton, Jeremiah Jack, and
George McNutt esqrs.

The following persons were elected a Grand Inquest for the
Body of Knox, County to Wit, John Trimble Foreman, William Kerr,
George Brook, John Patterson, Robert Black, Archibald Rhea, William
McNutt, James Anderson, James Harralson, William Doak, William
Richey, Peter Huffacre, Jester Huffacre, Samuel Henry, and James
Gillespie; who have been Sworn, received their charge and withdrew
to enquire of their presentments.___

David Greer appeared in Court, and took the Oath prescribed
by law for Attornies, He is therefore admitted.

The following Instrument of writing was proven by the Oath
of William Wallace a Subscribing witness thereto and admitted
to Record to Wit, ____

Territory S. W. of the River Ohio, Knox County.

I Gasper faught of Said County did Raise a false Report,
on Mary Walker, Young Woman, that I had Carnil knowledge of her
body, which Report I do hereby acknowledge to be false and Ground-
less given under my hand this 19th day of January 1793.

Witness		his
William Wallace	Gasper	X fautt
		mark

Rhea 2	:	ANNANIAS McCOY ...... Plaintiff	)	
48	:		)	
A. R.	:	vs	)	Origl atta.
	:		)	
	:	JOHN COWAN ...... Defendant	)	

This day came the Plaintiff by his attorney and the attachment
awarded, against the Defendants Estate, being returned executed on a
Sorrel horse; Wm. Lowry & Robt. Houston of this County comes into
Court, and undertakes for the Defendant, that in case he shall be
cast, in this Suit he Shall Satisfy and pay the condemnation, or
render his Body to prison in Execution for the Same or that they
the Said William Lowry and Robert Houston will do it for him.
Whereupon the Plaintiff filed his declaration; the Defendant filed
his plea and Issue being joined the Tryal thereof is referred untill
next Court.____

(Pg. 18)

Ordered that Polly Fillson an orphan, Six years of age be bound to James Sims, until She arrive to the age of Eighteen Years, and agreeably to the Said order Indentures are Signed and a Counterpart filed in the office.

Court adjourned until tomorrow Eight O'Clock.

TUESDAY JANUARY 22nd 1793.

Court met according to adjournment present James White, Samuel Newell, & James Cozby esquires, Justices of the Peace & C.

James White esquire is appointed Chairman for the Court.

David Campbell appeared and produced a Commission from Governor Blount, by which it appears that he is appointed a Justice of the peace for this County, who took an Oath to support the Constitution of the United States, and also the Oath of Office, and took his Seat accordingly.

Reece 74	:	WILLIAM DAVIDSON .... Plaintiff	)
J. H.	:		)
47	:	vs	) Appeal
	:		).
	:	ANDREW PAUL .... Defendant	)

This day came the parties by their Attornies, and the appeal not having been brought up, by the mutual consent, of the parties, and with the assent of the Court came also a Jury, to Wit, Joseph Kearns, Joseph Brooks, William Kerr, Samuel Brooks, Samuel Sterling, Henry Sterling, Alexander Campbell, Hugh Dunlap, William Lea, Paul Cunningham, Alexander Cavit, and Major Lea, who being elected, tryed, and Sworn, well and truly, to try the matter of controversy between the parties, upon their oath to Say, they find for the Plaintiff his Debt of Forty three Dollars and thirty three and one third cents, and Costs; Therefore it is considered by the Court that the Plaintiff do recover against the Defendant his Debt aforesaid with his costs by him about his Suit in this behalf expended & the Said Defendant in Mercy & C.

A. R. 4	:	SAMUEL THOMPSON .... Plaintiff	)
L. B.	:		)
J. H.	:	vs	) In Case.
26	:		)
	:	DAVID LINDSEY .... Defendant	)

This day came the parties by their attornies and thereupon came a Jury to Wit, John Cowan, James Robertson, Amos Bird, Joseph Lea, Samuel Samples, Peter Stout, John Rider, Charles Bleakly, John

Hicklin, John Regan, James Adair, David Wessels Howell, who being elected tryed and Sworn the truth to speak upon the issue joined (Pg. 19) upon their oath do Say, they find for the Plaintiff and assess his damages to Ten Dollars besides his costs; Therefore it is considered by the Court that the Plaintiff do recover against the Defendant, the damages aforesaid, in form aforesaid assessed, and his costs by him about his Suit in this behalf expended. And the Said Defendant in Mercy & C.

Court adjourned 'till tomorrow 9 O'Clock.

WEDNESDAY JANUARY 23rd 1793.

Wednesday Morning January 23rd 1793 Court met according to adjournment present John Kearnes, Luke Lea, and Thomas McCullough, esquires, Justices of the Peace & C.

A. R. 5	:	SAMUEL THOMPSON .... Plaintiff	)	
27	:		)	
L. B.	:	vs	)	In Case.
J. H.	:		)	Non assumpsit
	:	DAVID LINDSEY .... Defendant	)	

This day came the parties by their attornies and thereupon came a Jury to Wit; Samuel Henderson, James Miller, Zapher Tanery, William Reed, Major Lea, Joseph Lea, William Trimble, Joseph Brand, Adam Meek, William Rhea, Fuller Pruitt, and James King who being elected, tried and Sworn, the truth to Speak upon the Issue joined upon their Oath to Say that the Defendant did assume upon himself in manner and form as the Plaintiff against him hath complained and they do assess the Plaintiffs damages by occasion of the Defendants non performance of that assumption to Thirty three dollars and thirty three and one third Cents; besides his costs, Therefore it is considered by the Court that the Plaintiff recover against the Defendant the damages aforesaid, in form aforesaid assessed and his costs by him about his Suit in this behalf expended and the Said Defendant in Mercy & C.

D. A. 6	:	SOLOMON MARKS ....Plaintiff	)	
28	:		)	
Rhea.	:	vs	)	In Case.
A. O.	:		)	
	:	WILLIAM ROSEBERRY.......Defendant	)	

The Plaintiff not farther prosecuting, on motion of the Defendant, It is ordered that this Suit be dismissed and that the Defendant do recover against the Plaintiff his Costs by him about his Suit in this behalf expended.

<pre>
 5 :   UNITED STATES .... Plaintiff)
25 :   )
    :   vs   )   Petit Larceny
    :   )
    :   GASPER FAUGHT .... Defendant   )
</pre>

This day came John Rhea esquire Solicitor for the County,
and the Defendants by his attorney; and the Defendant being charged
pleads not guilty and thereupon came a Jury to Wit, William Kerr,
William Douglass, William Houston, James Morris, Solomon McCampbell,
(Pg. 20)   James McElwee, Benjamin Blackburn, Henry White, George
Wolf, Thomas Richey, William Haislet, and Hugh Dunlap who being
elected, tried and Sworn, well and truly to try the Issue of traverse,
the United States against Gasper Faught upon their Oath to Say the
Defendant is not guilty in manner and form as charged in the Bill
of Indictment; Therefore it is considered by the Court that he be
acquitted and discharged of the Petit Larceny aforesaid, and recover
against Henry Rhodes the prosecutor of the Said Indictment his
costs by him about his defence in this behalf expended, and it is
further ordered that the Said Henry Rhodes pay the other costs
accrueing on the Said Indictment.

<pre>
72 :   ADAM MEEK   .... Plaintiff)
45 :   )
    :   vs   .   )   Origl. Atta.
    :   )
    :   WILLIAM ALEXANDER .... Defendant)
</pre>

This day came the Plaintiff by his attorney; and the Defendant
in his proper person, comes into Court, and agrees to pay the Costs
of this Suit; and upon this the Plaintiff prays Judgement for his
costs and Charges by him about his Suit in this behalf expended.__

Therefore it is considered by the Court that the Plaintiff do
recover against the Said Defendant his costs by him about his Suit
in this behalf expended. And the Said Defendant is mercy & C. And
the Plaintiff not farther prosecuting; it is ordered that this Suit
be dismissed. ____

Samuel Hannah who is charged by Clary Ogden, of this County
Single Woman with being the Father of her Bastard Child, and Stands
bound to appear here and abide by and perform, the order of this Court -
concerning the Same, appeared; and thereupon it is adjudged that the
Said Samuel Hannah find Security to discharge and Save harmless the
Overseers of the Poor and the Inhabitants of this County from all
costs, charges and trouble whatsoever by reason of the Birth, Maintenance of, and bringing up of the Said Child. Whereupon the Said
Samuel Hannah with John Patterson and John Crawford his Securities
came into Court and acknowledged themselves to be Jointly and Severally
indebted to the Justices of the Peace of this County and their
Successors in Office in the Sum of One Hundred pounds; Yet upon this
condition that if the Said Samuel Hannah, Shall observe and perform
the above order of this Court against him the Same shall be void.

Court adjourned 'till tomorrow 9 O'Clock.

(Pg. 21)

THURSDAY JANUARY 24th 1793.

Thursday Morning January 24th, 1793. Court met according
to adjournment   present William Lowry, John Adair, and George
McNutt esquires Justices of the Peace & C.

Joseph Greer appeared and produced a Commission from
Governor Blount, by which it appears that he is appointed a Justice
of the Peace for this County, who took an Oath to Support the
Constitution of the United States, and also the Oath of Office; and
took his Seat accordingly._

A. R. 73 : WILLIAM HOUSTON .... Plaintiff)
  46   :   )
       :   vs   )   Origl. Atta.
       :   )
       : JACOB HICKMAN   .... Defendant)

George Colville Garnashee, being first Sworn Saith he owes
the Defendant nothing, that he hath not, nor had he at the time
he was Summoned Garnashee any effects of the Defendants in his
hands that he knows of no debts due to; or effects belonging to
the Defendant in the hands of any other person. The Plaintiff
not farther prosecuting by motion of the Defendant it is ordered
that this Suit be dismissed, and that the Defendant do recover
against the Plaintiff his costs by him about his Suit in this behalf expended. ____

A. R. : JOHN WALLACE .... Plaintiff)
  8   :   )
 29   :   vs   ) In Case
      :   )
      : DAVID SCOTT .... Defendant)

This day came the Plaintiff by his attorney and thereupon
came a Jury to Wit   John Gamble, Calvin Johnston, Samuel Sterling,
James Snodgrass, Moses Brooks, Annanias McCoy, Mathew Kerr,
John Kerr, David Walker, Hugh Johnston, William Lea, and Pierson
Brook who being Sworn, diligently to enquire of damages in this Suit,
upon their oath do Say that the Plaintiff hath Sustained damages by
occasion of the Defendants non performance of the Promise in the
declaration mentioned to amount of Eighty Seven dollars and fifty
Cents, besides his costs

Therefore it is considered by the Court that the Plaintiff
recover against the Defendant the damages aforesaid, in form aforesaid assessed, and his costs by him about his Suit in this behalf

expended. And the Said Defendant in Mercy & C. and the Plaintiff agrees to Stay the execution of this Judgment three Months.

(Pg. 22)

Rhea	:	JAMES ANDERSON .... Plaintiff	)	
10	:		)	
J. H.	:	vs	)	In Case.
49	:		)	
	:	ALEXANDER OUTLAW....... Defendant	)	

This day came the parties by their Attornies, and on motion of the Defendants, a Commission is awarded him to examine and take the Deposition of John Campbell, giving the Plaintiff legal notice of the time and place of executing the Same and the Tryal of the Issue is referred until next Court.

A. O.	:	SAMUEL STIRLING .... Plaintiff	)	
L. B.	:		)	
J. H. 13	:	vs	)	In Case
E. D.	:		)	Words
87	:	HUGH JOHNSTON)	)	
		&)	)	
		WILLIAM JOHNSTON) .... Defendants	)	

This day came the parties by their Attornies, and by their mutual consent and the assent of the Court, the Tryal of the Issue is referred until next Court.

A. O.	:	JAMES McELWEE .... Plaintiff	)	
18	:		)	
Rhea	:	vs	)	In Covn't.
L. B.	:		)	
50	:	HENRY STIRLING)	)	
		&)	)	
		JAMES STIRLING)....... Defendants	)	

This day came the parties by their attornies and by their mutual consent and with the assent of the Court the Trial of the Issue is referred until next Court.

A. O.	:	ABRAHAM RIFE .... Plaintiff	)	
19	:		)	
Rhea	:	vs	)	In Case
51	:		)	
	:	JAMES ANDERSON .... Defendant	)	

This day came the parties by their Attornies, and on motion of the Defendant a Commission is awarded him to examine and take the Deposition of Leeroy Taylor De bene esse. giving the Plaintiff legal notice of the time and place of executing the same and the Trial of the issue is referred until next Court._____

J. H.   :   WILLIAM KERR .... Plaintiff)
..O   :   )
A. R.   :   vs   )   In Case
30   :   )
         :   JOHN CUSICK .... Defendant)

This day came the parties by their attornies and thereupon
came a Jury to Wit, John Gamble, Calvin Johnston, Samuel Sterling,
James Snodgrass, James Gibson, Annanias McCoy, Adam Meek, Joseph
Cowan, David Walker, Hugh Johnston, William Lea & Pierson Brock
who being elected tried and Sworn the truth to speak
(Pg. 23)   upon the Issue joined upon their Oath do Say that
they find for the Defendant;   Therefore it is considered by the
Court that the Defendant do recover against the Said Plaintiff
his costs by him about his Suit in this Behalf expended.

J. H.   :   ALEXANDER OUTLAW .... Plaintiff)
22   :   )
A. R. Rhea :   vs   )   In Case
52   :   )
            :   WILLIAM LOWRY   .... Defendant)

This day came the parties by their attornies and on motion
of the Defendant, a Commission is awarded him to examine and take
the deposition of John Lowry giving the Plaintiff legal notice of
the time and place, of executing the Same, and the Trial of the
issue is referred until next Court.

Rhea   :   JOHN CHISOLM .... Plaintiff)
21   :   )
J. H. :   vs   )   In Case
31   :   )   Non Assumpsit.
       :   MAJOR LEA   .... Defendant)

This day came the parties by their attornies and thereupon
came a Jury to Wit, William Kerr, Jeremiah Jeffery, Henry Stirling,
John McNeill, George Colville, William Hannah, Thomas Gillespie,
John McAllister, Fuller Pruett, Joseph Brooks, Benjamin Grayson
and Thomas Robinson, who being elected, tried and Sworn the
truth to Speak upon the issue joined upon their oath do say that
the Defendant did not assume, and take upon himself in manner and
form as the Plaintiff against him hath complained, as in his pleadings he hath alledged; Whereupon the Plaintiff entered a rule to
Shew cause why the Said verdict Should be Set aside and a new trial
granted, which was argued and overruled; Therefore it is considered
by the Court that the Defendant do recover against the Plaintiff his
costs by him about his Suit in this behalf expended.

J. H.   :   ALEXANDER WILLSON .... Plaintiff)
23   :   )
A. R. Rhea :   vs   )   In Case
32   :   )
            :   WILLIAM LOWRY   .... Defendant   )

This day came the parties by their Attornies, and thereupon
came a Jury to Wit, John Gamble, Calvin Johnston, James Snodgrass,
Annanias McCoy, David Walker, Hugh Johnston, William Lea, Pierson
Brock, Joseph Shadden, John Thomas, Joseph Alexander & Abraham Pruitt
(Pg. 24) who being elected tried and Sworn, the truth to Speak
upon the Issue joined upon their Oath do Say that the Defendant did
assume upon himself in manner and form as the Plaintiff against him
hath complained, within three years next before the Suing out of the
original Writ, and they do assess the Plaintiffs damages by occasion
of the Defendants nonperformance of that assumption to One hundred
three Dollars and thirty three and one third Cents, besides his costs.
Therefore it is considered by the Court that the Plaintiff recover
against the Defendant the damages of aforesaid in form aforesaid
assessed and his costs by him about his Suit in this behalf expended
and the Said Defendant in Mercy & C.

J. H.	:	JOSEPH SEVEIR ....Plaintiff	)	
24	:		)	
Rhea	:	vs	)	In Case
53	:		)	
	:	HUGH DUNLAP ....Defendant	)	

This day came the parties by their Attornies, and the Plaintiff
having filed his declaration, the Defendant filed his Plea and Issue
being joined the Tryal thereof is referred until next Court._____

Rhea	:	JAMES ANDERSON	)	
25	:		)	
A. O.	:	vs	)	In Case
33	:		)	
	:	JOSEPH GREER	)	

The Plaintiff not farther prosecuting on motion of the Defendant it is ordered that this Suit be dismissed and that the Defendant
do recover against the Plaintiff his costs by him about his defence
in this behalf expended. ___

A. R.	:	DAVID FRAME .... Plaintiff	)	
26	:		)	
A. O.	:	vs	)	In Case
54	:		)	
	:	THOMAS BROWN .... Defendant	)	

This day came the parties by their attorneys and on
Motion of the Plaintiff, a Commission is awarded him to examine
and take the Depositions of his Witnesses, giving the Plaintiff
legal notice of the time and place of executing the Same, and the
tryal of the Issues is referred until next Court.

A. O. Rhea	:	WILLIAM COOPER .... Plaintiff	)	
30	:		)	
A. R.	:	vs	)	In Case
55	:		)	Plea, not
	:	JOHN PIPER &)	)	Guilty.
		SARAH PIPER) .... Defendants	)	
		)		

This day came the parties by their attornies and thereupon came a Jury to Wit, William Kerr, Jeremiah Jeffry, Henry Stirling, William Hannah, Thomas Gillespie, John McAllister, (Pg. 25) Fuller Pruitt, Joseph Brooks, Benjamin Grayson, John McNeill, Thomas Robertson, and Thomas Brown, who being elected tried and Sworn the truth to Speak upon the issue joined upon their oath do Say that the Defendants are guilty in manner and form as the Plaintiff against them hath complained and they do assess the Plaintiff's damages by occasion thereof to Seven Dollars and fifty Cents besides his Costs; Whereupon the Said Defendants Say the Court ought not to proceed to Judgement upon the Verdict aforesaid for the reasons following " that the words set forth in the Plaintiff's Declaration are insufficient in Law for to maintain his action against them wherefore they pray the Judgement of the Court thereon and that the verdict of the Jury in this cause may be arrested and Set aside, and because the Court will advise thereupon, day is given the parties aforesaid here until the next Court.

Court adjourned until Tomorrow 9 O'Clock.

FRIDAY JANUARY 25th 1793

Friday Morning January 25th 1793 Court met according to adjournment; present Jeremiah Jack, John Kearnes and John Adair, esquires Justices of the Peace & C.

A. O.	:	JOHN HICKLIN	.... Plaintiff	)	
32	:			)	
Rhea	:	vs		)	In Case
34	:			)	Non Assumpsit.
	:	DANIEL CARMICHAEL	.... Defendant	)	

This day came the parties by their attornies and thereupon came a Jury to Wit, John Thomas, Major Lea, Hugh Dunlap, James Haven, William McBroom, John Lacky, Moses Looney, John Trimble, John Carter, John Ish, Dennis Conner, and Fuller Pruitt who being elected, tried and Sworn the truth to Speak upon the Issue joined upon their oath do Say, that the Defendant did not assume and take upon himself in manner and form as the Plaintiff against him hath complained, as in his pleadings he hath alledged. Therefore it is considered by the Court that the Defendant do recover against the Plaintiff his costs by him about his Suit in this behalf expended.

J. H.	:	WILLIAM HOUSTON	.... Plaintiff	)	
33	:			)	
88	:	vs		)	Origl. Atta.
	:			)	In Covn't.
	:	JAMES CRESWELL	.... Defendant	)	

This day came the Plaintiff by his Attorney and the attachment awarded against the Defendants Estate, being returned Executed on One thousand Acres of land on the West Fork of Turkey Creek (Pg. 26) and the Defendant not appearing to replevy the Same although Solemnly called; It is ordered by the Court that the Plaintiff recover against the Defendant his Damages Sustained by the Occasion in the Declaration mentioned and his costs, But because it is unknown to the Court what those Damages are; It is ordered that the Same be enquired of by a Jury at the next Court.

A. O. Reece	:	WILLIAM DAVIDSON'S LESSEE........ Plaintiff	)	
———	:		)	
34	:	vs	)	Eject'mt.
D. G.	:		)	
H. L.	:	LANTY ARMSTRONG .... Defendant	)	
56	:			

This day came the parties by their Attornies and thereupon came a Jury to Wit; Major Lea, William McBroom, Hugh Dunlap, Moses Looney, Peter McNamee, Annanias McCoy, John Ish, David Looney, George Preston, William Murphy, John Singleton and Archibald Rhea, who being elected tried and Sworn the truth to Speak upon the Issue joined upon their Oath do Say that the Defendant is guilty in manner and form as the Plaintiff against him hath complained and they do assess the Plaintiffs damages by occasion thereof to Six Cents besides his costs; Whereupon the Defendant entered a rule to Shew cause why the Said Verdict Should be Set aside and a new trial granted, which was argued and Granted.

	:	UNITED STATES .... Plaintiffs	)	
3	:		)	
23	:	vs	)	A B
	:		)	
	:	DAVID ROBERTSON .... Defendant	)	

This day came John Rhea Solicitor for the County & the Defendant by his attorney; and the Defendant being charged, pleads not guilty, and thereupon came a Jury to Wit; David Scott, Abraham Pruitt, William Cooper, David Willson, John McFarland, Robert Miller, Peter McNamee, Stephen Duncan, Thomas Kearns, Thomas Reardon, Archibald Rhea, and Francis Amas, who being elected tried and Sworn, well and truly to try the issue of traverse The United States against David Robertson upon their Oath do Say that the Defendant is guilty in manner and form as charged in the Bill of Indictment; Therefore it is considered by the Court that for Such his Offence, he be fined in the Sum of Five Dollars and that he pay the costs of this prosecution.

James Cozby appeared in Court appeared in Court and acknowledged that he had received the amount of a Note of hand, given by James White to him for Thirty Pound Virginia Currency Some time in the Year 1787 which Note the Said James Cozby Says is lost or mislaid.

(Pg. 27)

James Cozby and Samuel Newell being chosen by the parties to
Wit John Ish, and John McAllister, to arbitrate a dispute in the
division of their lands do Say that the line dividing the Land
between John Ish and John McAllister Shall be as follows, that
it Shall be measured from McAllister's Spring at his improvement forty poles down the Branch, and that at the extermity, of
Said measurement a line Shall be drawn directly across between the
Improvements of Said Ish and McAllister which Shall be the line
dividing Said Lands the parties being Sworn to abide by the
opinion of the Parties .and the parties agreed that all former
disputes Shall cease.

Rhea	:	UNITED STATES	)	
2	:		)	
84	:	vs	)	Barratry
	:		)	
	:	JOSEPH VANCE	)	

Ordered that Process issue against Joseph Vance to cause him
to appear at the next Court, to answer the Indictment *this day* .
found against him by the Grand Jury.

Rhea	:	UNITED STATES .... Plaintiffs	)	
6	:		)	
85	:	vs	)	Contempt.
	:		)	
Rhea	:	GEORGE TEDFORD .... Defendant	)	
7	:			
86	:			

Rhea	:	UNITED STATES .... Plaintiff	)	
7	:		)	
86	:	vs	)	Contempt.
	:		)	
	:	JOHN LOWRY .... Defendant	)	

Ordered that Process Issue against George Tedford and
John Lowry to cause them to appear at the next Court to answer
the Indictments this day found against them by the Grand Jury.

Ordered that Robert Given, David Dearmond, & Samuel Stockton
be fined each the Sum of Sixty two and One half Cents for Contempt of the Court._____ And on the Prayer of the Said David
Dearmond and Samuel Stockton, their Fine and costs are Remitted.

	:	GEORGE AMERINE .... Plaintiff	)	
35	:		)	
35	:	vs	)	In Case
	:		)	
	:	WILLIAM HINDS .... Defendant	)	

The Plaintiff not farther prosecuting on motion of the
Defendant it is ordered that this Suit be dismissed and that
the Defendant do recover against the Plaintiff his Costs by him
about his defence in this behalf expended._____

(Pg. 28)

J. H.	:	SOLOMON MARKS	)	
36	:		)	
Rhea	:	vs	)	In Case.
252	:		)	
	:	ROBERT KING	)	

This day came the parties by their Attornies, and the Plaintiff
having filed his declaration, the Defendant filed his pleas, and Issues
being joined, the Trial thereof is referred until next Court.

J. H.	:	SOLOMON MARKS	)	
37	:		)	
	:	vs	)	In Case
	:		)	Trover
Rhea	:	DAVID CRAIG	)	
57	:		)	

This day came the parties by their attornies, and the Plaintiff having filed his declaration, the Defendant filed his plea,
and Issue being joined, the Trial thereof is referred until next
Court.

Rhea	:	JOSHUA SPEARS .... Plaintiff	)	
38	:		)	
58	:		)	
	:	vs	)	In Case
	:		)	
	:	GEORGE WALLACE .... Defendant	)	

This day came the Plaintiff by his attorney and filed his
declaration, and the Defendant having been arrested, and not
appearing though Solemnly called; on motion of the Plaintiff
by his attorney; It is ordered that Judgement be entered for
the plaintiff against the Said Defendant for what damages the
Plaintiff hath Sustained by occasion of the Defendants breach
of the promise in the Declaration mentioned. Which damages are to
be enquired of by a Jury at the next Court. _____

39	:	ELLIOTT GRILLS .... Plaintiff	)	
36	:		)	
	:	vs	)	In Case
	:		)	
	:	WILLIAM PORTER .... Defendant	)	

The Plaintiff not farther prosecuting, on motion of the
Defendant it is ordered that this Suit be dismissed and that the

Defendant do recover against the Plaintiff his Costs by him about
his defence in this behalf expended.

```
A. R.  :   JOHN KIRKPATRICK   .......  )
40     :                                )
37     :             vs                 )    In Case
       :                                )    Trover
       :   JAMES HENDERSON   .......    )
```

The Plaintiff not farther prosecuting, ~~by motion of the Defendant~~
It is ordered that this Suit be dismissed and that the Defendant do
recover against the Plaintiff his Costs by him about his Defence
in this behalf expended.

(Pg. 29)

```
A. R.  :   EDWARD HIGGINS         Plaintiff
41     :                                     )
113    :             vs                      )
       :                                     )
       :   SAMUEL WEAR &          )          )
       :   WILLIAM LOWRY  EXRS.   )          )    In Convenant.
Rhea   :   of JAMES WALKER deceased) Defendants )
J. H.  :   JAMES W. LACKEY &      )          )
       :   JOHN COWAN             )          )
```

This day came the parties by their attornies, and the
Plaintiff having filed his Declaration; time was given the Defend-
ants to plead, and the Sheriff having returned Samuel Wear and
John Cowan are not to be found within his County; on motion of the
Plaintiff by his Attorney an Alias Capias is awarded him to this
County against the Said John Cowan and an Alias Capias is awarded
him to Jefferson County against the Said Samuel Wear returnable
here at next Court.

```
A. O.  :   SAMUEL BOWMAN  ....... Plaintiff )
42     :                                     )
A. R.  :             vs                      )    T. V. A.
38     :                                     )
       :   HENRY SMITH  ....... Defendant    )
```

This day came the parties by their attornies and by
their mutual consent a Commission is awarded them, to examine
and take the deposition of William Thomas giving each other legal
notice of the time and place of executing the Same. The plaintiff
not farther prosecuting on motion of the Defendant it is ordered
that this Suit be dismissed and that the Defendant recover against
the Plaintiff his costs by him about his defence in this behalf
expended.

```
Rhea   :   JOSEPH SEVIER  .......Plaintiff  )
43     :                                    )
A. R.  :          vs                        )
59     :                                    )      Debt
       :   SAMUEL ACKLIN  )                 )
       :        &         )                 )
           SAMUEL NEWELL  )......Defendants )
```

This day came the Parties by their attornies and the Plaintiff having filed his declaration the Defendant filed his Plea and Issue being joined the trial thereof is referred until next Court.___

(Pg. 30)

```
Rhea   :   WILLIAM COOPER  FATHER  )
       :   & Next Friend of        ) ..... Plaintiff  )
       :   ELIZABETH COOPER        )                  )
       :                                              )  In Case
44     :            vs                                )  Words
A. R.  :                                              )
89     :   THOMAS KEARNS ................. Defendant  )
```

This day came the parties by their attornies & the Plaintiff having filed his declaration the Defendant filed his pleas, and Demurrer, and the Plaintiff having joined in Demurrer and ye. issues being joined the Trial and argument thereof is referred until next Court.

```
A. O.  :   WILLIAM COOPER  Father )
       :   and next Friend of     ) ....... Plaintiff  )
       :   ELIZABETH COOPER       )                    )
       :                                               )
45     :            vs                                 )  In Case
60     :                                               )
       :   THOMAS KEARNS &  )                          )
           MARGARET KEARNS  )        ....... Defendants )
```

This day came the Plaintiff by his attorney and having filed his declaration and the cause is continued untill next Court.

```
Rhea   :   WILLIAM COOPER  Father )
       :   and next Friend of     ) ......Plaintiff  )
       :   ELIZABETH COOPER       )                  )
46     :                                             )
       :            vs                               )  In Case
L. B.  :                                             )  Words
61     :   JAMES SMITH            ......Defendant    )
```

This day came the parties by their Attornies and the Plaintiff having filed his declaration the Defendant filed his plea and issues being joined the Trial thereof is referred until next Court.___

A. O.	:	WILLIAM COOPER Father and next Friend of ELIZABETH COOPER)	.... Plaintiff	)
47 62	:	vs		) In Case) Words
L. B.	:	JAMES SMITH) &) SARAH SMITH)	.... Defendants	)

This day came the parties by their Attornies and the Plaintiff having filed his declaration the Defendant filed his Pleas and the Issues being joined the Trial thereof is referred until next Court.

(Pg. 31)

A. R.	:	JOHN HACKETT) &) ROBERT LIGGIT)	.....Plaintiffs	)
48 114 Rhea.	:	vs		) In Case.
	:	DANIEL CARMICHAEL) &) ALEXANDER CARMICHAEL)	.....Defendants	)

This day came the parties by their Attornies and the Plaintiff having filed his declaration the defendant filed his pleas and Issues being joined the Trial thereof is referred until next Court.

Rhea	:	JOHN CHISOLM .... Plaintiff	)
49 662	:	vs	) In Case
	:	RICHARD HAMILTON .... Defendant	)

This day came the Plaintiff by his Attorney and filed his Declaration, and the Defendant having been arrested, and not appearing though Solemnly called, on motion of the Plaintiff by his attorney, It is ordered that Judgment be entered for the Plaintiff against the Said Defendant for what damages the Plaintiff has Sustained by occasion of the Fraud and Deceit in the declaration mentioned; which damages are to be enquired of by a Jury at the next Court.

Rhea	:	HENRY STERLING) &) JAMES STERLING)	...... Plaintiffs	)
50 A. O. 63	:	vs		) In Covenant
	:	JAMES McELWEE .... Defendants	)

This day came the parties by their Attorney and the Plaintiff
having filed his declaration the Defendant filed his plea and the
Plaintiff his replication thereto, and Issue being joined the Trial
thereof is referred untill next Court.

```
J. H.    :    SOLOMON MARKS  ......, Plaintiff  )
51       :                                      )
Rhea     :            vs                        )   In Case
64       :                                      )
         :    JOSEPH SEVIER  ....... Defendant  )
```

This day came the parties by their attornies and the Plaintiff having filed his declaration the Defendant filed his pleas and
Issues being joined the Tryal thereof is referred until next Court.

Court adjourned 'till tomorrow 7 O'Clock

(Pg. 32)

SATURDAY JANUARY 26th 1793.

Saturday Morning January 26th 1793 Court met according to
adjournment present Jeremiah Jack, John Kearnes, and John Adair
esquires Justices & C.____

```
A. O.    :    MAJOR LEA  ....... Plaintiff  )
52       :                                  )
Rhea     :          vs                      )   In Case.
65       :                                  )
         :    JOHN CHISOLM ....... Defendant )
```

This day came the parties by their Attornies and the Plaintiff
having filed his declaration the Defendant filed his pleas and
issues being joined the trial thereof is referred until next Court.

```
Rhea     :    JAMES ARMSTRONG  ....... Plaintiff  )
53       :                                        )
L. B.    :            vs                          )   In Case
90       :                                        )
         :    WILLIAM HENRY  ....... Defendant    )
```

This day came the Plaintiff by his attorney and filed his
declaration, and the Defendant having been arrested, and not appearing though Solemnly called, on motion of the Plaintiff by his attorney
It is ordered that Judgment be entered for the Plaintiff against
the Said Defendant for what damages the Plaintiff hath Sustained
by occasion of the Defendants Nonperformance of the assumption in
the declaration mentioned; which damages are to be enquired of by
a Jury at the next Court.____

Rhea : JAMES W. LACKEY .... Plaintiff)
54 :
L. B. : vs) In Covenant
66 :)
: WILLIAM HENRY .... Defendant)

This day came the Plaintiff by his attorney and filed his declaration, and the Defendant having been arrested, and not appearing though Solmnly called, on motion of the Plaintiff by his attorney, It is ordered that Judgement be entered for the Plaintiff against the Said Defendant, for what damages the Plaintiff hath Sustained by occasion of the Defendants Nonperformance of the Covenant, in the declaration mentioned; which damages are to be enquired of by a Jury at the next Court._____

(Pg. 33)

Reese : THOMAS WELCH .... Plaintiff)
55 :)
67 : vs) In Covenant
:)
: ALEXANDER MILLIKEN &)
JAMES COZBY .... Defendants)

This day came the Plaintiff by his attorney, and the Sheriff having returned not executed by order of the Plaintiff, On motion of the plaintiff by his Attorney an Alias Capias is awarded him returnable here at the next Court.

A. O. : WILLIAM COOPER)
Rhea : Father and next Friend of)....... Plaintiff)
J. H. : ELIZABETH COOPER))
:) In Case
56 : vs) Words
Reece :)
91 : JAMES KEARNS .... Defendant)

This day came the parties by their attornies & the Plaintiff having filed his declaration, the Defendant demurred thereto, and the Plaintiff joins in the Said demurrer, and the Argument thereof is referred until the next Court.____

A. R. : ALEXANDER CAVET .... Plaintiff)
57 :)
39 : vs) Debt.
:)
: SAMUEL SHIPLEY .... Defendant)

: WILLIAM COWAN .... Plaintiff)
58 :)
40 : vs) In
:) Case
: JOHN PAUL)
: ANDREW PAUL))
: JOSEPH WEAR &)............. Defendants)
JOHN WEAR))

The Plaintiffs not farther prosecuting; It is ordered that these Suits be dismissed._____

```
59   :   JACOB TARWATER ..... Plaintiff      )
J. H.:                                       )
41   :            vs                         )   In Case
     :                                       )
     :   JOHN PAUL  et alias ·....... Defendants )
```

The Plaintiff not farther prosecuting; On motion of the Defendants; It is ordered that this Suit be dismissed and that the Defendants do recover against the Plaintiff their costs by them about this defence in this behalf expended._____

(Pg. 34)

```
J. H.:   THOMAS BROWN   ....... Plaintiff )
L. B.:                                    )
60   :            vs                       )   In Case
Rhea :                                    )   T. V. A.
J. L.:   LITTLE PAGE SIMS....... Defendant )
172  :
```

This day came the parties by their attornies and the Plaintiff having filed his Declaration the Defendant filed his plea and Issue being joined the Trial thereof is referred until the next Court._____

```
J. H.:   THOMAS BROWN   ....... Plaintiff )
L. B.:                                    )
     :            vs                       )   In Case
61   :                                    )   Words
Rhea :   JOHN SHARKEY )                    )
144  :         &      )....... Defendants )
     :   JEAN SHARKEY )
```

This day came the parties by their attornies and the Plaintiff having filed his declaration the Defendant demurs to the first count thereof and the Plaintiff joins in Demurrer; and the Defendant having filed his pleas to the other counts, and the Issues being joined the argument of the Demurrer, and the Trial of the Issues are referred 'Till the next Court._____

```
J. H.:   MARGARET BROWN .................Plaintiff )
62   :                                              )
Rhea :            vs                                )   In Case.
92   :                                              )
     :   JOHN SHARKEY & JEAN SHARKEY .....Defendants )
```

This day came the Parties by their attornies and time is given the Plaintiff to File her declaration 'till next Court.___

```
A. R.  :   JAMES GIBSON  ....... Plaintiff   )
63     :                                     )
       :          vs                         )   In Case.
Rhea   :                                     )
68     :   JACOB CLEMAN  ....... Defendant   )
```

This day came the parties by their attornies and the plaintiff having filed his declaration the Defendant filed his plea and the plaintiff his replication thereto, and issue being joined the Trial thereof is referred untill next Court._____

```
A. R.      FRANCIS ROWAN   ........ Plaintiff   )
64                                              )
69              vs                              )   In Covenant.
                                                )
           WILLIAM OVERSTREET  ....... Defendant )
```

This day came the Plaintiff by his attorney and filed his declaration, and the Defendant having been arrested, and not appearing though Solemnly called. On motion of the Plaintiff by his Attorney, It is ordered that Judgment be entered for the Plaintiff against the Said Defendant, for what damages the Plaintiff hath Sustained by occasion of the Defendants Nonperformance of the Covenant in the Declaration mentioned; which damages are to be enquired of by a Jury at the next Court._____

(Pg. 35)

```
J. H.  :   THOMAS BROWN  ................. Plaintiff   )
L. B.  :                                               )
61     :          vs                                   )   In Case
Rhea   :                                               )   Words
144    :   JOHN SHARKEY & JEAN SHARKEY ... Defendants  )
```

Robert Rhea of this County comes into Court and undertakes for the Defendants, that in case they Shall be cast in this Suit, they Shall Satisfy and pay the condemnation, or render their bodies to prison in execution for the Same, or that he the Said Robert Rhea will do it for them._____

```
Rhea   :   RICHARD RIDER  ....... Plaintiff   )
65     :                                      )
115    :          vs                          )   In Covenant.
       :                                      )
       :   JOHN RIDER     ....... Defendant   )
```

This day came the Plaintiff by his attorney; and the Defendant having been arrested, and not appearing though Solemnly called, on motion of the Plaintiff by his attorney, It is ordered that Judgment be entered for the Plaintiff, against the Said Defendant for what damages the Plaintiff hath Sustained by occasion of the Defendants Nonperformance of the Covenant; Which damages are to be enquired of by a Jury at the next Court.

```
       :  CRAIN BRUSH    ....... Plaintiff  )
       :                                    )
66     :       vs                           )     In Case.
42     :                                    )
       :  CHARLES COLLINS ....... Defendant )
```

The Defendant Charles Collins in his proper person comes
into Court, and agrees to pay the Costs of this Suit, and upon this
the Plaintiff prays Judgment for his costs and charges by him about
his Suit in this behalf expended to be adjudged to him; Therefore
it is considered by the Court that the Plaintiff do recover against
the Said Defendant his costs by him about his Suit in this behalf
expended, And the Said Defendant in Mercy & C. And the Said Plaintiff not farther prosecuting It is ordered that this Suit be dismissed. ___

```
A. R.  :  JOHN PIPER & SARAH PIPER....... Plaintiffs )
  67   :                                             )
Rhea.  :              vs                             )   In Case
A. O.  :                                             )   Words
  93   :  WILLIAM COOPER .............. Defendant     )
```

This day came the parties by their Attornies and the
Plaintiff having filed his Declaration, the Defendant filed his
pleas and the Issues being joined, the Trial thereof is referred
untill next Court.

(Pg. 36)

```
       :  HUGH DUNLAP    ....... Plaintiff  )
68     :                                    )
43     :       vs                           )   T. V. A.
       :                                    )
       :  THOMAS BROWN   ....... Defendant  )
```

```
A. R.  :    YOUNG   ....... Plaintiff  )
       :                               )
69     :       vs                      )   In Case
Rhea   :                               )
44     :  JOHN THOMAS  ....... Defendant )
```

The Plaintiffs in these Suits not farther prosecuting
On Motion of the Defendants it is ordered that the Said Suite be
dismissed and that the Defendants do recover against the Said
Plaintiffs their costs by them about this Defence in their behalf
expended.

```
Reece   :  WILLIAM RITCHY ....... Plaintiff )
70 L.B. :                                   )
        :       vs                          )   In Detinue
94      :                                   )
        :  DAVID LINSEY ....... Defendant   )
```

This day came the parties by their attornies and the
Plaintiff having filed his declaration the Defendant filed his
pleas and the Issues being joined the Trial thereof is referred
'till next Court.

```
Rhea   :   WILLIAM LOVE  Assignee .....  Plaintiff )
71     :                                           )
Rhea   :            vs ·                           )  Debt.
70     :                                           )
       :   ARCHIBALD RHEA        ..... Defendant )
```

This day came the parties by their Attorneys and by their
mutual consent, and with the assent of the Court a Commission is
awarded them to examine and take the depositions of William Davis,
Thomas Cuppyhaver, Walter Crockett, Jesse Evans, and William
Love giving each other legal notice of the time and place of
executing the Same.

The Court proceeded to lay the County Tax for this Year
which is laid as follows:

On each hundred acres of land .... .10 cents
On each Pole .... .33 1-3

Ordered that the Sheriff do summons the following persons
to attend at the next Superior Court as Jurors.____

James White, John Chisolm, Thomas Gillespie Annanias McCoy,
John Patterson, Andrew Evans Junior, Joseph Greer, and William
Sloan.

Ordered that the Clerk of this County, purchase the following
Books for the use of the Court, to Wit, Irdell's revisal of the
Laws of North Carolina, Ruffheads Dictionary, Blackstones Commen-
tarys; and Such Blank Books as are necissary for the Records of
this Court.____

(Pg. 37)

Ordered that, the following Justices do take in and return
to next Court a list of the Taxables and Taxable property of the
respective Companies for which they are appointed.____

```
For Captain McGauheys Company        John Evans
    "       Blacks      "            Samuel Newell
    "       Ewins       "            William Lowry
    "       Tedfords    "            William Wallace
    "       Singletons  "            William Hamilton
    "       Henrys      "            David Craig
    "       Flennekins  "            Thomas McCullough
    "       Cozbys      "            James Cozby
    "       Gillespies  "            Jeremiah Jack
    "       Cox's       "            John Kearns
```

For Captain McGauheys Company (Continued)

"	Beairds	"	John Sawyers
"	Crawfords	"	James White
"	Menifees	"	Luke Lea
"	Campbell	"	John Hackett
"	Samples	"	George McNutt

Ordered that all Ordinaries in this County be rated as follows to Wit,

For Diett .... 16 Cents	For Rum per half pint.... 16 Cents
Corn per gallon .... 10 "	Wine per ditto .... 16 "
Oats per ditto .... 10 "	Beer per Quart ...... 8 "
Fodder per bundle ...... 3 "	Cyder per ditto .... 8 "
Whiskey per half pint... 8 "	Lodging per Night ... 6 "
Brandy per ditto .... 12 "	Pasturage per day ... 8 "

Samuel Newell esquire is appointed trustee for the County of Knox, who with Annanias McCoy his security entered into and acknowledged Bond in the Sum of two thousand two Hundred Dollars, conditioned for the due performance of his duty in office.

Court adjourned to Court in Course.

(Pg. 38)

MONDAY MAY 6th 1793.

At a Court of Pleas and Quarter Sessions began and held for the County of Knox, at the Court House in Knoxville on the first Monday in May 1793 present James White, Luke Lea, John Kearns, and John Evans esquires Justices & C & C.

The following persons were elected a Grand Inquest for the Body of this County, to Wit, William Leaky Foreman, William Boyd, Thomas Chapman, Samuel McCullough, William Davidson, Robert Gamble, Amos Byrd, William Houston, William Hannah, Henry White, William Roberts, William Reed, Peter Keener, and James Brook, who have been Sworn, received their charge, and withdrew to enquire of their presentments.

John Sevier Junior, John Lowry, and Samuel Mitchell, appeared and produced Licenses from Governor Blount authorizing them to practice as Attorneys in the Several Courts of Pleas and Quarter Sessions within this Territory who Severally took an Oath to Support the Constitution of the United States & also took the Oath prescribed by Law for Attornies they are therefore admitted.

John Rhea esquire appeared and is duly Sworn as Solicitor for this County.

Court adjourned until tomorrow 8 O'Clock

TUESDAY MORNING MAY 7th 1793

Court met according to Adjournment   present   Luke Lea,
John Evans and John Kearnes esquires justices & C & C.

Rhea	:	ANNANIAS McCOY .... Plaintiff	)	
2	:		)	
A.R.	:	vs	)	In Case
48	:		)	Non Assumpsit
	:	JOHN COWAN .... Defendant	)	

This day came the parties by their Attornies and thereupon
came a Jury to Wit, James Smith, William Cooper, John Heron,
David W. Howell, Godfrey Antrem, Henry Smith, Robert Rhea, Joshua
Spears, John Burden, James Anderson, Robert McNutt, and John
McIntire who being elected tried and Sworn the truth to Speak
upon the Issue joined upon their Oath do Say the Defendant did not
assume upon himself in manner and form   (Pg. 39)   as the
Plaintiff against him hath complained as in pleading he hath
alledged. Therefore it is considered by the Court that the
Plaintiff take nothing by his Bill, but for his false clamour
be in Mercy & C. and the Said Defendant go thereof without day
& recover against the Plaintiff his Costs by him about his
defence in this behalf expended. From which Judgment the Plaintiff prays an Appeal to the next Superior Court of Law to be holden
for the district of Hamilton at the Court House in Knoxville; hath
filed his reasons and entered into Bond with David Craig and
Jeremiah Jack his Securities in the Sum of One hundred & Fifty
Dollars with condition for the prosecution of the Said appeal
with effect, which appeal is allowed.

Rhea	:	JAMES ANDERSON .... Plaintiff	)	
10	:		)	
J. H.	:	vs	)	In Case
49	:		)	Non Assumpsit
	:	ALEXANDER OUTLAW .... Defendant	)	

This day came the parties by their attornies and thereupon
came a Jury to Wit, James Sterling, Andrew Cowan, John Dunlap,
Joseph Cowan, James Snodgrass, James Robertson, Thomas Stockton,
Michael Childers, Archibald Rhea, James Gibson, John Campbell, and
John McAmey who being elected tried and Sworn the truth to Speak
upon the issue joined upon their oath do Say the Defendant did
assume upon himself in manner and form as the Plaintiff against him
hath complained and they do assess the Plaintiffs damages by occasion
of the Defendants Nonperformance of that assumption to Forty Six
Dollars Sixty Six and two third Cents besides his costs. Therefore it is considered by the Court that the Plaintiff recover against
the Defendant the Damages aforesaid in form aforesaid assessed, and

his costs by him about his Suit in this behalf expended and the
Said Defendant in Mercy & C. From which Judgment the Defendant
prays an Appeal to the next Superior Court of law to be holden
for the district of Hamilton at the Court House in Knoxville;
hath filed his reasons and entered into Bond with John Chisolm
his Security in the Sum of Two hundred & Fifty Dollars with
condition for the prosecution of the Said appeal with effect,
Which appeal is allowed,   (Pg. 40)   Whereupon the Plaintiff
acknowledges that he has received Satisfaction for the Damages
aforesaid together with his attorneys fee, therefore as to
So much the Said Defendant is acquitted and discharged.

A. O.	:	ABRAHAM RIFE .... Plaintiff	)	
19	:		)	
Rhea	:	vs	)	In Case
51	:	-	)	Non assumpsit
	:	JAMES ANDERSON .... Defendant	)	

This day came the parties by their Attorneys and thereupon
came a Jury to Wit, Jester Huffacre, James Scott Robert Black,
George Stout, Hugh Bodkins, Christian Pickle, Andrew Kerr,
Henry Stirling, Major Lea, Benjamin Grayson, Joseph Lea, and William
Kerr, who being elected tried and Sworn the truth to Speak upon
the Issue joined upon their Oath do Say the Defendant did assume
upon himself in manner and form as the Plaintiff against him hath
complained and they do assess the Plaintiffs damages by occasion
of the Defendants Nonperformance of that assumption to Fourteen
Dollars and Seventy five Cents besides his costs; Whereupon the
Said Defendant Saith the Court ought not to proceed to Judgment
upon the Verdict aforesaid; and moved for liberty to file his
reasons, which motion is withdrawn; Therefore it is considered
by the Court that the Plaintiff do recover against the Defendant
the damages aforesaid, in form aforesaid assessed, and his costs
by him about his Suit in this behalf expended and the Said
Defendant in Mercy & C. Whereupon the Plaintiff acknowledges that
he has received Satisfaction for the damages aforesaid together
with his attorneys fee, therefore as to So much the Said Defendant is acquitted and discharged.

J. H.	:	ALEXANDER OUTLAW....... Plaintiff	)	
22	:		)	
A. R. Rhea	:	VS	)	In Case
52	:		)	
	:	WILLIAM LOWRY .... Defendant	)	

The Defendant William Lowry in his proper person comes
into Court and agrees to pay the Costs of this Suit and upon
this the Plaintiff prays Judgment for his costs & charges by him
about his Suit in this behalf expended to be adjudged   (Pg. 41)
to him; Therefore it is considered by the Court that the Plaintiff
do recover against the Said Defendant his costs by him about his
Suit in this behalf expended, and the Said Defendant in Mercy & C.
And the Said Plaintiff not farther prosecuting; It is ordered
that this Suit be dismissed.

A. R. :   DAVID FRAME .... Plaintiff)
26   :   )
A. O. :   vs   ) In Case Non assumpsit
54   :   ) Stat. Lim. Tender &
       :   THOMAS BROWN .... Defendant)   refusal.

This day came the parties by their Attornies and thereupon
came a Jury to Wit, James Smith, William Cooper, John Herron,
David W. Howell, Godfrey Antrim, Henry Smith, Joshua Spears,
John Cowan, Joseph Kearnes, David Scott, John Black, and Andrew
Cowan, who being elected tried and Sworn, the truth to Speak
upon the issues joined upon their Oath do Say the Defendant did
assume upon himself in manner and form as the Plaintiff against him
hath complained within three years next before the Suing out the
Original Writ; and that he did not tender as in pleading he hath
alledged, and they do assess the Plaintiffs damages by occasion
of the Defendants nonperformance of that Assumption to Four Dollars
and Interest from the date of the Note besides his costs; Whereupon
the Plaintiff releases the Interest in the verdict aforesaid mentioned And the Said Defendant Saith the Court ought not to proceed to Judgment upon the Verdict aforesaid for the reasons following
first, That it appears from the obligation that it was given in
the Year 1781 as also the Witness Said he thought it was about
nine or ten Years ago. Second That the time limited by law for
bringing actions on the case precluded the Plaintiff from any
recovery the action not having been instituted within the time
Specifyed by law. And the Said plea of the Defendant is arrest
of Judgment being argued and overruled It is considered by the
Court that the Plaintiff do recover against the Defendant Four
Dollars the damages in form aforesaid assessed, and his costs
by him about his Suit in this behalf expended, And the Said Defendant in mercy & C.

(Pg. 42)

A. O.   :   WILLIAM DAVIDSON'S LESSEE ..... Plaintiff)
Reece :   )
34   :   vs   ) Ejectmt.
D. G. :   )
H. L. :   LANTY ARMSTRONG   ..... Defendant)
56   :

This day came the parties by their attornies and thereupon
came a Jury to Wit, Joseph Lea, Joseph Looney, James Gibson,
John McIntire, James Anderson, Samuel Doak, David Walker, William
Murphy, John Chisolm, James McElwee, John Brady, and William Lea
who being elected, tried, and Sworn, the truth to Speak upon the
Issue joined upon their Oath do Say that the Defendant is guilty
in manner and form as the Plaintiff against him hath complained and
they do assess the Plaintiffs damages by occasion thereof to Six
Cents besides his costs; Therefore it is considered by the Court
that the Plaintiff recover against the Defendant his term yet to
come of and in the messuage and lands with the appurtenances in

the declaration mentioned together with his damages in form aforesaid assessed and his costs by him about his Suit in this behalf
expended. And the Said Defendant in Mercy & C. From which Judgment
the Defendant prays an appeal to the next Superior Court of law to
be holden for the District of Hamilton at the Court House in Knoxville;
hath filed his reasons and entered into Bond with Peter McNamee and
Jeremiah Jack his Securities in the Sum of Two Thousand Dollars with
Condition for the prosecution of the Said appeal with effect; Which
appeal is allowed.____

William Evans and James Blair Severally produced a Commission
from the Governor by which it appears they are appointed Constables
for this County who have entered into Bond to Wit, William Evans,
with James Anderson & Andrew Cowan his Securities and James
Blair with Joseph Black and William Lowry his Securities with
condition for the faithfull discharge of their duties in Office
who have been Severally Sworn as the Law directs.

On the presentment of the Grand Jury against Michael Foster
for misusasage of Francis Ogden an Orphan, It is ordered that
Hezekiah Jordan take into his possession the Said Orphan, and
bring him before this Court on the first day of the next Term.

For reasons appearing to the Court, James Brook, and Samuel
McCullough, are discharged from further attendance as Grand Jurors.

Court adjourned 'till tomorrow 8 O'Clock.

(Pg. 43)

WEDNESDAY MAY 8th 1793

Wednesday Morning May 8th 1793 Court met according to adjournment: Present James White, John Adair, & George McNutt
esquires Justices & C & C.

John Chisolm appeared, and produced a Commission from
Governor Blount; by which it appears that he is appointed
a Justice of the Peace for this County, who took an Oath to
Support the Constitution of the United States, and also the oath
of Office; and took his Seat accordingly.

6	:	UNITED STATES .... Plaintiff	)	
85	:		)	
	:	vs	)	Contempt.
	:		)	
	:	GEORGE TEDFORD .... Defendant	)	

$\frac{7}{86}$

:   UNITED STATES .... Plaintiff)
:   )
:   vs   ) Contempt.
:   )
:   JOHN LOWRY   .... Defendant)

This day came John Rhea Solicitor for the County and the Defendants George Tedford and John Lowry; and the Said Defendants having been Severally charged pleads not guilty. And now because they will not contend Severally withdraw their plea aforesaid and Say that they are guilty, in manner and form as in the Indictments against them is alledged and putteth themselves upon the Grace and Mercy of the Court; Therefore it is considered by the Court that for their Offence they be Severally fined in the Sum of One Dollar; and that they Severally pay the costs of the prosecution against them.

$\frac{2}{84}$

:   UNITED STATES .... Plaintiff)
:   )
:   vs   ) Barratry
:   )
:   JOSEPH VANCE   .... Defendant)

This day came as well the Solicitor for the County as the Said Defendant by his attorney; and the Said Defendant being charged pleads not guilty and thereupon came a Jury to Wit, Robert Wood, Major Lea, Adam Peck, Moses Looney, Moses Brooks, John Gamble, Thomas Kearns, James Anderson, Paul Cunningham, Joshua Spears, Joseph Lea, and Samuel Sterling; who being elected tried and Sworn the truth of and upon the premises to Speak upon their Oath do Say that the Defendant is not guilty as in pleading he hath alledged; Therefore it is considered by the Court, that he be acquitted and discharged of the Barratry aforesaid, and go thereof without day; and on Motion of the Said defendant; It is ordered that Charles Regan the Prosecutor pays the costs of this prosecution.

Samuel McGaughey, and James Gibson, are Sworn as Grand Jurors, in the place of James Brock & Samuel McCullough, who were discharged Yesterday.___

(Pg. 44)

$\frac{11}{558}$

:   UNITED STATES .... Plaintiffs)
:   )
:   vs   ) Petit Larceny
:   )
:   ZOPHER TANNERY .... Defendant)

Ordered that Process issue against Zopher Tannery to cause him to appear at the next Court, to answer the Indictment found against him by the Grand Jury.

	:	UNITED STATES .... Plaintiffs	)	
13	:		)	
83	:	vs	)	A B
	:		)	
	:	SAMUEL HINDMAN .... Defendant	)	

This day came as well the Solicitor for the County, as the
Said Defendant by his attorney; and the Said Defendant being charged
pleads not guilty and thereupon came a Jury to Wit, Elijah
Davis, John Sherrill, John Brady, Benjamin Grayson, David Adair,
Andrew Kerr, Joseph Rayney, John Sloan, Benjamin Blackburn, George
Stout, Thomas Richey, and James Mason, who being elected tried,
and Sworn the truth of and upon the premises to Speak upon their
Oath do Say that the Said Defendant is guilty in manner and form
as in the Indictment against him is alledged; Therefore it is con-
sidered by the Court that for Such his offence he be fined in the
Sum of One Dollar, and pay the costs of this prosecution.

	:	UNITED STATES .... Plaintiffs	)	
14	:		)	
	:	vs	)	Presentment.
202	:		)	
	:	MICHAEL FOSTER ......: Defendant	)	

Ordered that Process issue against Michael Foster, to cause
him to appear at the next Court to answer the Presentment of the
Grand Jury against him.

Court adjourned until tomorrow 8 O'Clock.

THURSDAY MAY 9th 1793

Thursday Morning May 9th 1793 Court met according to
Adjournment present James White, George McNutt, and John Adair
esquires Justices & C. & C. _____

A. O.	:	SAMUEL STERLING ..... Plaintiff	)	
L. B.	:		)	
	:	vs	)	In Case)
13	:		))	Words)
	:	HUGH JOHNSTON &) ..... Defendants	)	
J. H.	:	WILLIAM JOHNSTON)	)	Not Guilty
E. D.	:	)		Stat. Lim.
87	:			& Justification.

This day came the parties by their attornies and thereupon
came a Jury to Wit, James Gibson, Thomas Ritchy, Samuel Love,
Benjamin Blackburn, Paul Cunningham, Robert Christian, Jesse
Green, Joseph Vance, Robert Wood, Archibald Rhea, John Patterson,
and Major Lea, who being elected tried and Sworn the truth to
Speak upon the issues joined (Pg. 45) upon their Oath do Say

that the Defendants are Guilty in manner and form as the Plaintiff against them hath complained within Six Months next before the Suing out the original Writ; and that the words Spoken were of the Defendants own wrong, and without any justification therefor and they do assess the Plaintiffs damages by occasion thereof to Seven Dollars besides his Costs. Whereupon the Defendants entered a rule to Shew cause why the Said Verdict Should be Set aside and a new trial granted; which was argued and granted.

A. O.	:	JAMES McELWEE	.....	Plaintiff	)	In Covenant
18	:				)	
Rhea	:	vs			)	Covenant per-
L. B.	:				)	formed/
50	:	HENRY STERLING &			)	
		JAMES STERLING	.....	Defendants	)	

This day came the parties by their attorneys and thereupon came a Jury to Wit, William Sharp, Joseph Kearns, William Bails, Samuel Acklin, Robert Black, Benjamin Greyson, William Lea, Joshua Spears, Robert Rhea, Aquilla Johnston, Joseph Brooks, and Alexander Millikin, who being elected tried and Sworn the truth to Speak upon the issue joined upon their oath do Say that the Defendants have not performed the covenant in the Declaration mentioned but have broken the Same in manner and form as the Plaintiff against them hath complained and they do assess the Plaintiffs damages by occasion thereof to One Hundred and Sixty Dollars besides his costs; Therefore it is considered by the Court that the Plaintiff recover against the Said Defendants the damages aforesaid in form aforesaid assessed and his costs by him about his Suit in this behalf expended and the Said Defendants in Mercy & C.

J. H.	:	JOSEPH SEVIER	....	Plaintiff	)	
24	:				)	In Case.
Rhea	:	vs			)	Non Assumpsit.
53	:				)	Stat. of Gaming.
	:	HUGH DUNLAP	....	Defendant	)	

This day came the parties by their attornies, and thereupon came a Jury to Wit, John Therman, James Anderson, John Wallace, John Henry, George Preston, James Mason, John Patterson, James Gibson, Jessee Green, Joseph Vance, Archibald Rhea, and Major Lea, who being elected tried and Sworn the truth to Speak upon the issue joined upon their oath do Say that the Defendant did assume upon himself in manner and form as the Plaintiff against him hath complained, and that the Said Plaintiff is not barred from his recovery by the Statute of Gaming and they do assess the Plaintiffs damages by occasion of the Defendants Non performance of that assumption to Sixty six Dollars and Sixty six and two third cents besides his Costs; Therefore it is considered by the Court that the (Pg. 46) Plaintiff recover against the Defendant his damages aforesaid in form aforesaid assessed and his costs by him about his Suit in this behalf expended. And the Said Defendant in Mercy & C. From which Judgment the Defendant prays an Appeal to the

next Superior Court of law to be holden for the District of
Hamilton at the Court House in Knoxville; hath filed his reasons
and entered into Bond with James Anderson and Peter McNamee his
Securities in the Sum of Three hundred Dollars with condition for
the prosecution of the Said appeal with effect; which appeal is
allowed.

J. H.	:	SOLOMON MARKS .... Plaintiff	)	
37	:		)	
Rhea	:	vs	)	In Case Trover,
57	:		)	not Guilty.
	:	DAIVD CRAIG .... Defendant	)	

This day came the parties by their attornies, and thereupon
came a Jury to Wit, Thomas Ritchy, Samuel Stirling, Thomas
Reardan, William McNutt, Robert Black, Benjamin Grayson, William
Lee, Joshua Spears, Robert Rhea, Alexander Milliken, John Stirling,
and Joseph Kearns who being elected, tried and Sworn the truth to
Speak upon the issue joined upon their oath do Say the Defendant
is guilty of the Trover and conversion in manner and form as the
Plaintiff against him hath complained and that they do assess the
Plaintiffs Damages by occasion of the Said Trover and Conversion
to Ten Dollars besides his costs; Therefore it is considered by the
Court that the Plaintiff recover against the Defendant the Damages
aforesaid in form aforesaid assessed, and his costs by him about
his Suit in this behalf expended; And the Said Defendant in Mercy
& C. From which Judgment the Defendant prays an appeal to the
next Superior Court of law, to be holden for the District of
Hamilton at the Court House in Knoxville; hath filed his reasons,
and entered into Bond with William Lowry and Archibald Rhea his
Securities in the Sum of One hundred and Fifty Dollars, with condition for the prosecution of Said appeal with effect; which appeal
is allowed.___

J. H.	:	WILLIAM HOUSTON .... Plaintiff	)	
33	:		)	
88	:	vs	)	In Covenant
	:		)	
	:	JAMES CRESWELL .... Defendant	)	

This day came the Plaintiff by his attornoy and by his consent,
and with the assent of the Court, the enquiry of damages is referred
until next Court._____

(Pg. 47)

J. H.	:	SOLOMON MARKS .... Plaintiff	)	
36	:		)	
Rhea	:	vs	)	In Case
252	:		)	
	:	ROBERT KING .... Defendant	)	

This day came the parties by their attornies and by their
Mutual consent and with the assent of the Court the trial of the
Issues is referred untill next Court.

Court adjourned until tomorrow 8 O'Clock.

FRIDAY MAY 10th 1793.

Friday Morning May 10th 1793   Court met according to
adjournment   present   William Lowry, David Craig, & Samuel
Newell   esquires   Justices & C. & C.

| A. R.
41
Rhea
J. H.
113 | : EDWARD HIGGINS   ..... Plaintiff
:
:   vs
:
: SAMUEL WEAR et alias ..... Defendants |))) In Covenant)) |

This day came the parties by their attornies, and time is
given the Defendants to plead and the Sheriffs having returned
Samuel Wear & John Cowan not to be found within their Counties;
on motion of the Plaintiff by his attorney a Pluries Capias is
awarded him to Jefferson County against Samuel Wear, and a Pluries
Capias is awarded him to Washington County against John Cowan
returnable here at the next Court.

| Rhea
38
58 | : JOSHUA SPEERS   .... Plaintiff
:
:   vs
:
: GEORGE WALLACE   .... Defendant |))) In Case)) |

This day came the Plaintiff by his attorney and thereupon
came a Jury to Wit, John Therman, William Cooper, Archibald
Rhea, John Sloan, John Kearns, Samuel Stirling, Joseph Kearns,
John Stirling, Samuel Hindman, John Frazier, William Bails,
and James McElwee who being Sworn diligently to enquire of damages
in this Suit, upon their oath do Say that the Plaintiff hath Sustained damages by occasion of the Defendants Nonperformance of the
Promise in the declaration mentioned to amount of One Hundred,
and Six dollars, Sixty Six and two third Cents besides his Costs;
Therefore it is considered by the Court that the Plaintiff recover
against the Defendant the damages aforesaid in form aforesaid assessed,
and his costs by him about his Suit in this behalf expended. And
the Said Defendant in Mercy & C.

(Pg. 48)

| Rhea
43
A. R.
59 | : JOSEPH SEVIER   ..... Plaintiff
:
:   vs
:
: SAMUEL ACKLIN &)
: SAMUEL NEWELL   )..... Defendants |))) In Debt) Owe Nothing))) |

This day came the parties by their attornies and thereupon came a Jury to Wit, Aquilla Low, James Mason, Henry Sterling, Alexander Carmichael, Robert Armstrong, Hugh Dunlap, Godfrey Antrim, James Smith, Robert Black, John Black, James Anderson and Samuel Cowan who being elected tried and Sworn the truth to Speak upon the issue joined upon their oath do Say that the Defendants oweth nothing of the Debt in the Declaration mentioned, as in his pleading he hath alledged; Therefore it is considered by the Court that the Plaintiff take nothing by his Bill but for his false clamour be in mercy & C. and the defendants go hence without day and recover against the Plaintiff their costs by them about their defence in this behalf expended.

Rhea	:	WILLIAM COOPER	) ..... Plaintiff	)	
	:	Father and next Friend of	)	)	
	:	ELIZABETH COOPER	)	) In Case Words
44	:			) Not guilty,
A. R.	:	vs		) Justification
89	:			) and Demurrer
	:	THOMAS KEARNS	..... Defendant	to last count

This day came the parties by their attornies and the Defendants demurrer to the last count of the plaintiffs declaration being argued and Overuled; Thereupon came a Jury to Wit, Calvin Johnston, Alexander Milliken, Hugh Johnston, Samual Doake, William Kerr, Thomas Ritchey, John Sterling, Samuel Hindman, Andrew Richey, Peter McNamee, Robert Miller, and Archibald Rhea, who being elected tried and Sworn, the truth to Speak upon the issues joined upon their oath do Say the Defendant is not guilty as in pleading he hath alledged, Whereupon the Plaintiff entered a rule to Shew cause why the Said verdict Should be Set aside and a new trial granted which was argued and granted.

A. O.	:	WILLIAM COOPER	)..... Plaintiff	)	
	:	Father & next Friend of	)	)	
45	:	ELIZABETH COOPER :	)	)	
60	:			)	
	:	vs		) In Case
				) Words
		THOMAS KEARNES &		)	
		MARGARET KEARNES	..... Defendants	)	

The Plaintiff not farther prosecuting, On motion of the Defendants it is ordered that this Suit be dismissed & that the Defendants do recover against the Plaintiff their costs by them about their defence in this behalf expended.

(Pg. 49)

Rhea	:	WILLIAM COOPER Father & next Friend of	) Plaintiff	)	
	:	ELIZABETH COOPER	)	)	
46	:			) In
L. B.	:	vs		) Case
61	:			) Words
		JAMES SMITH		Defendant	)

A. O. : WILLIAM COOPER Father & next Friend of) ... Plaintiff)
     : ELIZABETH COOPER))
47 :)
L. B. :   vs)
    :)
    : JAMES SMITH & SARAH SMITH ....,..,, Defendants)

In Case   Words

The Plaintiff in these Suits not farther prosecuting on motion
of the Defendants it is ordered that the Said Suits be dismissed
and that the Defendants do recover against the Plaintiff their
costs by them about their defence in this behalf expended. Whereupon the Said Defendants acknowledge that they have received Satisfaction of the Plaintiff for their attorney's fees therefore as to
So Much the Said Plaintiff is acquitted.

A. R. : JOHN HACKETT and .... Plaintiffs)
48 : ROBERT LIGGITT)
Rhea :)
114 :   vs) In Case
    :)
    : DANIEL CARMICHAEL &)
    : ALEXANDER CARMICHAEL .... Defendants)

This day came the parties by their Attornies and by their
mutual consent and with the assent of the Court the trial of the
issues is referred until next Court._____

Rhea : JOHN CHISOLM .... Plaintiff)
49 :)
662 :   vs) In Case
    :)
    : RICHARD HAMILTON .... Defendant)

This day came the Plaintiff by his attorney and by his consent

Rhea : HENRY STIRLING & .... Plaintiffs)
50 : JAMES STIRLING)
A. O. :) In Covenant.
63 :   vs) Covenant
    :) performed
    JAMES McELWEE .... Defendant)

This day came the parties by their Attornies and thereupon
came a Jury to Wit, Hugh Dunlap, Aquilla Low, Godfrey Antrim,
Paul Cunningham, Robert Black, James Campbell, Robert Miller,
John Black, William Ritchy, Thomas Welch, Robert Rhea, &
Archibald Trimble (Pg. 50) who being elected tried and
Sworn, the truth to Speak upon the issue joined upon their oath
do Say the Defendant hath not performed the Covenant in the
declaration mentioned but hath broken the Same in manner and form
as the Plaintiff against him hath complained as the Said Plaintiff

by repplying hath alledged and they do 'assess the Plaintiffs damages by occasion thereof to Sixty Dollars besides their costs; Therefore it is considered by the Court that the Plaintiffs do recover against the Defendant the damages aforesaid in form aforesaid assessed and their costs by them about their Suit in this behalf expended. And the Defendant in mercy & C.

J. H.	:	SOLOMON MARKS .... Plaintiff	)	
51	:		)	In Case, Non assumpsit
Rhea	:	vs	)	Stat. Lim. Set off ___
64	:		)	
	:	JOSEPH SEVIER .... Defendant	)	

This day came the parties by their Attornies and thereupon came a Jury to Wit, Alexander Carmichael, Godfrey Antrim, Robert Black, James Campbell, John Black, William Cooper, William Ritchy, Thomas Welch, John Henry, Thomas Kearns, John Piper, and David Dermand who being elected tried and Sworn the truth to Speak upon the issues joined upon their Oath do Say that the Defendant did assume upon himself in manner and form as the Plaintiff against him hath complained within three years next before the Suing out the Writ of Capias in this Suit; and that the Said Defendant hath no Set off against the Same and they do assess the Plaintiffs damages by occasion of the Defendants Non-performance of that assumption to Seventy eight Dollars, Sixty Six & two third cents besides his costs; Therefore it is considered by the Court that the Plaintiff recover against the Defendant his damages aforesaid in form aforesaid assessed, and his costs by him about his Suit in this behalf expended and the Said Defendant in Mercy & C. From which Judgment the Defendant prays an appeal to the next Superior Court of law for the District of Hamilton to be holden at the Court House in Knoxville; hath filed his reasons and entered into Bond with Alexander Outlaw and John Sevier Junior his Securities in the Sum of Three hundred Dollars with condition for the prosecution of the Said appeal with effect; which appeal is allowed.____

(Pg. 51)

Constant Claxton produced a Commissioner from the Governor, by which it appears, he is appointed a Constable for the County of Knox, who entered into Bond with Luke Lea and Aquilla Low his Securities in the Sum of Six hundred and twenty five dollars, with condition for the faithful discharge of the duties of his Office; who hath been Sworn as the law directs.

A. O.	:	MAJOR LEA .... Plaintiff	)	
52	:		)	
Rhea	:	vs	)	In Case, Non
65	:		)	assumpsit
	:	JOHN CHISOLM .... Defendant	)	

This day came the parties by their Attornies, and thereupon came a Jury to Wit, James Campbell, John Stono, Hugh Dunlap, George Raulstone, John McNeill, John Trimble, James McElwee, Thomas Welch, James Anderson, William Henry, Thomas Kearns, and James Smith who being elected tried and Sworn the truth to Speak upon the issue joined upon their Oath do Say that the Defendant did assume upon himself in manner and form as the Plaintiff against him hath complained, and they do assess the Plaintiffs damages by occasion thereof to Forty Six dollars, Sixty Six & two third Cents, besides his costs; Therefore it is considered by the Court that the Plaintiff recover against the Defendant his damages aforesaid in form aforesaid assessed and his costs by him about his Suit in this behalf expended. And the Said Defendant in Mercy & C. From which Judgment the Defendant prays an appeal to the next Superior Court of law to be holden for the district of Hamilton at the Court House in Knoxville hath filed his reasons and entered into Bond with Alexander Outlaw & Alexander Carmichael his Securities in the Sum of Two hundred Dollars with condition for the prosecution of the Said appeal with effect; which appeal is allowed.

Rhea	:	JAMES ARMSTRONG .... Plaintiff	)	
53	:		)	
L. B.	:	vs	)	In case.
90	:		)	
	:	WILLIAM HENRY .... Defendant	)	

This day came the parties by their attornies and by their mutual consent and with the assent of the Court, the enquiry of damages is referred untill next Court.

Court adjourned 'till tomorrow 7 O'Clock.

(Pg. 52)

SATURDAY MAY 11th 1793.

Saturday Morning May 11th 1793   Court met according to adjournment   present   James White, John Adair, & George McNutt esquires Justices & C. & C.

Rhea	:	JAMES W. LACKEY .... Plaintiff	)	
54	:		)	
L. B.	:	vs	)	In Covenant.
66	:		)	
	:	WILLIAM HENRY .... Defendant	)	

This day came the Plaintiff by his attorney and the Defendant in his proper person, and the parties agree that the Plaintiff hath Sustained damages by occasion of the Defendants Nonperformance of the Covenant in the declaration mentioned, to Fifty four Dollars,

Thirty three and one third Cents besides his costs; Therefore it is considered by the Court that the plaintiff recover against the Defendant the damages agreed as aforesaid and his costs by him about his Suit in this behalf expended. And the Said defendant in Mercy & C. and the Plaintiff agrees to Stay the execution of this Judgment two Months.

```
Reece    :   THOMAS WELCH          ....... Plaintiff  )
55       :                                            )
‾67      :            vs                              )   In Covenant
         :                                            )
         :   ALEXANDER MILLIKEN &                     )
             JAMES COZBY            ....... Defendants )
```

The defendants Alexander Milliken and James Cozby in their proper persons comes into Court, and agrees to pay the Costs of this Suit, and upon this the Plaintiff prays Judgment for his costs and charges by him about his Suit in this behalf expended to be adjudged to him; therefore it is considered by the Court that the Plaintiff do recover against the Said Defendants his costs by him about his Suit in this behalf expended. And the Said Defendants in Mercy & C. And the Said Plaintiff not farther prosecuting; It is ordered that this Suit be dismissed.

```
A. O.    :   WILLIAM COOPER          )
Rhea     :   Father & next Friend of )..... Plaintiff )
J. H.    :   ELIZABETH COOPER        )                )
56       :                           )                )   In Case
Reece    :            vs             )                )   Words
91       :                           )                )
             JAMES KEARNS            ..... Defendant  )
```

This day came the parties by their Attornies and the Demurrer of the Defendant, to the Plaintiffs declaration being argued It seems to the Court that the Said Declaration and the matters therein contained is Sufficient in law to maintain the Action aforesaid; Whereupon the Defendant moved for liberty to plead over, which was argued and overruled; Therefore it is considered by the Court that the Said Demurrer be overruled and that the Plaintiff recover against the   (Pg. 53)   the Defendand Such damages as he hath Sustained by occasion of the Speaking of the words in the Declaration mentioned; Which damages are to be enquired of by a Jury at the next Court.

```
J. H.    :   THOMAS BROWN          ....... Plaintiff )
L. B.    :                                           )
60       :            vs                             )   T. V. A.
Rhea     :                                           )
J. L.    :   LITTLE PAGE SIMS      ....... Defendant )
172      :
```

This day came the Parties by their attornies and by their consent and with the Assent of the Court the trial of the Issue is referred until next Court.____

J. H.	:	THOMAS BROWN	...... Plaintiff	)
L. B.	:			)
61	:	vs		) In Case
Rhea	:			) Words
144	:	JOHN SHARKEY &	)	)
		JEAN SHARKEY	) ...... Defendants	)

This day came the parties by their attornies and by their mutual consent and with the assent of the Court; the argument of the Demurrer, and the trial of the issues are referred 'till next Court.____

J. H.	:	MARGARET BROWN	...... Plaintiff	)
62	:			)
Rhea	:	vs		) In Case.
·92	:			)
	:	JOHN SHARKEY &	)	)
		JEAN SHARKEY	) ...... Defendants	)

This day came the parties by their attornies, and time is given the Plaintiff to file her declaration, 'till next Court.

A. R.	:	JAMES GIBSON	...... Plaintiff	)
63	:			)
Rhea	:	vs		) In Case
68	:			)
	:	JACOB CLEMAN	...... Defendant	)

The Defendant in his proper person comes into Court, and agrees to pay the Clerk's and his Attorney's fee and the Plaintiff not farther prosecuting It is ordered that this Suit be dismissed.

A. R.	:	FRANCIS ROWAN	...... Plaintiff	)
64	:			)
69	:	vs		) In Covenant
	:			)
	:	WILLIAM OVERSTREET	...... Defendant	)

The Plaintiff not farther prosecuting, on motion of the Defendant It is ordered that this Suit be dismissed and that the Defendant recover against the Plaintiff his costs by him about his defence in this behalf expended.____

(Pg. 54)

Rhea	:	RICHARD RIDER	...... Plaintiff	)
65	:			)
115	:	vs		) In Covenant
	:			)
	:	JOHN RIDER	...... Defendant	)

This day came the Plaintiff by his attorney and by his consent and with the assent of the Court, the enquiry of damages is referred until next Court.

```
A. R.  :   JOHN PIPER &                              )
67     :   SARAH PIPER      ....... Plaintiffs      )
A. O.  :                                             )
Rhea   :        vs                                   )   In Case
93     :                                             )     Words
       :   WILLIAM COOPER   ....... Defendants      )
```

This day came the parties by their attornies and by their mutual consent and with the assent of the Court the trial of the issues is referred until next Court.

```
Reece  :   WILLIAM RITCHEY  ....... Plaintiff       )
70     :                                             )
L. B.  :        vs                                   )   In Detinue
94     :                                             )
       :   DAVID LINDSEY    ....... Defendant        )
```

This day came the parties by their attornies and by their mutual consent, and with the assent of the Court the trial of the issues is referred until next Court.

```
Rhea   :   WILLIAM LOVE  Assignee  ....... Plaintiff )
71     :                                             )   In Debt
Rhea   :        vs                                   )   Owe nothing.
70     :                                             )
       :   ARCHIBALD RHEA         ....... Defendant  )
```

This day came the plaintiff and Defendant by their attorneys and thereupon came a Jury to Wit; James King, Major Lea, John Trimble, John Stirling, Andrew Ritchey, Robert Miller, Hugh Johnston, Alexander Milliken, Calvin Johnston, James Mason William Reed, and Thomas Ritchey who being elected tried and Sworn the truth to Speak upon the Issue joined upon their Oath do Say that the Defendant oweth nothing of the Debt in the declaration mentioned; as in his pleading he hath alledged; Therefore It is considered by the Court that the Plaintiff take nothing by his Bill but for his false clamour be in Mercy & C. and the Defendant go hence without day and recover against the Plaintiff his costs by him about his defence in this behalf expended.

Hugh Lawson White appeared and was duly Sworn Deputy Clerk of this County. ____

(Pg. 55)

```
A. O.  :   WILLIAM COOPER              ..... Plaintiff )
Rhea   :   Father and next Friend of                  )
30     :   ELIZABETH COOPER                            )
A. R.  :                                               )   Plea in
55     :        vs                                     )   arrest of
       :                                               )   Judgment
       :   JOHN PIPER  and                             )
       :   SARAH PIPER               ..... Defendants )
```

This day came the parties by their attorneys and the Plea of
the Defendant in arrest of Judgment being argued and overruled; It
is considered by the Court that the Plaintiff recover against the
Defendant Seven Dollars, Fifty Cents the damages by the Jury in this
case formerly assessed; and his costs by him about his Suit in this
behalf expended; And the Said Defendants in mercy & C. From which
Judgment the Defendants pray an appeal to the next Superior Court
of law to be holden for the district of Hamilton at the Court House
in Knoxville; hath filed their reasons and entered into Bond with
Security conditioned for the prosecution of the Said appeal with
effect; which appeal is allowed.

John Hackett appeared and entered into Bond with James White
and George McNutt his Securities; in the Sum of Five hundred Dollars;
with condition for the faithful Execution of the duties of his
office as Coroner. ____

Thomas Chapman appeared and entered into Bond, with John Chisolm
his Security, in the Sum of Five hundred Dollars; with condition
for the faithful collection, and payment of certain Monies therein
mentioned.

Robert Houston produced a Commission appointing him Sheriff for
this County, who entered into a Bond, with Charles McClung, John
Hackett, and James White his Securitys, in the Sum of Twelve Thousand
Five Hundred Dollars, with condition for the faithfull execution
of the duties of his office as Sheriff. And also entered into Bond
with James Cozby and George McNutt his Securities in the Sum of
One Thousand Dollars; with condition for the faithful collection
of the County Tax; for the present Year; and for the payment thereof,
as the law directs, & was qualified accordingly.

Charles McClung entered into Bond, with James Cozby and Robert
Houston his Securities, in the Sum of Five Hundred Dollars; with
condition for the faithful collection of Monies arising from fines,
and forfeitures; Taxes on law proceedings, on the probate of Deeds;
and on issuing Marriage, and Ordinary licenses and for the payment
thereof agreeably to law._____

(Pg. 56)

William Meek produced a Commission from the Governor; by
which it appears he is appointed a Constable for this County; who
entered into Bond with Jeremiah Jack and James White his Securities,
in the Sum of Six hundred and Twenty five Dollars; with condition
for the faithful discharge of the duties of his office; who hath
been Sworn as the law directs.__

Ordered that the Sheriff do pay the Clerk of this County
Fifty dollars for exofficio Services; out of the Money he may receive for the County Taxes for the past Year.___

Ordered that the Sheriff do retain in his own hands Sixty
Seven dollars part of the County Tax for his exofficio Services
for the past Year.

Ordered that the Clerk do receive from the Sheriff Twelve
Dollars for his Services in respect of County Taxes for the present
Year.___

```
A. R.  :   JOHN TODD     ....... Plaintiff  )
75     :                  .                 )
A. O.  :        vs                          )  In Case
173    :                                    )
       :   JOHN McAMY    ....... Defendant  )
```

This day came the parties by their attornies and the plaintiff having filed his declaration the Defendant filed his plea
and the issue being joined the trial thereof is referred until
next Court.

```
A. O.  :   JOHN RUSSELL   ....... Plaintiff  )
76     :           .                         )
Rhea   :        vs                           )  In Case
95     :                                     )
       :   JAMES ANDERSON  ....... Defendant )
```

This day came the parties by their Attornies and the Plaintiff
having filed his declaration, the Defendant filed his pleas and the
issue being joined the trial thereof is referred 'till next Court;
and on motion of the Plaintiff a Commission is awarded him, to
examine & take the deposition of Christopher Haines, giving the
Defendant legal notice of the time and place of executing the Same.

```
J. H.  :   GEORGE BOWERMAN ....... Plaintiff  )
A. O.  :                                       )
77     :              vs                        )  T. V. A.
A. R.  :                                       )
96     :   JOHN ISH      ....... Defendant     )
```

This day came the parties by their Attornies & the Plaintiff
having filed his declaration the Defendant filed his pleas and
the issues being Joined the trial thereof is referred until next
Court. _____

```
A. O.  :   CHARLES McCLOUD  ....... Plaintiff  )
78     :                                        )
97     :              vs                         )  In Case.
       :                                        )
       :   WILLIAM WALKER   ....... Defendant   )
```

This day came the Plaintiff by his Attorney and having filed
his declaration and the Defendant having been arrested and not
appearing though Solemnly called   (Pg. 57)   on motion of the

Plaintiff by his attorney; It is ordered that Judgment be
entered for the Plaintiff against the Said Defendant for what
damages the Plaintiff hath Sustained by occasion of the Defendant's
Non performance of the assumption in the declaration mentioned
which damages are to be enquired of by a Jury at the next Court.

A. R.	:	JAMES EWING	.... Plaintiff	)	
79	:			)	
71	:	vs		)	In Case
	:			)	
	:	WILLIAM LOWRY esqr.	.... Defendant	)	

The Plaintiff not farther prosecuting; It is ordered that this
Suit be dismissed; Note John Bradley appeared and assumes
payment of the Costs;

A. O.	:	GEORGE PAGE by .... Plaintiff	)	
	:	JAMES PAGE his	)	
80	:	next Friend	)	
72	:		)	
	:	vs	)	In Case
			)	Words
	:	MICHAEL CARTER .... Defendant	)	

The parties appeared and each agree to pay their own
Costs; & The Plaintiff not farther prosecuting; It is ordered
that this Suit be dismissed.

A. O.	:	JACOB TARWATER	..... Plaintiff	)	
Rhea	:			)	
81	:	vs		)	In Covenant
J. H.	:			)	
A. R.	:	ANDREW PAUL Admr. &c of	)	
116	:	JAMES PAUL deceased	) ..... Defendants	)	

This day came the parties by their attornies and the Plaintiff
having filed his Declaration the Defendant filed his pleas and
the Plaintiff his replication thereto and the issues being joined
the trial thereof is referred until next Court.

Rhea	:	JOHN FEE	.... Plaintiff	)	
82	:			)	
J. H.	:	vs		)	In Case
A. R.	:			)	
174	:	ANDREW PAUL Admr.of	)	
	:	JAMES PAUL deceased	) .... Defendant	)	

This day came the parties by their Attornies and the Plaintiff
having filed his declaration the Defendant filed his pleas, and the
issues being joined the trial thereof is referred until next Court.

A. O.   :   WILLIAM COOFER .... Plaintiff)
83   :   )
L. B. 98:   vs   )   In Case
)
            GODFREY ANTRIM · .... Defendant)

    This day came the parties by their attorneys and the plaintiff having filed his Declaration the Defendant filed his plea and the issue being joined the trial thereof is referred 'till next Court._

(Pg. 58)

Rhea   :   JOHN LOWRY   .... Plaintiff)
84   :   )
J. H. :   vs   )   In Covenant
A. R. :   )
99   :   ROBERT BLACKBURN   )
                        &   )
            BENJAMIN BLACKBURN .... Defendants)

    This day came the parties by their attornies and the Plaintiff having filed his declaration the Defendant filed his plea and the issue being joined the trial thereof is referred until next Court._

Rhea   :   DAVID SCOTT   .... Plaintiff)
85   :   )
A. R. :   vs   )   In Case
100   :   )
       :   ·JOHN WALLACE .... Defendant   )

    This day came the parties by their attornies and the Plaintiff having filed his declaration the Defendant filed his Plea and the issue being joined the trial thereof is referred untill next Court._ ·

Rhea   :   THOMAS KING Assignee of) ... Plaintiff)
86   :   STOCKLEY DONALSON   )   )
J. H. :   )
101   :   vs   )   In Case
       :   )
       :   JOSEPH BEAIRD   ... Defendant   )

    This day came the Plaintiff, by his attorney and having filed his declaration the cause is continued until next Court. _____

Rhea   :   JOHN LIDDY & FLORA LIDDY   ..... Plaintiffs)
87   :   )
73   :   vs   )   In Case
       :   )
       :   NICHOLAS HALE & SARAH HALE ..... Defendants)

    The Plaintiffs not farther prosecuting; It is ordered that this Suit be dismissed.

```
A. O.  :   ROBERT STEPHENSON  .....  Plaintiff  )
88     :                                        )
J. H.  :           vs                           )   In Case
288    :                                        )
       :   BENJAMIN BLACKBURN  .....  Defendant )
```

This day came the parties by their attornies, and the Plaintiff having filed his declaration, the Defendant filed his Pleas and the issues being joined the trial thereof is referred until next Court.

```
Rhea   :   ROBERT GRAY   .......  Plaintiff  )
89     :                                     )
J. L.  :           vs                        )   In Covenant
143    :                                     )
       :   JOHN WALLACE  .......  Defendant  )
```

This day came the parties by their attornies; and the Plaintiff having filed his declaration the Defendant filed his Plea, and the issue being joined the trial thereof is referred until next Court.

```
Rhea   :   JOHN CHISOLM  .......  Plaintiff  )
90     :                                     )
J. H.  :         vs                          )   In Case
102    :                                     )
       :   MAJOR LEA    .......  Defendant   )
```

This day came the parties by their attornies, and the Plaintiff having filed his Declaration, the Defendant filed his plea and the Issue being joined the trial thereof is referred until next Court.

(Pg. 59)

```
A. O.  :   JOHN MISSEY  .......  Plaintiff   )
91     :                                     )
74     :           vs                        )   In Covenant
       :                                     )
       :   JOHN STOUT  .......  Defendant    )
```

The Defendant in his proper person appeared, and agrees to pay the costs of this Suit, and upon this the Plaintiff prays that his costs and charges by him about his Suit in this behalf expended may be adjudged to him; Therefore it is considered by the Court that the Plaintiff recover against the Said Defendant his costs by him about his Suit in this behalf expended; And the Said Defendant in Mercy & C. And the Plaintiff not farther prosecuting; It is ordered that this Suit be dismissed.

```
       :   ROBERT FERGUSON  .......  Plaintiff  )
92     :                                        )
75     :           vs                           )   In Case.
       :                                        )
       :   GEORGE ROULSTONE  .......  Defendant )
```

The Plaintiff not farther prosecuting; It is ordered that
this Suit be dismissed.

```
          :   JOSEPH LEA & AMY LEA  .......  Plaintiffs  )
  93      :                                              )
  ‾76     :                  vs                          )   In Covenant
          :                                              )
          :   JAMES RANDOLPH       .......  Defendant    )
```

The Plaintiffs not farther prosecuting; It is ordered that
this Suit be dismissed.

```
  J. H.   :   ANDREW PAUL  .......  Plaintiff   )
  94      :                                     )
  A. R.   :                  vs                 )   In Case
  77      :                                     )
          :   JOHN FEE   ........  Defendant    )
```

The Plaintiff not farther prosecuting; It is ordered that
this Suit be dismissed.

```
  J. H.   :   JAMES KING       .......  Plaintiff   )
  95      :                                          )
  Rhea    :                  vs                      )   In Case
  117     :                                          )
          :   WILLIAM McCORMACK   .......  Defendant )
```

This day came the parties by their Attornies, and the Plaintiff
having filed his declaration, the Defendant filed his Plea and the
issue being joined the trial thereof is referred until next Court.

```
  A. O.   :   WILLIAM COX     .......  Plaintiff    )
  96      :                                          )
  A. R.   :                  vs                      )   In Case
  Rhea    :                                          )
  175     :   WILLIAM TRIMBLE  .......  Defendant    )
```

This day came the parties by their Attornies, and the Plaintiff having filed his declaration the Defendant filed his plea, and
the issue being joined the trial thereof is referred 'till next Court.

```
  J. L.   :   THOMAS TAYLOR  .......  Plaintiff   )
  97      :                                        )
  Rhea    :                  vs                    )   A B
  103     :                                        )
          :   SAMUEL HYNMAN  .......  Defendant    )
```

This day came the parties by their attornies, and the
Plaintiff having filed his declaration the Defendant filed
his pleas and the issues being joined the trial thereof is
referred 'till next Court.

(Pg. 60)

```
Rhea   :   ROBERT BOYD  .......  Plaintiff  )
98     :                                    )
118    :          vs                        )   A B
       :                                    )
       :   DAVID WOOD   .......  Defendant  )
```

This day came the Plaintiff by his attorney and having
filed his Declaration, and the Defendant having been arrested
and not appearing though Solemnly called; on Motion of the Plaintiff by his attorney; It is considered by the Court that the
Plaintiff recover against the Defendant Such damages as he hath
Sustained by occasion of the Trepass, Assault and Battery; in the
declaration mentioned which damages are to be inquired of by a Jury
at the next Court.

```
A. R.  :   GEORGE SAMPLE  .......  Plaintiff  )
99     :                                      )
Rhea   :          vs                          )   In Covenant.
119    :                                      )
       :   JAMES GEALEY  .......  Defendant   )
```

This day came the parties by their attornies; and by their
Mutual consent and with the assent of the Court the cause is
continued until the next Court.

```
A. R.  :   GEORGE SAMPLE  .......  Plaintiff  )
100    :                                      )
Rhea   :          vs                          )   In Covenant
120    :                                      )
       :   JAMES GEALEY  .......  Defendant   )
```

This day came the parties by their Attornies; and by their
Mutual consent and with the assent of the Court the cause is
continued until next Court.

```
       :   JAMES GEALEY  .......  Plaintiff  )
101    :                                     )
78     :          vs                         )   In Case
       :                                     )
       :   JOHN COULTER  .......  Defendant  )
```

The Plaintiff not farther prosecuting it is ordered that
this Suit be dismissed.

```
Rhea   :   JOHN CHISOLM  .......  Plaintiff  )
102    :                                     )
176    :          vs                         )   In Case
       :                                     )
       :   JOHN CHISOM   .......  Defendant  )
```

This day came the Plaintiff by his Attorney, and having filed his declaration, the cause is continued until next Court.

```
        :   JOHN LYLE      ....... Plaintiff  )
103     :                                      )
79      :        vs                            )   In Case
        :                                      )
        :   WILLIAM BURK    ....... Defendant  )
```

The Plaintiff not farther prosecuting It is ordered that this Suit be dismissed.

```
Rhea    :   DANIEL WILSON    ....... Plaintiff  )
104     :                                        )
145     :        vs                              )   In Covt.
        :                                        )
        :   NICHOLAS HOLMES  ....... Defendant   )
```

This day came the Plaintiff by his Attorney and the Sheriff having returned that the Defendant is not to be found in his County; on motion of the Plaintiff by his Attorney a Judicial Attachment is awarded him against the Estate of the Said Defendant; returnable here at the next Court.

(Pg. 61)

```
A. R.   :   MATTHEW HOUSTON  ....... Plaintiff  )
105     :                                        )
121     :        vs                              )   In Case
        :                                        )
        :   ROBERT HOUSTON   ....... Defendant   )
```

This day came the Plaintiff by his Attorney, and the Sheriff having returned that the Defendant is not to be found in his County; on motion of the Plaintiff by his Attorney; and Alias Capias is awarded him returnable here at the next Court._____

```
Rhea    :   NATHANIEL and SAMUEL COWAN ... Plaintiffs )
106     :                                              )
A. R.   :              vs                               )  In Case.
122     :                                              )
        :   ROBERT THOMPSON           ... Defendant   )
```

This day came the Plaintiffs by their attorney and the Sheriff having returned that the Defendant is not to be found in his County; on motion of the Plaintiffs by their Attorney; an Alias Capias is awarded them returnable here at the next Court._____

```
A. R.   :   MARGARET BROWN ..... Plaintiff  )
107     :                                     )
L. B.   :        vs                           )   In Detinue
Rhea    :                                     )
123     :   WILLIAM HENRY  ..... Defendant   )
```

This day came the parties by their attornies and the Plaintiff having filed his declaration the Defendant filed his Plea and the issue being joined, the trial thereof is referred until next Court._____

Reece	:	PETER McNAMEE	....	Plaintiff	)	
108	:				)	
Rhea	:	vs			)	Original Attach-
104	:				)	ment
	:	ARTHUR COODY	....	Defendant	)	

This day came the Plaintiff by his Attorney & filed his declaration. And Titus Ogden Garnashee being first Sworn Saith he owes the Defendant nothing, that he hath not, nor had he at the time he was Summoned Garnashee any effects of the Defendants in his hands, that he knows of no debts due to; or effects belonging to the Defendant in the hands of any other person; And the Cause is continued 'till next Court.

	:	ANDREW THOMPSON	....	Plaintiff	)	
109	:				)	
80	:	vs			)	Appeal
	:				)	
	:	ROBERT RHEA	....	Defendant	)	

The Defendant Robert Rhea in his proper person appeared and agrees to pay the costs of this Suit, and upon this the Plaintiff not farther prosecuting It is ordered that this Suit be dismissed.

(Pg. 62)

A. R.	:	HUGH L. WHITE	:	Plaintiff	)	
110	:		:		)	
Rhea	:	vs	:		)	Appeal
81	:		:		)	
	:	ROBERT DOUGLASS	:	Defendant	)	

This day came the parties by their attornies & having been fully heard; It is considered by the Court that the Judgment of the Justice of Peace be confirmed; And that the Plaintiff recover against the Defendant Six dollars and his costs by him about his Suit in this behalf expended.

A. R.	:	SAMUEL PAXTON	....	Plaintiff	)	
111	:				)	
82	:	vs			)	Origl. Attd._____
	:				)	
	:	JAMES WALLACE &			)	
	:	JAMES WILLSON	....	Defendants	)	

Joseph Tedford, & James Tedford Garnashees being first Sworn Say; they owe the defendants nothing, that they have not nor had they, at the time they were Summoned Garnashees any effects of the Defendants in their hands, that they know of no debts due to; or effects belonging to the Defendants in the hands of any other person. The Plaintiff not farther prosecuting It is ordered that this Suit be dismissed, and that the Defendants do recovor against the Plaintiff their costs by them about their Suit in this behalf expended.

A. R. :   WILLIAM RICE .... Plaintiff)
112   :   )
Rhea :   vs   )   In Case
124   :   )
      :   JOHN THOMAS .... Defendant)

This day came the parties by their Attornies, and the Plaintiff having filed his Declaration the Defendant filed his Pleas and the Plaintiff his replication thereto and the Issues being joined the trial thereof is referred until next Court.

COURT ADJOURNED 'TILL COURT IN COURSE

(Pg. 63)

MONDAY AUGUST 5th 1793

At a Court of Pleas and Quarter Sessions began and held for the County of Knox, at the Court House in Knoxville on the first Monday of August 1793. present James White, George McNutt and John Sawyers esquires Justices & C. & C.

Robert Houston esquire Sheriff & C. returned that he had executed our Writ of Venire Facias to him directed upon the following persons, to Wit, John Singleton, John Cain, William McNutt Junior George Ewing, John Beaird, Paul Cunningham Senior, Warner Martin, John Dearmand Junior, John Dearmand, John Sterling, Senior, Moses Looney, Joseph Looney Senior, George Hays, Thomas Ritchy, Nicholas Nail, Nicholas Gibbs, Andrew McCampbell, William McCampbell, David Hailey, Moses Justice, George Sample, Jesse Bounds; Samuel Samples, Moses Brooks, William Reed, R. C., Thomas Inglis; Thomas Gillespie, William Hazlet, William Walker, Hugh Beard, Charles Bleakly, Robert Armstrong, Charles Diviny, Christian Pickle, Joseph Evans, David Eagleton, & Josias Gamble; Out of which Venire the following persons were elected a Grand Inquest for the Body of this County to Wit, Joseph Looney Senior Foreman, William McNutt, John Dearmond, Junior, Moses Brooks, John Cain, John Singleton, William Hazlet, John Sterling Senior, Robert Armstrong, Thomas Ritchy, Charles Diviny, Christian Pickle, George Hays, Thomas Inglis, Joseph Evans, William Walker, and Paul Cunningham, who have been Sworn received their charge and withdrew to enquire of their presentments;

(Venire)   (Grand Jury)

Rhea	:	WILLIAM COOPER .... Plaintiff	)	
	:	Father & next Friend of	)	
44	:	ELIZABETH COOPER	)	In Case, Words,
A. R.	:		)	Not guilty,
89	:	vs	)	Justification.
	:		)	
	:	THOMAS KEARNS ... Defendant	)	

This day came the parties by their Attorneys and thereupon came a Jury to Wit, Josias Gamble, William McCampbell, David Eagleton, William Murphy, Alexander McMillin, Major Lea, Peter Mowry, Samuel Crawford, John Dyer, Little Page Sims, William Regan, and John Lowe who being elected tried and Sworn the truth to Speak upon the Issues joined upon their Oath do Say that the Defendant is guilty of Speaking the Words in manner and form as the Plaintiff against him hath complained, and that the Words Spoken were of the Defendants own wrong, and without any Justification therefor (Pg. 64) and they do assess the Plaintiffs damages by occasion thereof to Three Dollars ~~besides his costs~~ Therefore it is considered by the Court; that the Plaintiff recover against the Defendant his Damages aforesaid in form aforesaid assessed and three Dollars for his costs by him about his Suit in this behalf expended. And the Defendant in Mercy & C.

Note, The Demurrer to the last Count of the Plaintiffs declaration that was argued and overruled at last Court after the Jury was Sworn in the above cause was again argued and Overruled.

Court adjourned 'till tomorrow 9 O'Clock.

TUESDAY AUGUST 6th 1793

Tuesday Morning August 6th 1793 Court met according to adjournment present James White, George McNutt, and John Sawyers esquires & C. & C.

Ordered that John Fothergill Turner, be bound apprentice to George Roulstone, to learn his Art and Mystery of printing and agreeably to the Said order Indentures are Signed and a Counterpart filed in the Office.

A. O.	:	SAMUEL STIRLING .... Plaintiff	)	
L. B.	:		)	
13	:	vs	)	In Case Words
J. H.	:		)	not guilty
E. D.	:	HUGH JOHNSTON &	)	Stat. Lim. &
87	:	WILLIAM JOHNSTON .... Defendants	)	Justification

This day came the parties by their Attornies and thereupon came a Jury to Wit; Andrew McCampbell William McCampbell, George Samples, James Anderson, Archibald Trimble, Robert Wood, William Coker, John Thomas, John Patterson, Little Page Sims, William Trimble, and James Milliken who being elected tried and Sworn the truth to Speak

upon the issue joined, upon their Oath do Say that the Defendants
are guilty of Speaking the Words in manner and form as the Plaintiff
against them hath complained within Six Months next before the
Suing out the Writ of Capias in this Suit; and that the words Spoken
were of the Defendants own Wrong and without any Justification
therefor; and they do assess the Plaintiffs damages by occasion
thereof to Four Dollars Sixty Six and two third Cents; Therefore
It is considered by the Court that the Plaintiff recover against the
(Pg. 65)   Defendants his damages aforesaid in form afore-said
assessed and Four dollars, Sixty Six and two third Cents for his
costs by him about his Suit in this behalf expended; And the Defendants in Mercy & C.

```
J. H.  :   WILLIAM HOUSTON  ....... Plaintiff )
33     :                                      )
88     :              vs                      )  In Covenant
       :                                      )
       :   JAMES CRESWELL  ........ Defendant )
```

This day came the plaintiff by his attorney and thereupon
came a Jury to Wit Andrew MCCampbell, William McCampbell, George
Samples, James Anderson, Archibald Trimble Robert Wood, William
Coker, John Thomas, John Patterson, Littlepage Sims, William
Trimble, and James Milliken, who being elected tried and Sworn
diligently to enquire of damages in this Suit upon their Oath
do Say that the Plaintiff hath Sustained damages by occasion of the
Defendants non performance of the Covenant in the Declaration
Mentioned to amount of Six Hundred Sixty Six dollars, Sixty Six
and two third Cents besides Costs, Therefore It is considered
by the Court that the Plaintiff recover against the Defendant his
damages aforesaid in form aforesaid assessed & his costs by him
about his Suit in this behalf expended; And the Said Defendant
in Mercy & C. And it is ordered that the One Thousand acres of
land upon which the attachment was levied be exposed to public
Sale as the law directs to Satisfy this Judgment.

```
J. H.  :   SOLOMON MARKS  ....... Plaintiff )
36     :                                     )
Rhea   :              vs                     )  In Case
252    :                                     )
       :   ROBERT KING  ....... Defendant    )
```

This day came the parties by their Attornies and by their mutual
consent and with the assent of the Court the Trial of the Issues
is referred until next Court.

```
A. R.  :   EDWARD HIGGINS       ....... Plaintiff )
41     :                                          )
Rhea   :              vs                          )  In Covenant
J. H.  :                                          )
113    :   SAMUEL WEAR et alias ....... Defendants )
```

This day came the parties by their attornies & the Defendants filed their pleas and the Issues being joined the Trial thereof is referred until next Court. ____

(Pg. 66)

```
A. R.  :   JOHN HACKETT &
48     :   ROBERT LIGGETT      ..... Plaintiffs  )
Rhea   :                                         )
114    :          vs                             )   In Case
       :                                         )
           DANIEL CARMICHAEL &                   )
           ALEXANDER CARMICHAEL..... Defts.      )
```

This day came the parties by their Attornies and by their Mutual consent and with the assent of the Court the trial of the issues is referred until next Court.____

```
Rhea   :   JOHN CHISOLM    ....... Plaintiff  )
49     :                                       )
662    :        vs                             )   In Case
       :                                       )
       :   RICHARD HAMILTON ....... Defendant  )
```

This day came the Plaintiff by his attorney and by his consent and with the assent of the Court the enquiry of damages is referred until next Court.____

```
Rhea   :   JAMES ARMSTRONG  ........ Plaintiff  )
53     :                                         )
L. B.  :        vs                               )   In Case
90     :                                         )
       :   WILLIAM HENRY    ....... Defendant    )
```

This day came the Plaintiff by his attorney and the Defendant in his proper person, and the parties agree that the Plaintiff hath Sustained Eighty one Dollars, twelve and half cents damages besides his costs by occasion of the Defendants Non performance of the assumption in the declaration mentioned; Therefore it is considered by the Court that the Plaintiff recover against the Defendant the damages agreed as aforesaid and his costs by him about his Suit in this behalf expended; And the Said Defendant in Mercy & C. and the Plaintiff agrees to Stay the execution of this Judgment three Months. ____

```
A. O.  :   WILLIAM COOPER
Rhea   :   Father & next Friend of
J. H.  :   ELIZABETH COOPER    ....... Plaintiff  )
56     :                                           )
Reece  :        vs                                 )   In Case
91     :                                           )   Words
           JAMES KEARNS        ........ Defendant  )
```

This day came the Plaintiff by his attorney and thereupon
came a Jury to Wit, Abram Ghormley, James Sterling, Andrew Kerr,
George Berry, Joseph Baker, John Low, Henry Stirling Samuel
Henderson, John Smith, Robert Patterson, Hugh Johnston and
John Wallace who being elected tried and Sworn diligently to
enquire of damages in this Suit upon their Oath do Say that
(Pg. 67) the Plaintiff hath Sustained one penny damage by
occasion of the Defendants Speaking of the Words in the Declara-
tion mentioned Therefore it is considered by the Court that the
Plaintiff recover against the Defendant his damage aforesaid in form
aforesaid assessed and One penny for his costs by him about his
Suit in this behalf expended. And the Said Defendant in Mercy & C.

J. H.	:	THOMAS BROWN	.... Plaintiff	)	
L. B.	:			)	
60	:	vs		)	T. V. A.
Rhea	:			)	
J. L.	:	LITTLE PAGE SIMS	.... Defendant	)	
172	:				

This day came the parties by their attornies and by their
mutual consent and with the assent of the Court the Trial of the
issue is referred until next Court._____

J. H.	:	THOMAS BROWN	.... Plaintiff	)	
L. B.	:			)	
61	:	vs		)	In Case
Rhea	:			)	Words
144	:	JOHN SHARKEY &		)	
	:	JEAN SHARKEY	.... Defendants	)	

This day came the parties by their attornies, and the argument
of the Demurrer, and the trial of the issues are referred 'till next
Court. Ordered that the Defendants pay the costs of this continuance.

J. H.	:	MARGARET BROWN	.... Plaintiff	)	
62	:			)	
Rhea	:	vs	....	)	In Case
92	:			)	
	:	JOHN SHARKEY &	.... Defendants	)	
		JEAN SHARKEY			

The Plaintiff not farther prosecuting it is ordered that this
Suit be dismissed.

Rhea	:	RICHARD RIDER	.... Plaintiff	)	
65	:			)	
115	:	vs		)	In Covenant
	:			)	
	:	JOHN RIDER	.... Defendant	)	

This day came the Plaintiff by his attorney and by his
consent and with the assent of the Court the enquiry of damages is
referred until next Court._____

ⱱ

COURT adjourned 'till tomorrow 9 O'Clock.

(Pg. 68)

WEDNESDAY AUGUST 7th 1793

Wednesday Morning August 7th 1793 Court met according to adjournment present John Adair, James Cozby & William Lowry esquires Justices & C. & C.

A. R.	:	JOHN PIPER and	.... Plaintiffs	)	
67	:	SARAH PIPER		)	
A. O.	:			)	
Rhea	:	vs		)	In Case, Words
93	:			)	not guilty
		WILLIAM COOPER	.... Defendant		Stat. Lim.
					Justification

This day came the parties by their Attornies and thereupon came a Jury to Wit; William McCampbell, George Sample, Josias Gamble, Peter Huffacre, William Bales, Little Page Sims, Robert Black, William Reid Major Lea, William Stookton, Elliot Grills and James Cunningham, who being elected tried and Sworn, the truth to Speak upon the issues Joined upon their Oath do Say that the Defendant is guilty of Speaking the Words in manner and form as the Plaintiffs against him hath complained within Six months next before the Suing out the Writ of Capias in this Suit, and that the Words Spoken were of the Defendants own Wrong and without Justification therefor and they do assess the Plaintiffs damages by occasion thereof to two Dollars; Therefore it is considered by the Court that the Plaintifffs recover against the Defendant their damages aforesaid, in form aforesaid assessed and two dollars for their costs by them about their Suit in this behalf expended; And the Said Defendant in Mercy & C.

Reece	:	WILLIAM RITCHEY	.... Plaintiff	)	
70	:			)	
L. B.	:	vs		)	In Detinue
94	:			)	
	:	DAVID LINDSEY	.... Defendant	)	

The Plaintiff not farther prosecuting It is ordered that this Suit be dismissed. Whereupon the Defendant acknowledges that he has received Satisfaction of the Plaintiff for his Attorney's fee; therefore as to So much the Said Plaintiff is acquitted.

A. R.	:	JOHN TODD	.... Plaintiff	)	
75	:			)	
A. O.	:	vs		)	In Case
173	:			)	
	:	JOHN McAMEY	.... Defendant	)	

This day came the parties by their Attornies, and the Trial
of the issue is referred until next Court. Ordered that the Plaintiff pay the costs of this continuance.

(Pg. 69)

A. O.	:	JOHN RUSSELL .... Plaintiff	)	
76	:		)	
Rhea	:	vs	)	In Case
95	:		)	
	:	JAMES ANDERSON .... Defendant	)	

This day came the Plaintiff by his attorney; and the Defendant
in his proper person relinguishing his former plea, the parties agree
that the Plaintiff has Sustained Forty Dollars damages besides his
costs; by occasion of the Defendants nonperformance of the assumption in the declaration mentioned; Therefore it is considered by the
Court that the Plaintiff recover against the Defendant his damages
agreed as aforesaid; and his costs by him about his Suit in this behalf expended; And the Said Defendant in Mercy & C. And the Plaintiff agrees to Stay the execution of this Judgment three Months.

J. H.	:	GEORGE BOWERMAN .... Plaintiff	)	
77	:		)	
A. R.	:	vs	)	T. V. A.
96	:		)	
	:	JOHN ISH .... Defendant	)	

This day came the parties by their Attornies and thereupon
came a Jury to Wit, Joseph Kearns, John Lacky, Samuel Thompson,
George Berry, Robert Blackburn, John Wallace, David Scott, James
McElwee, Joseph Vance, John Patterson, Matthew Kerr, and John McAmey;
who being elected tried and Sworn the truth to Speak upon the issues
joined upon their Oath do Say, that the Defendant is guilty of the
Trespass, Assault and Battery in manner and form as the Plaintiff
against him hath complained and that the Said Tresspass Assault and
Battery, was of the Defendants own wrong and without any Such cause
as in pleading he hath alledged, and they do assess the Plaintiffs
damages by occasion thereof to Eight Dollars besides his costs
Therefore it is considered by the Court that the Plaintiff recover
against the Defendant the damages aforesaid in form aforesaid assessed and his costs by him about his Suit in this behalf expended; And
the Said Defendant in Mercy & C.

A. O.	:	CHARLES McCLOUD .... Plaintiff	)	
78	:		)	
97	:	vs	)	In Case enquiry
	:		)	
	:	WILLIAM WALKER .... Defendant	)	

This day came the Plaintiff by his Attorney and thereupon
came a Jury to Wit, William Hitchcock, Charles Regan, Joseph
Beaird, Samuel Stirling, William Cooper, Andrew Paul, Henry

Sterling, William Lea, William Trimble, Thomas Kearns, Joseph Lea, &
(Pg. 70)   James Campbell who being elected tried and Sworn
diligently to enquire of damages in this Suit upon their Oaths do
Say that the Plaintiff hath Sustained Seven dollars, Sixty Seven Cents
damages besides his Costs by occasion of the Defendants nonperformance
of the Assumption in the Declaration mentioned;   Therefore it is considered by the Court that the Plaintiff recover against the Defendant
his damages aforesaid in form aforesaid assessed and his costs by
him about his Suit in this behalf expended; And the Said Defendant
in Mercy & C.

A. O.	:	JACOB TARWATER		...... Plaintiff	)	
Rhea	:		)		)	
81	:	vs	)		)	In
J. H.	:		)		)	Covenant
A. R.	:	ANDREW PAUL Admr. of	)		)	
116	:	JAMES PAUL deceased	)	..... Defendant	)	

This day came the parties by their Attornies and by their
mutual consent, and with the assent of the Court the Trial of the
issues is referred 'till next Court.

Rhea	:	JOHN FEE		Plaintiff	)	In Case
82	:				)	Non Assum-
J. H.	:	vs			)	psit,
A. R.	:				)	accord and
174	:	ANDREW PAUL Admr. of	)		)	Satisfaction,
		JAMES PAUL deceased	)....... Defendant		)	release, no
						assets,

This day came the parties by their Attornies and thereupon
came a Jury to Wit, William Hitchcock, Charles Regan, Joseph Beaird,
Samuel Sterling, William Cooper, James Scott, Henry Sterling,
William Lea, William Trimble, Thomas Kearns, Joseph Lea, and
James Campbell who being elected tried and Sworn the truth to Speak
upon the issues joined upon their Oath do Say the Defendants
intestate did assume upon himself in manner and form as the Plaintiff
against him hath complained, and that the Said Intestate in his life
time or the Said Defendant Since the Death of his Instestate, hath
not made accord & Satisfaction, nor hath the Defendant a release as in
his pleading the Said Defendant hath alledged, and they do assess the
Plaintiffs damages by occasion of the Nonperformance of the assumption
in the Declaration mentioned to Sixty Dollars besides his costs;
Whereupon the Defendant entered a rule to Shew cause why the Said
Verdict Should be Set aside and a new trial granted, which was argued
and Granted.

(Pg. 71)

A. R.　：　JOHN WALLACE　.......　Plaintiff　)
141　：　　　　　　　　　　　　　　　　　　　)
255　：　　　　　　vs　　　　　　　　　　　　) Original Attach-
　　：　　　　　　　　　　　　　　　　　　　) ment,. Case
　　：　JAMES BRIANT　.......　Defendant　)

　　Barclay McGhee　Garnashee　being first Sworn, Saith he is indebted
to the Defendant, **Five Shillings** and three pence　Virginia currency
that he hath not, nor had he at the time he was Summoned Garnashee
any effects of the Defendants in his hands, that he knows of no
other debts due to, or effects belonging to the Defendant in the
hands of any other person.

　　Robert Houston　Garnashee, being first Sworn Saith he oweth
the Defendant nothing　that he hath not, nor had he, at the time
he was Summoned Garnashee, any effects of the Defendants in his
hands, that he knows of no debts due to, or effects belonging to the
Defendant in the hands of any other person;

　　James Tedford, and John Franklin　who were Summoned to appear
here to declare an oath, what they are Severally indebted to the
Defendant, or what effects they have, or had in their hands, at the
time they were Summoned Garnashees; and what Debts they know to be
due to, or effects belonging to the Defendant in the hands of any
other person; and who that Person is;＿＿＿　Being Solemnly called
came not, therefore it is considered by the Court, that the Plaintiff
recover against the Said James Tedford and John Franklin Severally
the amount of the Plaintiffs demand against the Said Defendant, and
also his costs; unless they appear at our next Court; and Shall
Shew Sufficient cause why this Judgment Should not be confirmed and
it is ordered a Scire Facias issue against them.＿＿＿

　　Abraham Ghormly appeared and produced a Commission from Governor
Blount, by which it appears that he is appointed a Justice of the
Peace for the County who took an Oath to Support the Constitution
of the United States and also the Oath　　Office, and took his Seat
accordingly.＿＿＿

　　　　Court adjourned 'till tomorrow 9 O'Clock.

(Pg. 72)

　　　　　　　　THURSDAY　AUGUST　8th　1793

　　Thursday Morning　August 8th　1793　Court met according to
adjournment　present　James White, John Adair, and John Sawyers
esquires　Justices & C. & C.＿＿＿

A. O.   :   WILLIAM COOPER .... Plaintiff)
83   :   )
L. B.   :   vs   )   In Case
98   :   )   Non Assumpsit
          :   GODFREY ANTRIM .... Defendant)

This day came the parties by their Attornies and thereupon
came a Jury to Wit;. Andrew Paul, William Davidson, Thomas Eldridge,
Archibald McKilip, James McElwee, Thomas Rogers, Annanias McCoy,
Major Lea, Jacob Tarwater, Richard Hail, David Walker, and William
Snodgrass who being elected tried and Sworn the truth to Speak upon
the issue joined upon their oath do Say that the Defendant did not
assume upon himself in manner and form as the plaintiff against him
hath complained, as in pleading he hath alledged; Therefore it is
considered by the Court that the Plaintiff take nothing by his Bill
but for his false clamour be in mercy & C. And the Defendant go hence
without day and recover against the Plaintiff his costs by him about
his defence in this behalf expended.

Rhea   :   JOHN LOWRY   .... Plaintiff)
84   :   )
J. H.   :   vs   )   In Covenant
A. R.   :   )   Covenant per-
99   :   ROBERT BLACKBURN   )   formance
          :   &   .... Defendants)
                BENJAMIN BLACKBURN

This day came the parties by their Attornies and thereupon
came a Jury to Wit; George Sample, George Patterson, Jonathan
Douglass, Robert Given, Richard Low, Samuel Hindman, John Lea, William
Ritchy, John Chism, Alexander Richey, John Patterson, and Taylor
Townsend, who being elected tried & Sworn the truth to Speak upon
the issue joined upon their oath do Say the Defendants hath not performed the Covenant in the Declaration mentioned, but hath broken
the Same in manner and form as the Plaintiff against them hath complained, and they do assess the Plaintiffs damages by occasion thereof to Twenty dollars, besides his costs; Therefore It is considered
by the Court that the Plaintiff recover against the Defendants his
damages aforesaid in form aforesaid assessed, and his costs by him
about his Suit in this behalf expended. And the Said Defendants in
Mercy & C.

Note, The Defendants prayed a new trial, but withdrew their Motion.

(Pg. 73)

Rhea   :   DAVID SCOTT .... Plaintiff)
85   :   )
A. R.   :   vs   )   In Case
100   :   )
          :   JOHN WALLACE .... Defendant)

The Plaintiff not farther prosecuting It is ordered that this
Suit be Dismissed.

This day came the parties by their attornies and thereupon came a Jury to Wit Michael Foster, William Trimble, William Lea, Archibald McKilip, James McElwee, Thomas Rogers, Ananias McCoy, Major Lea, Jacob Tarwater, Richard Hail, David Walker and Archibald Rhea who being elected tried and Sworn the truth to Speak upon the issue joined upon their Oath do Say the writing obligatory declared on is the deed of the Defendant in manner and form as the Plaintiff against him hath complained & they do assess the Plaintiffs damages to Thirty two dollars besides his costs; Whereupon the Plaintiff entered a rule to Shew cause why a new trial Should be granted; Which was argued and Granted. Ordered that the Plaintiff pay the costs of the attendance of Archibald Taylor, a Witness on his Behalf.

(Pg 74)

Rhea	:	JOHN CHISOLM .... Plaintiff	)	
90	:		)	
J. H.	:	vs	)	In Case
102	:		)	Performance
	:	MAJOR LEA .... Defendant	)	

This day came the parties by their attornies and thereupon came a Jury to Wit, George Sample, George Patterson, Jonathan Douglass, Samuel Hindman, William Ritchy, Alexander Ritchy, John Patterson, Taylor Townsend, Robert Black, Nathaneil Cowan, John Thomas, and Jonathan Darden; who being elected tried and Sworn, the truth to Speak upon the issue joined upon their Oath do Say that the Defendant hath performed the assumption in the Declaration mentioned as in pleading he hath alledged   Therefore it is considered by the Court that the Plaintiff take nothing by his Bill, but for his false clamour be in Mercy & C. And the Defendant go hence without day, and recover against the Plaintiff his costs by him about his defence in this behalf expended. From which Judgment the Plaintiff prays an appeal to the next Superior Court of Law & C. Which motion is withdrawn.

William McBroom, Joseph West, William Aclin, & William Cowan, being Summoned to attend this Court this day as Jurymen, were Solemnly called, but came not; Therefore it is considered by the Court, that for their Contempt, they be Severally fined One Dollar and fifty Cents and may be taken.

Court adjourned until tomorrow 9 O'Clock.

FRIDAY AUGUST 9th 1793

Friday Morning, August 9th 1793   Court met according to adjournment   present John Sawyers, John Adair, and George McNutt, esquires Justices & C. & C.

```
J. H.   :   JAMES KING        ....... Plaintiff )
95      :                                       )
Rhea    :            vs                         )   In Case
117     :                                       )
        :   WILLIAM MCCORMICK ....... Defendant )
```

This day came the parties by their attornies and by their Mutual consent and with the assent of the Court the trial of the Issue is referred 'till next Court.

(Pg. 75)

```
A. O.   :   WILLIAM COX       ....... Plaintiff )
96      :                                       )
A. R.   :            vs                         )   In Case
Rhea    :                                       )
175     :   WILLIAM TRIMBLE   ....... Defendant )
```

This day came the parties by their attornies and by their consent and with the assent of their Court the trial of the Issue is referred until next Court.

```
J. S.   :   THOMAS TAYLOR     ....... Plaintiff )
97      :                                       )
Rhea    :            vs                         )   A B
103     :                                       )
        :   SAMUEL HINDMAN    ....... Defendant )
```

This day came the parties in their proper persons, and they agree to pay the costs mutually between them. The Plaintiff not farther prosecuting; It is ordered that this Suit be dismissed.

```
Rhea    :   ROBERT BOYD       ....... Plaintiff )
98      :                                       )
118     :            vs                         )   A B
        :                                       )
        :   DAVID WOOD        ....... Defendant )
```

This day came the Plaintiff by his Attorney and by his consent and with the assent of the Court an enquiry of damages is referred until next Court.

```
A. R.   :   GEORGE SAMPLE     ....... Plaintiff )
99      :                                       )
Rhea    :            vs                         )   In Covenant
119     :                                       )
        :   JAMES GAILEY      ....... Defendant )
```

This day came the parties by their Attornies and by their Mutual consent and with the assent of the Court the cause is continued 'till next Court. _____

```
A. R.    :   GEORGE SAMPLE   ....... Plaintiff )
100      :                                     )
Rhea     :           vs                        )   In Covenant
120      :                                     )
         :   JAMES GAILEY    ....... Defendant )
```

This day came the parties by their Attornies & by their Mutual consent & with the assent of the Court the cause is continued until next Court.

```
Rhea     :   JOHN CHISOLM    ....... Plaintiff )
         :                                     )
102      :           vs                        )   In Case
176      :                                     )
         :   JOHN CHISOM     ....... Defendant )
```

This day came the Plaintiff by his Attorney and by his consent and with the assent of the Court the cause is continued until next Court. _____

(Pg. 76)

```
Rhea     :   DANIEL WILLSON  ....... Plaintiff )
104      :                                     )
145      :           vs                        )   In Cov't.
         :                                     )
         :   NICHOLAS HOLMES ....... Defendant )
```

On Motion of the Plaintiff by his attorney an Alias Judicial attachment is awarded him against the Estate of the Defendant returnable here at the next Court.

```
A. R.    :   MATTHEW HOUSTON  ....... Plaintiff )
105      :                                      )
121      :           vs                         )   In Case
         :                                      )
         :   ROBERT HOUSTON   ....... Defendant )
```

The Defendant in his proper person appeared and agreed to pay the costs of this Suit, and upon this the Plaintiff prays that his costs and Charges by him about his Suit in this behalf expended may be adjudged to him; Therefore it is considered by the Court that the Plaintiff recover against the Said Defendant his costs by him about his Suit in this behalf expended. And the Said Plaintiff not farther prosecuting It is ordered that this Suit be dismissed.

Stay Execution three months.

```
Rhea     :   NATHANIEL & SAMUEL COWAN ..... Plaintiff )
106      :                                             )
A. R.    :           vs                                )   In Case
122      :                                             )
         :   ROBERT THOMPSON          ..... Defendant )
```

This day came the parties by their attornies and the Plaintiffs having filed their Declaration the Defendant filed his Plea, and the issue being joined the trial thereof is referred untill next Court.

A. R.	:	MARGARET BROWN .... Plaintiff)	
107	:	)	
L. R.	:	vs)	In Detinue
Rhea	:	)	
123	:	WILLIAM HENRY .... Defendant)	

This day came the parties by their Attornies and by their mutual consent and with the assent of the Court the Trial of the issue is referred until Thursday of next Court.

Reece	:	PETER MCNAMEE .... Plaintiff)	
108	:	)	
Rhea	:	vs)	Original
104	:	)	Attachment
	:	ARTHUR COODY .... Defendant)	

The Plaintiff not farther prosecuting; It is ordered that this Suit be dismissed._____

(Pg. 77)

A. R.	:	WILLIAM RICE .... Plaintiff)	
112	:	)	
Rhea	:	vs)	In Case
124	:	)	
	:	JOHN THOMAS .... Defendant)	

This day came the parties by their attornies & by their mutual consent and with the assent of the Court the trial of the Issues is referred until next Court.

11	:	UNITED STATES .... Plaintiffs)	
558	:	)	
	:	vs)	Petit Larceny
	:	)	
	:	ZAPHER TANNERY .... Defendant)	

This day came John Rhea esquire Solicitor for the County and the Sheriff having returned the Defendant not to be found in his County an Alias Capias is awarded to Hawkins County returnable here at the next Court.

236 . 15	:	Ordered that Process issue against Christina
559 . 16	:	Amerine, and James Bunch to cause them to appear at
	:	the next Court; to answer the Indictments found
	:	against them by the Grand Jury.

14 :   UNITED STATES .... Plaintiff)
202 :
    :   vs   )   Presentment
    :
    :   MICHAEL FOSTER .... Defendant)

This day came John Rhea esquire Solicitor for the County and the Sheriff having returned the Defendant is not to be found in his County; an Alias Capias is awarded against the Defendant returnable here at the next Court.

Ordered that the Sheriff do Summons the following persons to attend at the next Superior Court as Jurors to Wit._____

Robert Armstrong, George McNutt, John Chisolm, James White, Jeremiah Jack, John Adair, David Campbell, John Kain, Moses Brooks, Thomas Gillespie, Major Lea, John Sawyers, David Craig, John Houston, Alexander Kelley, William Hamilton, Thomas McCullough, William Lowry, James Houston, Samuel Newell, James Cozby, William Wallace, Joseph Black & Samuel McGaughery.

Ordered that Samuel Cowan, John McNutt & Hugh Dunlapp, be patrollers for the District of Captn Stones Company and be cited by a Constable to appear before a Justice of the Peace to take the Oath prescribed by Law._____

(Pg. 78)

Peter McNamee produced a Commission from Governor Blount, by which it appears that he is appointed a Constable for this County, who hath entered into Bond with Securities with condition for the faithfull discharge of the duties of his office who hath been Sworn as the law directs;

J. Rhea :   JOHN CHISOLM   .... Plaintiff)
113   :
A. O.   :   vs   )   In Case
146   :
        :   JOSEPH SEVIER .... Defendant)

This day came the parties by their Attorneys; and the Plaintiff having filed his Declaration the Defendant filed his Plea and the issue being joined the trial thereof is referred until next Court.___

J. Rhea :   JOHN SOMMERVILLE .... Plaintiff)
114   :
A. O.   :   vs   )
125   :
        :   JOSEPH SEVEIR   .... Defendant)

This day came the parties by their attorneys; and the Plaintiff having filed his Declaration, the Defendant filed his plea and the issue being joined the trial thereof is referred untill next Court.

A. R. : ROBERT THOMPSON .... Plaintiff)
115   :   )
253   :   vs   ) In Case
Rhea   :   )
       : JOHN MCALLISTER .... Defendant)

    This day came the Plaintiff by his attorney and the Sheriff having returned that the Defendant is not to be found in his County on Motion of the Plaintiff by his attorney an Alias Capias is awarded him returnable here at the next Court.

L. B. : GODFREY ANTRIM .... Plaintiff)
116   :   )
A. O. :   vs   ) In Case
126   :   )
       : WILLIAM COOPER .... Defendant)

    This day came the parties by their Attornies and the Plaintiff having filed his declaration the Defendant filed his plea and the issue being joined the trial thereof is referred 'till next Court._____

J. L. : JAMES W. LACKEY .... Plaintiff)
117   :   )
A. O. :   vs   ) In Case
127   :   )
       : BENJAMIN BLACKBURN .... Defendant)

    This day came the parties by their Attornies and the Plaintiff having filed his declaration, the Defendant filed his Plea and the issue being joined the trial thereof is referred until next Court.___

J. Rhea : ALEXANDER CARMICHAEL ..... Plaintiff)
118   :   )
A. O.   :   vs   ) In Case
254   :   )
        : JOSEPH SEVEIR   ..... Defendant)

    This day came the parties by their Attornies & the Plaintiff having filed his declaration, the Defendant filed his plea & issue being joined the trial thereof is referred 'till next Court.

(Pg. 79)

J. Rhea : DAVID SMITH   .... Plaintiff)
119   :   )
147   :   vs   ) In Case
        :   )
        : DAVID FORRESTER .... Defendant)

    This day came the Plaintiff by his attorney, and the Sheriff having returned that the Defendant is not to be found in his County on motion of the Plaintiff by his attorney an alias Capias is awarded him returnable here at the next Court._____

```
D. G.   :   SAMUEL EVANS      ....... Plaintiff )
120     :                                        )
128     :            vs                          )   In Case
        :                                        )
        :   DAVID FORRESTER  ....... Defendant   )
```

This day came the Plaintiff by his attorney, and the Sheriff having returned that the Defendant is not to be found in his County on motion of the Plaintiff by his attorney an Alias Capias is awarded him returnable here at the next Court.

```
A. O.   :   JACOB SMELSER  ....... Plaintiff )
121     :                                     )
Rhea    :            vs                       )   In Covenant
129     :                                     )
        :   THOMAS KING    ....... Defendant  )
```

This day came the parties by their attornies & the Plaintiff having filed his declaration the Defendant prays Oyer of the Writing obligatory aforesaid and to him it is read & C. he prays likewise Oyer of the condition of the Same Writing and to him it is read in these Words to Wit, "The Condition of the above obligation is Such that if the above bound Thomas King do make and convey unto the Said Jacob Smelser his heirs & C. a good and Sufficient State title to Six hundred acres of land lying nearly opposite to the head of one prong of Turkey Creek on the waters of clinch, to be land of a good quality well timbered and watered, the Title to the aforesaid land to be made as Soon as a Title can be obtained from the State of North Carolina then this obligation to be void, or else to remain in full force power and virtue in law."... which being read and heard, the Said Defendant filed his pleas and the issues being joined the trial thereof is referred until next Court.

```
J. Rhea :   JOHN WHITE     ....... Plaintiff )
122     :                                     )   In Case
148     :            vs                       )
        :                                     )
        :   JOHN THOMAS   ....... Defendant   )
```

This day came the Plaintiff by his attorney and having filed his declaration the cause is continued is continued untill next Court.____

(Pg. 80)

```
J. Rhea :   SAMUEL COWAN &    ) ..... Plaintiff )
123     :   NATHANIEL COWAN   )                 )
H. L.   :                                       )
149     :            vs                         )   In Debt
        :                                       )
            JAMES CALLISON       ..... Defendant )
```

This day came the parties by their attorneys and the Plaintiffs having filed their declaration the Defendant filed a plea in abatement and the argument thereof is referred until next Court.

J. H. :	SOLOMON MARKS .... Plaintiff)	
124 :	)	
Rhea :	vs)	In Debt
150 :	)	
:	WILLIAM ROSEBERRY....... Defendant)	

This day came the parties by their Attorneys and by their mutual consent and with the assent of the Court the Cause is continued 'till next Court.

:	JOSEPH BAKER .... Plaintiff)	
125 :	)	
106 :	vs)	In Case
:	)	
:	STEPHEN DUNCAN .... Defendant)	

The Defendant in his proper person appeared and agrees to pay the costs of this Suit and upon this the Plaintiff prays that his costs and charges by him about his Suit in this behalf expended be adjudged to him; Therefore It is considered by the Court that the Plaintiff recover against the Said Defendant his costs by him about his Suit in this behalf expended. And the Said Defendant in Mercy & C. And the Plaintiff not farther prosecuting, It is ordered that this Suit be dismissed.

H. L. :	JOHN STONE .... Plaintiff)	
126 :	)	
130 :	vs)	In Case
:	)	
:	JAMES MCCLAIN .... Defendant)	

This day came the Plaintiff by his attorney and having filed his declaration, and the Defendant having been arrested, and not appearing though Solemnly called; On motion of the Plaintiff by his attorney It is considered by the Court that the Plaintiff recover against the Defendant Such damages as he hath Sustained by occasion of the Defendants Nonperformance of the assumption in the Declaration mentioned, which damages are to be enquired of by a Jury at the next Court.

Rhea :	SAMUEL HINDMAN .... Plaintiff)	
127 :	)	
H. L. :	vs)	In Case
131 :	)	
:	GEORGE ROULSTONE .... Defendant)	

This day came the parties by their attorneys & the Plaintiff having filed his declaration the Defendant filed his pleas and the issues being joined the trial thereof is referred 'till next Court.

(Pg. 81)

```
H. L.   :   JOSEPH WEST   ....... Plaintiff )
128     :                                   )
Rhea    :           vs                      )   In Case
105     :                                   )
        :   JOSEPH JEANS  ....... Defendant )
```

This day came the parties by their Attorneys & the Plaintiff having filed his Declaration, the Defendant filed a plea in abatement, which was argued; And because it Seems to the Court that the Said Plea and the matter therein contained are not Sufficient in law to abate the Plaintiffs writ; It is considered by the Court that the plea aforesaid be overruled: From which Judgment the Defendant prays an appeal to the next Superior Court of law to be holden for the District of Hamilton at the Court House in Knoxville hath filed his reasons, and entered into Bond with Alexander Carmichael and John Chisolm with condition for the prosecution of the Said appeal with effect which appeal is allowed. _____

```
J. Rhea :   BARNEY HAINEY  ....... Plaintiff )
129     :                                    )
A. R.   :           vs                       )   In Case
132     :                                    )
        :   DAVID WALKER  ,..... Defendant   )
```

This day came the parties by their Attorneys; and the Plaintiff having filed his declaration the Defendant filed his Plea and the issue being joined the trial thereof is referred until next Court.

```
D. G.   :   JAMES STEWART  ....... Plaintiff )
130     :                                    )
133     :           vs                       )   In Case
        :                                    )
        :   PETER MCNAMEE  ....... Defendant )
```

This day came the Plaintiff by his attorney & having filed his declaration, the Defendant also came in his proper person, and the parties agree that the Plaintiff hath Sustained damages by occasion of the Defendants Nonperformance of the assumption in the declaration mentioned to Forty eight Dollars, Sixty Six and two third Cents besides his costs. Therefore it is considered by the Court that the Plaintiff recover against the Defendant the Damages agreed as aforesaid and his costs by him about his Suit in this behalf expended. And the Said Defendant in Mercy & C. And the Plaintiff agrees to Stay the Execution of this Judgment three Months.

(Pg. 82)

```
J. Rhea :   HIS EXCELLENCY  THE GOVERNOR & C. ... Plaintiff )
131     :                                                   )
107     :                        vs                         )   In DEBT
        :                                                   )
        :   BENJAMIN M. WALLACE .................. Defendant )
```

The Plaintiff not farther prosecuting; It is ordered that this
Suit be dismissed._____ Note, no Costs Demanded._____

```
A. O.  :   ANNE MILLS        ....... Plaintiff  )
132    :                                        )
J. H.  :          vs                            )   In Case
177    :                                        )
       :   ANDREW PAUL & C.   ....... Defendant )
```

This day came the Plaintiff by his attorney and the Sheriff having
returned that the Defendant is not to be found in his County, on motion
of the Plaintiff by his attorney an Alias Capias is awarded him returnable here at the next Court.

```
A. O.  :   JOHN HUTCHISON    ....... Plaintiff  )
133    :                                        )
J. H.  :          vs                            )   In Case
567    :                                        )
       :   ANDREW PAUL & C.  ....... Defendant  )
```

This day came the Plaintiff by his Attorney and the Sheriff
having returned that the Defendant is not to be found in his County;
On motion of the Plaintiff by his Attorney an Alias Capias is awarded
him returnable here at the next Court._____

```
J. H.  :   ANDREW PAUL & C.  ....... Plaintiff  )
134    :                                        )
J. L.  :          vs                            )   In Case.
L. B.  :                                        )   Trover
178    :   JOSEPH WEAR        ....... Defendant )
```

This day came the parties by their Attorneys and the Plaintiff
having filed his Declaration the Defendant filed his plea and the
issue being joined the trial thereof is referred untill next Court. __

```
S. M.  :   JAMES ALLISON     ....... Plaintiff  )
135    :                                        )
J. H.  :          vs                            )   In Covenant
L. B.  :                                        )
356    :   ABRAHAM SWAGERTY,  ....... Defendant )
```

This day came the Plaintiff by his Attorney and the Sheriff
having returned that the Defendant is not to be found in his County.
On Motion of the Plaintiff by his attorney an Alias Capias is awarded him returnable here at the next Court.

```
       :   WILLIAM COOPER  Father & )
       :   next Friend of           )  ....... Plaintiff  )
       :   ELIZABETH COOPER         )                     )
       :                            )                     )
156    :          vs                )                     )   In Case
L. B.  :                            )                     )   Words
108    :   JAMES SMITH ..................... Defendant    )
```

The Plaintiff not farther prosecuting; It is ordered that this
Suit be dismissed; and that the Plaintiff pay to the Defendant his costs

(Pg. 83)

	:	JOHN FRYAR	....	Plaintiff	)	
137	:				)	
A. O.	:	vs			)	Appeal
151	:				)	
	:	WILLIAM SNEED	....	Defendant	)	

This day came the parties by their Attornies and by their
mutual consent and with the assent of the Court the Cause is continued until next Court.

H. L.	:	JAMES GAILEY		....	Plaintiff	)	
138	:					)	
	:	vs				)	In Case
D. G.	:					)	
152	:	JOHN LINNEY &	)	....	Defendants	)	
		ROBERT CUSICK	)				

This day came the parties by their attorneys and the Plaintiff
having filed his declaration the Defendants filed their plea and the
issue being joined the trial thereof is referred 'till next Court.

A. O.	:	WILLIAM LOWRY	....	Plaintiff	)	
	:				)	
139	:	vs			)	Appeal
A. R.	:				)	
134	:	WILLIAM REGAN	....	Defendant	)	

This day came the parties by their Attorneys and by their
mutual consent and with the assent of the Court, the cause is
continued untill next Court.

J. L.	:	WILLIAM LOWRY	....	Plaintiff	)	
140	:				)	
	:	vs			)	In Case
A. O.	:				)	
205	:	GEORGE WOODS	....	Defendant	)	

This day came the parties by their Attornies, and the Plaintiff
having filed his declaration the Defendant filed his Plea and the
issue being joined the Trial thereof is referred 'till next Court.

A. R.	:	JOHN WALLACE	....	Plaintiff	)	
141	:				)	
255	:	VS			)	Original
	:				)	Attachment,
	:	JAMES BRIANT	....	Defendant	)	Case

This day came the Plaintiff by his attorney and having filed his
declaration the cause is continued 'till next Court.

```
Rhea    :   DAVID CRAIG    ....... Plaintiff ·)
142     :                                    )
J. H.   :          vs                        )  Original
179     :                                    )    attachment
        :   SOLOMON MARKS ....... Defendant  )
```

Samuel Newell & Samuel Acklin of this County
(Pg. 84) came into Court, and undertake for the Defendant that
in case he Shall be cast in this Suit, he Shall Satisfy and pay the
condemnation, or render his body to prison, in execution for the Same,
or that they the Said Samuel Newell and Samuel Acklin will do it for
him. Whereupon the Defendant filed a Plea in abatement._____

Note, The papers of this Suit were handed into the Office
the first day of the term, by Benjamin Pride and taken out again
and returned   "Executed by Benj. Pride.

COURT adjourned 'till COURT in COURSE.

MONDAY NOVEMBER 4th 1793

Monday November 4th 1793

At a Court of Pleas and Quarter sessions began
and held for the County of Knox, at the Court House in Knoxville
on the first Monday of November 1793, present James White,
John Evans, and William Hamilton esquires Justices & C & C.

Robert Houston esquire Sheriff & C. returned that he
had executed our Writ of Veniro Facias to him directed upon the
following persons to Wit; Charles Regan, Alexander Cunningham,
Andrew Evans, Robert McAmey, William Lea, Joseph Lea, Archibald
McKillip, James McElwee, Samuel Stirling, John Gamble, Samuel
Love, Joseph Brooks, James Robertson, Daniel McDonald, James
Brock, Alexander Campbell, James Gealy, Abner Witt, Archibald Trimble,
John McAmey, William Doake, Nicholas Bartlett, John Craig, John
Sherrell, and John Bradly.

Out of which Venire the following persons were elected a grand
Inquest for the body of this County to Wit; Andrew Evans, Fore-
man, Charles Regan, Alexander Cunningham, William Lea, Joseph Lea,
James McElwee, Samuel Love, Joseph Brooks, Dan'l. McDonald, James
Brock, Alexander Campbell, James Gealey, Abner Witt, Archibald
Trimble, and John McAmey, who have been Sworn received their
charge and withdrew to enquire of their presentments.

(Pg. 85)

```
L. B.   '   STEPHEN RENFRO  ......, Plaintiff  )
143     '                                      )
135     '          vs                          )  In Trover
        '                                      )
        '   JAMES SPENCE    ....... Defendant  )
```

This day came the Plaintiff by his Attorney and the
Defendant in his proper person acknowledges Service of the Writ
and by their Mutual consent, and with the assent of the Court
also came a Jury to Wit, John Craig, John Sherrell, John Bradly
John Wood, Joseph Wear, James Stirling, Jonathan Douglass,
Matthew Kerr, Michael Foster, David Mitchell, John Crawford
and William Reed; who being elected tried and Sworn well and
truly to try the matter of controversey between the parties upon
their Oath do Say they find for the Plaintiff and assess his damages to Forty Dollars besides his costs; Therefore it is considered
by the Court that the Plaintiff recover against the Defendant his
damages aforesaid in form aforesaid assessed and his costs by him
about his Suit in this behalf expended. And the Said Defendant in
Mercy & C.

William Kerr produced a Commission from Governor Blount,
by which it appears that he is appointed a Constable for this
County, who entered into Bond with Matthew Kerr and Jonathan
Douglass his Securities in the Sum of Six hundred and twenty
five dollars; with condition for the faithful discharge of the
duties of his office; who hath been Sworn as the law directs.

Court adjourned 'till tomorrow 9 O'clock.

TUESDAY NOVEMBER 5th 1793.

Tuesday Morning November 5th 1793 Court met according to
Adjournment present James White, John Evans; and William
Hamilton esquires Justices & C. & C.

A. R.	'	EDWARD HIGGINS .... Plaintiff)	
41	'		)
Rhea	'	vs	) In Covenant
J. H.	'		)
113	'	SAMUEL WEAR and	)
		WILLIAM LOWRY Exors. of	)
		JAMES WALKER deceased	) ...... Defendants)
		JAMES W. LACKEY and	)
		JOHN COWAN	)

This day came the parties by their Attornies and thereupon came
a Jury to Wit, Nicholas Robertson, John   (Pg. 86)   Kearnes,
John Sharkey, Thomas Cox, Joseph Cowan, John Wear, John Craig,
John Sherrell, John Erwin, John Williams, John Conelly, and James
Williams who being elected tried and Sworn the truth to Speak
upon the issues joined upon their Oath do Say they find the Issues
for the Plaintiff and assess his damages to Ninety dollars besides
his Costs; Therefore it is considered by the Court that the Plaintiff
recover against the Defendants his damages aforesaid in form aforesaid assessed and his costs by him about his Suit in this behalf
expended.

J. H.	'	THOMAS BROWN ....: Plaintiff	)	
L. B.	'		)	
61	'	vs	)	In Case
Rhea	'		)	Words
144	'	JOHN SHIRKY &)	)	
		JEAN SHIRKY).......... Defendants	)	

This day came the parties by their Attornies and the Defendants Demurrer to the first count of the Plaintiffs declaration being argued and overruled, on affidavit of the Defendants the trial of the issues is referred until next Court.

Rhea	'	RICHARD RIDER .... Plaintiff	)	
65	'		)	
115	'	vs	)	In Covenant
	'		)	
	'	JOHN RIDER .... Defendant	)	

This day came the Plaintiff by his attorney and thereupon came a Jury to Wit; James Harrell, Samuel Henderson & Andrew Cowan, William Sharp, William Snoddy, John Thomas, James Gillespie, William Reed, Archibald Lackey, William Cooper, Robert Blackburn, and James Scott, who being elected tried and Sworn, diligently to enquire of damages in this Suit, upon their Oath do Say that the Plaintiff hath Sustained damages by occasion of the Defendants Nonperformance of the Covenant in the Declaration mentioned to One Cent damages besides his costs; Therefore it is considered by the Court that the Plaintiff recover against the Defendant his damages aforesaid in form aforesaid assessed and his costs by him about his Suit in this behalf expended. And the Said Defendant in Mercy & C.

A. R.	'	JOHN TODD .... Plaintiff	)	
75	'		)	
A. O.	'	vs	)	In Case:
173	'		)	Non assumpsit.
	'	JOHN MCAMEY .... Defendant	)	

This day came the parties by their Attornies and thereupon came a Jury to Wit James Harrill, Samuel Henderson, Major Lea, William Sharp, Solomon Harrison, John Thomas, James Gillespie, William Reed, Archibald Lackey, Robert Boyd (Pg. 87) Robert Blackburn, and George Berry who being elected tried and Sworn the truth to Speak upon the issue joined upon their oath do Say, that the Defendant did not assume upon himself in manner and form as the Plaintiff against him hath complained as in pleading he hath alledged. Whereupon the Plaintiff entered a rule to Shew cause why the Said verdict Should be Set aside and a new trial granted which was argued and Granted.

Court adjourned 'till tomorrow 9 O'Clock.

WEDNESDAY NOVEMBER 6th 1793

Wednesday Morning November 6th 1793 Court met according to Adjournment present John Sawyers, John Adair, and John Kearnes esquires Justices & C. & C.

J. H.   '   SOLOMON MARKS .... Plaintiff)
36   '   )
Rhea   '   vs   ) In Case;
252   '   ) Non Assumpsit
          '   ROBERT KING   .... Defendant) Tender & Refusal

    This day came the parties by their Attornies and thereupon came a Jury to Wit; Aquilla Low, Thomas Millican, Andrew McCampbell, William Kerr, Henry Swisher, John Black, James Callison, George Greer, Stephen Byrd, Humphry Montgomery, Jeremiah McClain, and Robert Trimble who being elected, tried, and Sworn the truth to Speak upon the issue joined upon their Oath do Say that the Defendant did not assume upon himself in manner and form as the Plaintiff against him hath complained as in pleading he hath alledged. Whereupon the Plaintiff entered a rule to Shew cause why the Said verdict Should be Set aside and a New Trial granted, which was argued & Granted.

A. R.   '   JOHN HACKETT & ROBERT LIGGITT .... Plaintiffs)
48   '   )
Rhea   '   vs   )
114   '   )
          '   DANIEL CARMICHAEL & ALEXANDER CARMICHAEL ... Defendants)

                                              In Case:
                                              Non assumpsit,
                                              Sett off & no
                                              partnership.

    This day came the parties by their Attornies and thereupon came a Jury to Wit; Aquilla Low, Thomas Millican, Andrew McCampbell, William Kerr, Henry Swisher, John Black, James Callison, George Greer, Stephen Byrd, Humphry Montgomery, Richard Mynatt, and Robert Trimble who being elected tried and Sworn the   (Pg. 88)   truth to Speak upon the Issue joined upon their Oath do Say that the Defendants did not assume upon themselves in manner and form as the Plaintiffs against them have complained as in pleading they have alledged. Therefore it is considered by the Court that the Plaintiffs take nothing by their Bill but for their false clamour be in Mercy & C: And the Defendants go hence without day and recover against the Plaintiffs their costs by them about their Suit in this behalf expended.

Rhea   '   JOHN CHISOLM   .... Plaintiff)
49   '   )
662   '   vs   ) In Case
          '   )
          '   RICHARD HAMILTON .... Defendant)

This day came the Plaintiff by his Attorney and by his consent, and with the Assent of the Court, the enquiry of damages is referred until next Court.

J. H.	'	THOMAS BROWN .... Plaintiff	)	
L. B.	'		)	
60		vs	)	A B
Rhea	'		)	
J. L.	'	LITTLE PAGE SIMS .... Defendant	)	
172	'			

This day came the parties by their Attornies and by their Mutual consent and with the assent of the Court, the Trial of the issue is referred until next Court.

A. O.	'	WILLIAM LOWRY .... Plaintiff	)	
139			)	
A. R.	'	vs	)	Appeal
134	''		)	
	'	WILLIAM REAGAN .... Defendant	)	

This day came the parties by their Attornies and thereupon came a Jury to Wit, Elliot Grills, Robert Black, John Patterson, William Cooper, William Lackey, Augusta Wilson, David Dermond, Samuel McGauhoy, David Caldwell, Paul Cunningham, John Trimble, and David Walker, who being elected, tried and Sworn, well and truly to try the matter of controversy between the parties upon their Oath do Say they find for the Defendant, It is therefore considered by the Court that the Plaintiff take nothing by his plaint aforesaid, but for his false clamour be in Mercy & C. and the Said Defendant go hence without day and recover against the Plaintiff his costs by him about his defence in this behalf expended.

(Pg. 89)

On Petition of Sundry, the Inhabitants of Knoxville, it is ordered that the upper Mill Dam of James White be broke drown, against the first day of July next, and that the Petition of James McCullough for liberty to build a Mill on Second Creek be not Granted.

Court adjourned 'till tomorrow 9 O'Clock.

THURSDAY NOVEMBER 7th 1793

Thursday Morning November 7th 1793 Court met according to Adjournment present James White, George McNutt and William Hamilton esquires Justices & C. & C.

```
Rhea    '   JOHN FEE  ....................  Plaintiff  )
82      '                                              ) .
J. H.   '        vs                                    )   In Case
A. R.   '                                              )
174     '   ANDREW PAUL  Admr. of  )                   )
        '   JAMES PAUL  deceased   ) ...... Defendant  )
```

This day came the parties by their Attornies and by their
mutual consent, and with the assent of the Court the Trial of the
issues is referred until next Court._____

```
A. O.   '   ROBERT STEPHENSON  ....... Plaintiff  )
88      '                                          )
J. H.   '        vs                                )   In Case
288     '                                          )
        '   BENJAMIN BLACKBURN  ....... Defendant  )
```

Mary Stephenson Executrix, and Edward Stephenson Executor,
of Robert Stephenson deceased by their attorny revives this Suit,
and by the Mutual consent of the parties and with the assent of
the Court the Trial of the Issues is referred 'till next Court.

```
Rhea    '   ROBERT GRAY  ....... Plaintiff  )
89      '                                    )
J. S.   '        vs           ..             )   In Covenant
143     '                                    )
        '   JOHN WALLACE  ....... Defendant  )
```

This day came the Plaintiff by his Attorney and the Defendant
in his proper person, and the Said Defendant relinquishing his
former Plea, the parties agree that the Plaintiff hath Sustained
damages by occasion of the Defendants Non performance of the Covenant in the Declaration mentioned to Forty dollars & Fifty Cents
besides his costs; Therefore it is considered by the Court that the
Plaintiff recover against the Defendant the Damages agreed as aforesaid and his costs by him about his Suit in this behalf expended.
And the Said Defendant in Mercy & C._____

(Pg. 90)

```
J. H.   '   JAMES KING  ........ Plaintiff  )
95      '                                    )
Rhea    '        vs                          )   In Case
117     '                                    )
        '   WILLIAM MCCORMACK  ....... Defendant  )
```

The Plaintiff not farther prosecuting; It is ordered that
this Suit be dismissed. Note, Stockley Donelson assumes payment
of the Costs.

A. O.	'	WILLIAM COX	.... Plaintiff	)	
96	'			)	
A. R.	'	vs		)	In Case
Rhea	'			)	
175	'	WILLIAM TRIMBLE	.... Defendant	)	

This day came the parties by their Attornies and by their Mutual consent and with the assent of the Court the trial of the issue is referred until next Court.

Rhea	'	ROBERT BOYD	.... Plaintiff	)	
96	'			)	
118	'	vs		)	A B
	'			)	
	'	DAVID WOOD	.... Defendant	)	

This day came the Plaintiff by his attorney and thereupon came a Jury to Wit Major Lea, George Berry, John Gamble, John Linney, Richard Mynatt, Amos Lird, Stephen Byrd, James Callison, Alexander McMillin, David Walker, John McIntire, and Robert Williams who being elected tried and Sworn diligently to enquire of damages in this Suit upon their Oath do Say that the Plaintiff hath Sustained damages by occasion of the Tresspass assault and Battery in the declaration mentioned to Thirty Dollars besides his costs; Therefore it is considered by the Court that the Plaintiff recover against the Defendant his damages aforesaid in form aforesaid assessed and his costs by him about his Suit in this behalf expended. And the Said Defendant in Mercy.

A. R.	'	GEORGE SAMPLE	.... Plaintiff	)	
99	'			)	
Rhea	'	vs		)	In Covenant
119	'			)	
	'	JAMES GEALEY	.... Defendant	)	

The Defendant James Gealey in his proper person appeared and agrees to pay the costs of this Suit and upon this the Plaintiff prays that his Costs and charges by him about his Suit in this behalf expended may be adjudged to him. Therefore it is considered by the Court that the Plaintiff recover against the Said Defendant his costs by him about his Suit in this behalf expended. And the Said Defen-   (Pg. 91)   dant in Mercy & C. And the Plaintiff not farther prosecuting, it is ordered that this Suit be dismissed.

A. R.	'	GEORGE SAMPLE	.... Plaintiff	)	
100	'			)	
Rhea	'	vs		)	In Covenant
120	'			)	
	'	JAMES GEALEY	.... Defendant	)	

The Defendant James Gealey in his proper person appeared and agrees to pay the costs of this Suit, and upon this the Plaintiff prays that his costs and charges by him about his Suit in this behalf expended may be adjudged to him. Therefore it is considered by the Court that the Plaintiff recover against the Said Defendant his costs by him about his Suit in this Behalf expended. And the Said Defendant in Mercy & C. And the Said Plaintiff not farther prosecuting, It is ordered that this Suit be dismissed.

Rhea			
102		JOHN CHISOLM .... Plaintiff	)
176			) In Case
		vs	)
			)
		JOHN CHISOM .... Defendant	)

This day came the Plaintiff by his Attorney and the Defendant having been arrested and not appearing though Solemnly called, on motion of the Plaintiff by his Attorney, It is considered by the Court that the Plaintiff recover against the Defendant Such damages as he hath Sustained by occasion of the Defendants nonperformance of the assumption in the declaration mentioned; which damages are to be enquired of by a Jury at the next Court.

Rhea		NATHANIEL & SAMUEL COWAN .... Plaintiffs	)
106			) In Case
A. R.		vs	) Plea.
122			) Payment
		ROBERT THOMPSON .... Defendant	)

This day came the parties by their Attornies and thereupon came a Jury to Wit Solomon Harrison, James Davis, Moses Justice, James Gailey, Thomas Flipping, Thomas Millican, Robert Blackburn, William Roberts, John McAllister, John Bradley, Hugh Forgey, and John Steel who being elected tried and Sworn the truth to Speak upon the issue joined upon their Oath do Say the Defendant hath not paid the Sum in the Plaintiffs declaration mentioned and they do assess the Plaintiffs damages by occasion thereof to Fifty four dollars & forty five Cents, besides their Costs, Therefore it is considered by the Court that the Plaintiffs recover against the Defendant the damages aforesaid in form aforesaid assessed and their costs by them about their Suit in this behalf expended. And the Said Defendant in Mercy & C.

(Pg. 92)

A. R.		MARGARET BROWN .... Plaintiff	)
107			)
L. B.		vs	) In detinue
Rhea			) Non detinet
123		WILLIAM HENRY .... Defendant	)

This day came the parties by their Attornies and thereupon
came a Jury to Wit, Solomon Harrison, James McElwee, Moses Justice,
James Gealey, Thomas Flipping, Thomas Millican, Robert Blackburn,
William Roberts, John McAllister, John Bradley, Hugh Forgey, and
John Steel who being elected tried and Sworn the truth to Speak
upon the issue joined upon their oath do Say that the Defendant
doth detain the Negro Slave Nance in the Declaration mentioned in
manner and form as the Plaintiff against him hath complained, and
that the Said Negro Slave Nance is of the price of Three hundred
Dollars and they do assess the Plaintiffs damages by occasion of the
detention aforesaid to Five dollars besides her costs. Therefore
it is considered by the Court that the Plaintiff recover against the
Said Defendant the Negro Slave Nance aforesaid if She may be had
but if not then the price aforesaid of her; together with her
damages aforesaid in form aforesaid assessed and her costs by her
about her Suit in this behalf expended. And the Said Defendant
in Mercy & C.

A. R.	'	WILLIAM RICE .... Plaintiff	)	
112	'		)	
Rhea	'	vs	)	In Case
124	'		)	
	'	JOHN THOMAS .... Defendant	)	

The Plaintiff not farther prosecuting, It is ordered that
this Suit be dismissed and that the Plaintiff pay to the Defendant
his costs.

Court adjourned 'till tomorrow 9 O'Clock.

FRIDAY NOVEMBER 8th 1793

Friday Morning November 8th 1793   Court met according to
Adjournment   present   John Sawyers, John Evans and Thomas
McCullough   esquires   Justices & C. & C.

A. O.	'	JACOB TARWATER .... Plaintiff	)	
Rhea	'		)	
81	'	vs	)	
J. H.	'		)	In
A. R.	'	ANDREW PAUL admr. of)	)	Covenant
116	'	JAMES PAUL deceased) .... Defendant	)	

This day came the parties by their Attornies and thereupon
came a Jury to Wit; John Cochran, James McElwee, John Sharkey
(Pg. 93)   William Lea, Thomas Gillespie, John Gamble, Samuel
Hindman, John Bradley, George Berry, Archibald Lackey, Thomas
Millican and Ananias McCoy who being elected tried and Sworn
the truth to Speak upon the issue joined upon their Oath do Say
the Deed tendered is not agreeable to the Covenant, and they do
assess the Plaintiffs damages by occasion of the Nonperformance

of the Covenant, in the declaration mentioned to Four Hundred
Dollars, besides his costs. Therefore it is considered by the
Court that the Plaintiff recover against the Defendant his Damages
aforesaid in form aforesaid assessed and his costs by him about
his Suit in this behalf expended. And the Said Defendant in Mercy &C.

Rhea		DANIEL WILLSON .... Plaintiff	)	
104	'		)	
145	'	vs	)	In Covenant
	'		)	
	'	NICHOLAS HOLMES .... Defendant	)	

Moses Justice Garnashee being first Sworn Saith that there
is in his possession a Note for Six pounds Virginia currency or
thereabouts the property of Nicholas Holmes and that he owes
the Defendant Fifteen pounds in trade by a note of hand, which note
he is informed is in the possession of James Gealey; that he knows
of no other debts due to, or effects belonging to the Defendant
in the hands of any other person, And the Defendant not appearing
to replevy the Same although Solemnly called; It is considered
by the Court that the Plaintiff recover against the Defendant Such
damages as he hath Sustained by occasion of the Defendants Nonperformance of the Covenant in the Declaration (heretofore filed)
mentioned; which damages are to be enquired of by a Jury at the
next Court.

Rhea	'	JOHN CHISOLM .... Plaintiff	)	
113	'		)	
A . O.	'	vs	)	In Case
146	'		)	
	'	JOSEPH SEVIER .... Defendant	)	

This day came the parties by their attornies and by their
mutual consent and with the assent of the Court the trial of the
Issue is referred until next Court.

Rhea	'	JOHN SOMMERVILLE .... Plaintiff	)	
114	'		)	
A. O.	'	vs	)	In Case
125	'		)	Non Assumpsit
	'	JOSEPH SEVIER .... Defendant	)	

This day came the parties by their Attornies and thereupon
came a Jury to Wit; Samuel McGaughey, Moses Justice, Abraham
Swagerty, George Greer, John Patterson, Major Lea,   (Pg. 94)
James Jeffery, Thomas Flipping, Jacob Tarwater, Joseph West,
James Gealey, and Alexander McMullin, who being elected tried
and Sworn the truth to Speak upon the issue joined upon their
Oath do Say that the Defendant did assume upon himself in manner
and form as the Plaintiff against him hath complained ~~within three~~
~~years next before the Suing out the Writ of Capias in this Suit~~
and they do assess the Plaintiffs damages by occasion of the De-

fendants non performance of that assumption to Thirty dollars and
twenty Seven Cents besides his costs. Therefore it is considered
by the Court that the Plaintiff recover against the Defendant
his damages aforesaid in form aforesaid assessed and his Costs by
him about his Suit in this behalf expended and the Said Defendant
in Mercy & C.

A. R.	'	ROBERT THOMPSON .... Plaintiff	)	
115	'		)	
Rhea	'	vs	)	In Case
253	'		)	
	'	JOHN MCALLISTER .... Defendant	)	

This day came the Plaintiff by his Attorney and having
filed his declaration and the Defendant having been arrestid,
and not appearing though Solemnly called, on motion of the
Plaintiff by his Attorney, it is ordered that Judgment by
default be entered against him. Whereupon the Said Defendant
by his Attorney appeared and by the mutual consent of the parties
and with the assent of the Court the Judgment by default is Set
aside, and the Defendant craves Oyer, and filed his plea, and
the issue being joined the trial thereof is referred until next
Court.

L. B.	'	GODFREY ANTRIM .... Plaintiff	)	
116	'		)	
A. O.	'	vs	)	In Case
136	'		)	
	'	WILLIAM COOPER .... Defendant	)	

The Plaintiff not farther prosecuting; It is ordered that
this Suit be dismissed. Note John Williams assumes payment of
Costs.

J. L.	'	JAMES W. LACKEY .... Plaintiff	)	
117	'		)	
A. O.	'	vs	)	In Case
127	'		)	Infamy
	'	BENJAMIN BLACKBURN .... Defendant	)	

This day came the parties by their Attornies and thereupon
came a Jury to Wit, Samuel McGaughey, Abraham Swagerty, George
Greer, John Patterson, Major Lea, Thomas Flipping, Jacob Tarwater,
Joseph West, James Gealey, Alexander McMullen, James Miller and
Allen Gillespie who being elected tried and Sworn the truth
to Speak upon the issue joined upon their Oath do Say   (Pg. 95)
that the Defendant was of full age at the time of making the
assumption in the declaration mentioned, and they do assess the
plaintiffs damages by occasion of the Defendants nonperformance
of that assumption to Ten dollars besides his costs; Therefore it is
considered by the Court that the Plaintiff recover against the
Defendant his damages aforesaid in form aforesaid assessed, and
his costs by him about his Suit in this behalf expended. And
the Said Defendant in Mercy & C.____ .

Rhea   '   ALEXANDER CARMICHAEL .... Plaintiff   )
118   '   )
A . O.   '   vs   )   In Case;
254   '   )   Non Assumpsit
        '   JOSEPH SEVIER .... Dofendant   )

     This day came the parties by their Attornies and thereupon
came a Jury to Wit, Abraham Swagerty, George Greer, John
Patterson, Thomas Flipping, Joseph West, Alexander McMullin,
James Miller, Allen Gillespie, David Walker, William Lackey,
John Renfroe, and Moses Justice, who being elected tried and
Sworn the truth to Speak upon the Issue joined went out of
court to consult of their verdict and after Some time returned
into Court, and declared they could not agree in their verdict,
by consent of the parties and with the assent of the Court One
of the Jurors aforesaid was with drawn, and the rest of the
Said Jurors from rendering their Verdict discharged and the
cause is continued 'till next Court for a now trial to be had
thereon.

Rhea   '   DAVID SMITH   .... Plaintiff   )
119   '   )
<u>147</u>   '   vs   )   In Case
        '   )   Continued.
        '   DAVID FORRESTER .... Defendant   )

D. G.   '   SAMUEL EVANS   .... Plaintiff   )
120   '   )
<u>128</u>   '   vs   )   In Case
        '   )
        '   DAVID FORRESTER .... Defendant   )

     The Sheriff having returned that the Defendant is not to
be found in his County; The Plaintiff not farther prosecuting
it is ordered that this Suit be dismissed.

A. O.   '   JACOB SMELSER   .... Plaintiff   )
121   '   )
Rhea   '   vs   )   In Covenant
129   '   )
        '   THOMAS KING   .... Defendant   )

     This day came the parties by their Attornies and thereupon
came a Jury to Wit, John Cochran, James McElwee, John Sharkey,
John Gamble, Samuel Hindman, John Bradley, Archibald Lacky,
Thomas Millican, Ananias McCoy, George   '(Pg. 96)   George
Woods, William Blackburn and George Berry, who being elected
tried and Sworn the truth to Speak upon the issues joined upon
their Oath do Say, the writing obligatory declared on, is the
Deed of the Defendant in manner and form as the Plaintiff
against him hath complained, and that the Said Defendant hath not
performed the Same and they do assess the Plaintiffs damages

by occasion thereof to Five hundred and fifty dollars besides his Costs; Therefore it is considered by the Court that the Plaintiff recover against the Defendant his damages aforesaid in form aforesaid assessed and his costs by him about his Suit in this behalf expended. And the Said Defendant in Mercy & C. From which Judgment the Defendant prays an Appeal; which rule is withdrawn, and the Said Plaintiff acknowledges that he hath received Satisfaction of Robert King for the damages aforesaid; and the parties each agree to pay their own Attorney and the Plaintiff agrees to pay three of the Witnesses and the Court charges they agree to pay equally between them.

Rhea	'	JOHN WHITE .... Plaintiff	)	
122	'		)	
148	'	vs	)	In Case
	'		)	
	'	JOHN THOMAS .... Defendant	)	

This day came the Plaintiff by his Attorney and the Defendant having been arrested, and not appearing though Solemnly called, on motion of the Plaintiff by his attorney It is considered by the Court that the Plaintiff recover against the Defendant Such damages as he hath Sustained by occasion of the Defendants Nonperformance of the assumption in the declaration mentioned which damages are to be enquired of by a Jury at the next Court.

Rhea	'	SAMUEL COWAN &		
123	'	NATHANIEL COWAN .... Plaintiff	)	
H. L.	'		)	
149	'	vs	)	In Debt.
	'		)	
		JAMES CALLISON .... Defendant	)	

This day came the parties by their Attornies, and by their mutual consent and with the assent of the Court, the Defendant withdraws his plea in abatement and filed his Pleas and the issues being joined the Trial thereof is referred until next Court.___

(Pg. 97)

J. H.	'	SOLOMON MARKS .... Plaintiff	)	
124	'		)	
150	'	vs	)	In Debt
Rhea	'		)	Continued
	'	WILLIAM ROSEBERRY .... Defendant	)	

Court adjourned 'till tomorrow 9 O'Clock.

SATURDAY NOVEMBER 9th 1793

Saturday Morning November 9th 1793 Court met according to
Adjournment present James White, John Adair and John Evans esquires
Justices & C. & C. ____

The following persons are appointed Inspectors for the
ensuing Election to Wit, George McNutt, Thomas Gillespie &
James White.

H. L.	'	JOHN STONE	.... Plaintiff	)	
126	'		4	)	
130	'	vs		)	In Case
	'			)	
	'	JAMES McCLAIN	..... Defendant	)	

This day came the Plaintiff by his Attorney and thereupon
came a Jury to Wit, David Walker, Samuel Flenekin, George Greer,
William Black, George Woods, Allen Gillespie, Abraham Swagerty,
Joseph West, John McNeill, James McCullough, Samuel Hindman, and
Matthew Bell, who being elected tried and Sworn diligently to
enquire of damages in this Suit upon their Oath do Say that the
Plaintiff hath Sustained damages by occasion of the Defendants
Non performance of the assumption in the declaration mentioned
to Thirty four dollars and Ninety two Cents besides his costs;
Therefore it is considered by the Court that the Plaintiff recover against the Defendant his damages aforesaid in form aforesaid assessed and his costs by him about his Suit in this behalf
expended. And the Said Defendant in Mercy & C.

Rhea	'	SAMUEL HINDMAN	.... Plaintiff	)	
127	'			)	
H. L.	'	vs		)	In Case
131	'			)	
	'	GEORGE ROULSTONE	.... Defendant	)	

The parties appeared and each agree to pay their own Costs,
and the Plaintiff not farther prosecuting: It is ordered that
this Suit be dismissed.____

(Pg. 98)

Rhea	'	BARNEY HANEY	.... Plaintiff	)	
129	'			)	
A. R.	'	vs		)	In Case .
132	'			)	
	'	DAVID WALKER	.... Defendant	)	

By the Consent of the parties, by their Attornies all matters
in difference between them in this Suit are referred to the final
determination of John Hackett, John Chisolm, Luke Lea, James White
and Alexander Kelley, the award of any three of them thereupon to be
made the Judgment of the Court and the Same is ordered accordingly.

The Arbitrators to whom the determination of matters in
difference between the parties were Submitted returned the award

in these words: " Knox County Territory South of Ohio   We the Arbitrators appointed to Settle a dispute Subsisting between Barney Haney Plaintiff and David Walker Defendant, the Defendant pay two dollars and half and Plaintiff pay costs; James White, Luke Lea, Alexander Kelly, John Hackett. Therefore it is considered by the Court that the Plaintiff recover against the Defendant the Two Dollars and a half in the Said award mentioned, and that the Plaintiff pay to the Defendant his costs.

A. O.	'	ANNE MILLS	.... Plaintiff	)	
132	'			)	
J. H.	'	vs		)	In Case
177	'			)	
	'	ANDREW PAUL admr. of)		)	
		JAMES PAUL deceased)	.... Defendant	)	

This day came the parties by their Attornies and time is given the Plaintiff to file her declaration 'till next Court.

A. O.	'	JOHN HUTCHINSON	.... Plaintiff	)	
133	'			)	
J. H.	'	vs		)	In Case
567	'			)	
	'	ANDREW PAUL Adm. of)		)	
		JAMES PAUL deceased)	.... Defendant	)	

This day came the parties by their Attornies and time is given the Plaintiff to file his declaration 'till next Court.

(Pg. 99)

J. H.	'	ANDREW PAUL & C.	.... Plaintiff	)	
134	'			)	
J. L.	'	vs		)	In Case,
J. B.	'			)	Trover
178	'	JOSEPH WEAR	.... Defendant	)	

This day came the parties by their Attornies and on motion of the plaintiff by his Attorney and at his Costs the tryal of the issue is referred until next Court. Note, Dams, filled in Novo. fourth day of the Term.

S. M.	'	JAMES ALLISON	.... Plaintiff	)	
135	'			)	
J. H.	'	vs		)	In Court
L. B.	'			)	
356	'	ABRAHAM SWAGERTY	.... Defendant	)	

This day came the parties by their Attornies and the Plaintiff having filed his declaration the Defendant filed his Pleas and the Issues being joined the tryal thereof is referred 'till next Court.

```
137        '    JOHN FRYER      ....... Plaintiff )
A. O.      '                                      )
151        '         vs                           ) Appeal
           '                                      )
           '    WILLIAM SNEED   ....... Defendant )
```

This day came the Plaintiff in his proper person & the
Defendant by his Attorney and by their mutual consent & with the
assent of the Court the cause is continued 'till next Court.

```
H. L.      '    JAMES GAILEY              ..... Plaintiff )
138        '                                              )
D. G.      '         vs                                   ) In Case
152        '                                              )
           '    JOHN LINNEY & ROBERT CUSICK ..... Defendants )
```

This day came the parties by their Attornies and by their
mutual consent and with the assent of the Court the tryal of the
Issue is referred 'till next Court.

```
J. L.      '    WILLIAM LOWRY .......... Plaintiff )
140        '                                        )
A. O.      '         vs                             ) In Case
205        '                                        )
           '    GEORGE WOODS  ....... Defendant     )
```

This day came the parties by their Attornies and thereupon
came a Jury to Wit David Walker, Samuel Flenniken, George Greer,
William Black, Allen Gillespie, Joseph West, John McNeill, James
McCullough, Samuel Hindman, Mathew Bell, John Finley, and Jeremiah
McCarter who being elected, tried and Sworn, the truth to Speak
upon the issue joined went out of Court, to consult of their Verdict,
and after Some time returned into Court and declared they could not
agree in their verdict by consent of the parties and with the assent
of the Court one of the Jurors aforesaid   (Pg. 100)   was withdrawn, and the rest of the Said Jurors from rendering their Verdict
discharged, and the Cause is continued 'till the next Court for a
new trial to be had thereon.

```
A. R.      '    JOHN WALLACE    ....... Plaintiff )
141        '                                       )
255        '         vs                            ) Origl. Atta.
           '                                       ) Case
           '    JAMES BRIANT    ....... Defendant  )
```

James Tedford Garnashee being first Sworn Saith that he
hath in his possession a Gun the property of James Briant, that
he owes the Defendant nothing, that he hath not, nor had he at the
time he was Summoned Garnashee any other effects of the Defendants
in his hands, that he knows of no debt due to, or effects belonging
to the Defendant in the hands of any other person. Whereupon
John Franklin being again Solemnly called came not; therefore on
motion of the Plaintiff by his Attorney, It is ordered that an
Alias Scire Facias issue against him.

Rhea | DAVID CRAIG .... ` Plaintiff)
142 |
J. H. | vs) Original
179 | Attachment
| SOLOMON MARKS .... Defendant)

This day came the parties by their Attornies and the Defendant withdraws his plea in abatement and filed his pleas to the Action and the issues being joined, on Motion of the Defendant by his Attorney and at his Cost, the tryal thereof is referred until next Court.

Rees | WILLIAM DAVIDSON .... Plaintiff)
144 |
J. H. | vs) In Case
136 |
| ANDREW PAUL & C. .... Defendant)

The Plaintiff not farther prosecuting, It is ordered that this Suit be dismissed, and that the Plaintiff pay to the Defendant his Costs.

A. O. | JOHN EVANS .... Plaintiff)
L. B. |
145 | vs) In Case
A . R. |
153 | HENRY MULVENEY .... Defendant)

This day came the parties by their Attornies and with the assent of the Court they agree to plead and try at the next term.

H. L. | JAMES HUBBARD &
146 | MARGARET CARNES .... Plaintiffs)
137 |
| vs)
|) In Debt
| JAMES JORDAN,))
| JOHN CARNES &) .... Defendants)
| JAMES CARNES))

This day came the Plaintiffs by their Attorney and the Defendants James Jordan, & John Carnes in their proper persons and the Said Defendants acknowledge the Plaintiffs Action for One hundred thirty one Dollars & twenty Cents (Pg. 101) therefore with the assent of the Plaintiffs It is considered by the Court that they recover against the Said Defendants the Said One hundred, thirty one Dollars & twenty Cents, and their Costs by them in this behalf expended and the Said Defendants in Mercy & C.

```
A. R.    '    JAMES BLAIR          .......... Plaintiff )
147      '                                              )
J. H.    '         vs                                   )  In Case
180      '                                              )
         '    ANDREW THOMPSON &   )                     )
         '    ROBERT THOMPSON     ) ..........; Defendants )
```

  This day came the parties by their Attornies & the Plaintiff
having filed his Declaration the Defendants filed their pleas and
the Issues being joined the Tryal thereof is referred until next
Court.

```
Rhea     '    SAMUEL FLANAGAN  ..................... Plaintiff )
149      '                                                     )
Reese    '         vs                                          ) In
256      '                                                     ) Covenant
         '    JOHN SEVIER & ADAM MEEK  Exors & C.  ... Defendts. )
```

  This day came the parties by their Attornies and the Plaintiff
having filed his declaration the Defendants filed their plea and
the Cause is continued until the next Court. ___

```
A. R. 150   '    JAMES FORGY  adm. of                   )
J. H. 206   '    JOHN FORGY  deceased ....... Plaintiff )
            '                                           )
            '         vs                                )  In Case
            '                                           )
            '    JOSEPH BEARD .............. Defendant  )
```

  This day came the parties by their Attornies and the Plaintiff
having filed his declaration the Defendant filed his Plea and the
cause is continued until the next Court.

```
Rhea     '    STOCKLEY DONELSON ....... Plaintiff )
151      '                                        )
A. R.    '         vs                             )  In Case
181      '                                        )
         '    ELLIOTT GRILLS    ....... Defendant )
```

  This day came the plaintiff by his Attorney and having
filed his declaration, and the Defendant having been arrested and
not appearing though Solemnly called, on motion of the Plaintiff
by his attorney It is considered by the Court that the Plaintiff
recover against the Defendant Such damages as he hath Sustained
by occasion of the Defendants Nonperformance of the assumption
in the Declaration mentioned, which damages are to be enquired of
by a Jury at the next Court. But the Plaintiff agrees that this
Judgment may be Set aside if the Defendant appears and pleads
previous to the Second day of next Term.   .

A. R.   '   THOMAS EMBREE .... Plaintiff)
152   '   )
S. M. '   vs   )   In Case
Rhea '   )
257   '   JOHN CHISOLM .... Defendant)

      This day came the parties by their Attornies and the Plaintiff having filed his declaration the Defendant filed his Plea and the Issue being joined the Trial thereof is referred 'till next Court.___

D. G. '   SAMUEL TATE .... Plaintiff)
153   '   )
S. M. '   vs   )   In Case
Rhea '
207   '   JOHN CHISOLM .... Defendant)

      This day came the parties by their Attornies and the Plaintiff having filed his Declaration the Defendant filed his plea and the Issue being joined the trial thereof is referred until the next Court.___

A. R. '   WILLIAM JOHNSTON .... Plaintiff)
W. C. '   )   In Case
154   '   vs   )
J. H. '
A. O. '   ANDERSON ASHBURN .... Defendant)
208   '

      This day came the parties by their Attornies, and with the assent of the Court they agree to plead & try at the next Term.___

A. R. '   AMOS BIRD .... Plaintiff)
155   '   )
154   '   vs   )   In Case
      '   )
      '   DAVID WILLSON .... Defendant)

      This day came the Plaintiff by his Attorney and having filed his declaration, and the Defendant having been arrested and not appearing though Solemnly called, on motion of the Plaintiff by his Attorney, It is considered by the Court that the Plaintiff recover against the Defendant Such damages as he hath Sustained by occasion of the Defendants Nonperformance of the Assumption in the Declaration mentioned; which damages are to be enquired of by a Jury at the next Court.___

L. B. '   JOHN FRAZER .... Plaintiff)
156   '   )
155   '   vs   )   In Debt.
      '   )
      '   DAVID WILLSON &)   )
           NATHANIEL LYONS) .... Defdt.)

This day came the Plaintiff by his Attorney and the Sheriff having returned; the Capias executed on David Willson and Nathaniel Lyons not to be found in his County; the Plaintiff filed his declaration and on motion, an Alias Capias is awarded the Plaintiff to Jefferson County against the Said Nathaniel Lyons returnable here at the next Court._____

(Pg. 103)

Rhea		HUGH DUNLAP &			
157	'	GEORGE GREER	.... Plaintiffs	)	
138	'			)	
	'	vs		)	In Case
	'			)	
		WILLIAM MILLAR	.... Defendant	)	

The Plaintiffs not farther prosecuting It is ordered that this Suit be dismissed and that the Plaintiffs pay to the Defendant his Costs.

Rhea	'	SAMUEL FINLEY	.... Plaintiff	)	
158	'			)	
J. Love	'	vs		)	A B
258	'			)	
	'	JOHN BIRD	.... Defendant	)	

This day came the parties by their Attornies and the Plaintiff having filed his declaration the Defendant filed his pleas and the Issues being joined the Trial thereof is referred until next Court._____

Rhea	'	HUGH DUNLAP	.... Plaintiff	)	
159	'			)	
Reese	'	vs		)	In Debt
209	'			)	
	'	PETER McNAMEE	.... Defendant	)	

This day came the parties by their Attornies and the Plaintiff having filed his Declaration the Defendant filed his pleas and the Issues being joined the Trial thereof is referred until next Court.

160	'	HUGH DUNLAP	.... Plaintiff	)	
	'			)	
	'	vs		)	T. V. A.
	'			)	
	'	JAMES DOUGHERTY	.... Defendant	)	

The Plaintiff not farther prosecuting It is ordered that this Suit be dismissed; And that the Plaintiff pay to the Defendant his Costs. _____ Note the costs paid._____

A. R.   '   JOHN McCAULEY .... Plaintiff)
161   '   )
J. L.   '   vs   )   In Case
210   '   )
         '   WILLIAM LOWRY .... Defendant)

This day came the Plaintiff by his Attorney and the Sheriff haing returned that the Defendant is not to be found in his County; On Motion of the Plaintiff by his Attorney an Alias Capias is awarded him against the Said Defendant returnable here at the next Court. _____

(Pg. 104)

J. L.   '   CHARITY GARRISON .... Plaintiff)
162   '   )
140   '   vs   )   In Tresspass
         '   )
         '   JOHN WALLACE .... Defendant   )

The Plaintiff not farther prosecuting; It is ordered that this Suit be dismissed and that the Plaintiff pay the Costs of this Suit. _____

J. L.   '   CHARLES REGAN   .... Plaintiff)
163   '   )
Rhea   '   vs   )   In Case
L. B.   '   )
238   '   DANIEL CARMICHAEL .... Defendant)

This day came the Plaintiff by his Attorney and the Sheriff having returned the Writ of Capias too late came to hand On motion of the Plaintiff by his Attorney an Alias Capias is awarded him against the Said Defendant returnable here at the next Court.

         '   WILLIAM Q. HALL .... Plaintiff)
164   '   )
no Exr. '   vs   )   In Case
         '   )
         '   LARKINS WISDOM .... Defendant)

The Plaintiff not farther prosecuting It is ordered that this Suit be dismissed ____ Note John Kean assumes payment of Costs.

A. O.   '   JAMES McELWEES LESSEE........ Plaintiff)
165   '   )
Rhea   '   vs   )   In Ejectment
182   '   )
         '   FEN .... Defendant)

James Sterling on his motion is admitted Defendant in this Suit in the room of the Said Fen, and thereupon by his Attorney

he comes and defends the force and Injury when & C. And pleads
not guilty, confesses the Lease, entry and ouster, in the declaration Supposed and puts himself upon the Country. And the Plaintiff likewise, and the trial of the Issue is referred 'till the next
Court.

166	HENRY WHITTENBERGER .... Plaintiff	)	
L. B.	vs	)	Origl.
151		)	Attachment
	JOHN BROWN .... Defendant	)	

Continued until the next Court. ___

(Pg. 105)

J. H.	WILLIAM COBB .... Plaintiff	)	
167		)	
211	vs	)	Origl. Attachment
		)	
	WILLIAM COX .... Defendant	)	.

    This day came the Plaintiff by his Attorney and the attach-
ment having been returned levied on two horse Creatures the 23rd
day of October 1793 and the Court being Satisfied that the
property attached is perishable; Therefore it is ordered that
the Same be exposed to public Sale, after giving legal notice of
the time and place, and that the money arising therefrom be deposited in the hands of the Clerk of this Court, there to wait the event
of this Suit; ___ Unless the Said Defendant Shall replevy the Same
within Sixty days after the time of levying the Said attachment.

A. R.	SAMUEL BARTON .... Plaintiff	)	
168		)	
157	vs	)	In Debt
		)	
	JOHN COWAN &)	)	
	JOSEPH BIRD) .... Defendants	)	

    This day came the Plaintiff by his Attorney and the Sheriff
having returned the Writ of Capias not executed; On motion of the
Plaintiff by his attorney an Alias Capias is awarded him against
the Defendants returnable here at the next Court.

H. L.	LANTY ARMSTRONG .... Plaintiff	)	
169		)	
158	vs	)	In Case
		)	
	BENJAMIN BLACKBURN .... Defendant	)	

    This day came the Plaintiff by his Attorney and the Sheriff
having returned that the Defendant is not to be found in his County;
On motion of the Plaintiff by his Attorney an Alias Capias is
awarded him against the Defendant returnable here at the next
Court.

L. B.   '   ISAAC BULLARD assignee ` .... Plaintiff)
170   '   )
T42   '   vs   ) In Debt
               '   )
               '   WILLIAM HENRY .... Defendant   )

    This day came the Plaintiff by his Attorney & the Defendant in his proper person and the Defendant acknowledgs the Plaintiffs action for Twenty two dollars and fifty Cents   (Pg. 106) Therefore with the assent of the Plaintiff It is considered by the Court that the Plaintiff recover against the Defendant the Said Twenty two Dollars and fifty Cents and his costs by him in this behalf expended And the Said Defendant in Mercy & C. and the Plaintiff agrees to Stay the execution of this Judgment three months, and acknowledges that he has received Satisfaction of the Defendant for his Attorneys fees, therefore as to So much the Said Defendant is acquitted and discharged.

Reese   '   WILLIAM DAVIDSON .... Plaintiff   )
171   '   )
J. L.   '   vs   ) In Covenant
321   '   )
               '   WILLIAM LOWRY   .... Defendant   )

    This day came the Plaintiff by his Attorney and the Sheriff having returned the Writ of Capias not executed, On motion of the Plaintiff by his Attorney an Alias Capias is awarded him against the Defendant returnable here at the next Court. _____

Rhea   '   TITUS OGDEN   .... Plaintiff)
172   '   )
357   '   vs   ) In Case
               '   )
               '   EZEKIEL HENRY &)   )
                     WILLIAM HENRY   ) .... Defdts.   )

    This day came the Plaintiff by his Attorney and having filed his declaration, the death of the Plaintiff is Suggested in abatement: whereupon It is ordered that a Notice issue to Bryant McCabe administrator of Titus Ogden deceased to appear at next Court, to revive and prosecute this Suit.

Reese   '   LEWIS TINER .... Plaintiff)
173   '   )
Rhea   '   vs   ) Appeal
212   '   )
               '   HUGH DUNLAP .... Defendant   )

    This day came the parties by their Attornies and by their mutual consent and with the assent of the Court the Cause is continued until next Court. _____

```
558   11  '              Ordered that Process issue against
202   14  '        Zapher Tannery, Christiana Amerine, James
236   15  '        Bunch, and Michael Foster, to cause them to
559   16  '        appear at the next Court, to answerr the
          '        Indictments found against them by the
                   Grand Jury.
```

Court adjourned 'till Court in Course.

MONDAY FEBRUARY 3rd 1794

At a Court of Pleas and Quarter Sessions began
and held for the County of Knox at the Court house in Knoxville
on the first Monday of February 1794 present James White,
Samuel Newell and John Chisolm esquires Justices & C. & C. ___

Robert Houston esquire Sheriff & C. returned that he had
executed our Writ of Venire Facias to him directed upon the follow-
ing persons to Wit, James Stirling, George Preston, William McNutt
Senior James Anderson, James Adair, Amos Bird, George Hays, William
Robertson, George Walker, Miles Chapman, Obadiah Bounds, Pearson
Brook, James Harralson, Robert Patterson, James Millikin, Thomas
Ray, David Scott, William Rhea, James King, George Brook, and
William Gillespie.

Out of which Venire the following persons were elected a
Grand Inquest for the Body of this County to Wit, William Gillespie,
Foreman, James Stirling, George Preston, William McNutt Senior
James Adair, Amos Bird, William Robertson, George Walker, Miles
Chapman, Obadiah Bounds, Robert Patterson, James Millikin, Thomas
Ray, David Scott, William Rhea, James King, George Brook, and James
Harrelson who have been Sworn received their charge and withdrew
to enquire of their presentments.

Thomas Hardin produced a Commission from Governor Blount by
which it appears that he is appointed a Constable for this County
who entered into Bond with Thomas McCulloch his Security in the
Sum of Six hundred and twenty five Dollars; with condition for the
faithful discharge of the duties of his office; who hath been Sworn
as the law directs.

Court adjourned 'till tomorrow 9 O'Clock.

TUESDAY FEBRUARY 4th 1794

Tuesday Morning February 4th 1794 Court met according to
Adjournment present James White, Samuel Newell and John Chisolm
esquires Justices & C. & C.

(Pg. 108)

J. H.	!	SOLOMON MARKS .... Plaintiff	)		
36	!		)		
Rhea	!	vs	)	In Case	
252	!		)		
	!	ROBERT KING .... Defendant	)		

This day came the parties by their Attornies and by their mutual consent and with the assent of the Court the trial of the Issue is referred 'till next Court.____

The Petition of James Harralson & C. for liberty to keep a Public Ferry on Holston River, was preferred to Court, and argument of Council being heard thereon, It is ordered that the Said Petition be dismissed.

Rhea	!	JOHN CHISOLM .... Plaintiff	)
49	!		)
662	!	vs	) In Case
	!		)
	!	RICHARD HAMILTON .,..... Defendant	)

This day came the Plaintiff by his Attorney and by his consent, and with the assent of the Court, the enquiry of damages is referred until next Court.

J. H.	!	THOMAS BROWN .... Plaintiff	)
L. B.	!		)
60	!	vs	) A B
Rhea	!		)
J. L.	!	LITTLE PAGE SIMS .... Defendant	)
172	!		

This day came the parties by their Attornies and on affidavit of the Defendant the trial of the Issue is referred until next Court.__

J. H. L. B.	!	THOMAS BROWN .... Plaintiff	)
61	!		)
Rhea	!	vs	) In Case
144	!		) Words
	!	JOHN SHIRKY and)	)
		JEAN SHIRKY) .... Defendant	)

The Defendant John Shirky in his proper person appeared and agrees to pay the Costs of this Suit, and upon this the Plaintiff prays that his Costs and charges by him about his Suit in this be-half expended may be adjudged to him; Therefore It is considered by the Court that the Plaintiff recover against the sd. Defendants his costs by him about his Suit in this behalf expended and the Plaintiff not farther prosecuting It is ordered that this Suit be dismissed.

A. R.   '   JOHN TODD   .... Plaintiff   )
75   '   )
A. O..   '   vs   )   In Case
173   '   )
        '   JOHN McAMY   .... Defendant   )

      This day came the parties by their Attornies and thereupon came a Jury to Wit, Joseph Wear, John Irwin, James Gibson, David Mitchell, William Lacky, Samuel Henderson John Thurman, (Pg. 109)   David Miller, Stephen Renfro, John Hunt, Ananias McCoy, and Acquilla Johnston, who being elected tried and Sworn the truth to Speak upon the Issue joined upon their oath do Say that the Defendant did not assume upon himself in manner and form as the Plaintiff against him hath complained, as in pleading he hath alledged. Whereupon on the motion of the Plaintiff and for reasons appearing to the Court the Said Verdict is Set aside and It is ordered that the Plaintiff pay all former costs of this Suit and that a new trial be had at next Court, 'till which time the cause is continued.

D. G.   '   JOHN LINNEY   .... Plaintiff   )
174   '   )
A. R.   '   vs   )   Appeal
159   '   )
        '   JAMES McOLLOCK   .... Defendant   )

      This day came the parties by their Attornies and thereupon came a Jury to Wit, Abraham Swagerty, James McElwee, Archibald McKillip, Robert Black, Little Page Sims, Anderson Ashburn, Michael Foster, Joseph Looney, Thomas Dickson, David Caldwell, Robert Thompson and John Hunt who being elected tried and Sworn well and truly to try the matter of controversy between the parties upon their Oath do Say they find for the Plaintiff Sixteen Dollars, Seventy Seven Cents besides his cost, Whereupon the Plaintiff is put under a rule to Shew cause why a new trial Should not be granted which was argued and discharged, Therefore it is considered by the Court that the Plaintiff recover against the Defendant the Said Sixteen dollars Seventy Seven Cents and his costs by him about his Suit in this behalf expended, and the Said Defendant in Mercy & C.

            Court adjourned 'till tomorrow 9 O'Clock.

              WEDNESDAY FEBRUARY 5th 1794

      Wednesday Morning February 5th 1794 Court met according to adjournment present James White, John Adair and George McNutt esquires Justices & C. & C.

212
220 | To the Worshipful the Justices of the Peace
   | for the County of Knox in Court assembled at February
   | Term 1794, The Petition of Adam Meek and John Sevier
   | Executors of the Estate of Isaac Taylor deceased
   | Humbly Sheweth that by virtue of a Warrant dated
October 21st 1783 and a Survey thereon had a Grant
was issued bearing date the 29th day of July 1793
to James   (Pg. 110)   Gibson and Isaac Taylor
for Six hundred and forty acres of land on the North Side of French
Broad being the Same land on which James Gibson and Alexander
Campbell now lives, that by the decease of the Said Isaac Taylor,
the Said tract of land is vested in the Said James Gibson and the
heirs of Isaac Taylor as tenants in Common; that the Said Isaac
Taylor in his life time Sold and gave his bond to convey part of
Said Tract of land to Alexander Campbell, that the Executors
of the Said Estate (altho authorized by the Will of Said Taylor
to execute conveyances to those persons to whom the Said Taylor
had given bonds) are unable to comply with the bond given to the
Said Alexander Campbell by reason that the Said tract of land yet
remains undivided and the Said Gibson refuses to make Such a division as will do Justice to the Heirs of Said Isaac Taylor in the
opinion of the Said Executors. Your Petitioners therefore pray
that agreeable to the laws in Such case made and provided Your
Worships would nominate and appoint Commissioners to divide and
appropriate the Said tract of land between the Said Gibson and
your Petitioners as Executors of Said Isaac Taylor agreeable to
law allowing to Said Gibson the benefit of his improvement on
the upper end of Said Tract and to your petitioners the benefit
of the improvements on the lower end of the Same, and the division
to be made as if the whole was unimproved land And your petitioners
Shall ever pray _____ Adam Meek Exr. & John Sevier Exr.

Upon hearing the aforesaid Petition read It is ordered
that a Copy thereof be delivered to James Gibson and a Notice to
appear at next Court, and Shew cause if any he hath or can, why
Commissioners Should not be appointed to make partition of the
tract of land in the Said petition mentioned agreeably to the
prayer of the Petitioners.

Rhea | JOHN FEE .... Plaintiff)
82 |)
J. H. | vs   )   In Case
A. R. |)
174 | ANDREW PAUL Admr. of }   )
       | JAMES PAUL decd.   } .... Defendant)

This day came the parties by their Attornies and thereupon
came a Jury to Wit, John Irwin; James Gibson; David Mitchell,
William Lacky, Samuel Henderson, John Thurman, David Miller, Stephen
Renfroe, John Hunt, Ananias McCoy, Acquilla Johnston, and David
Willson who being elected tried and Sworn the truth to Speak upon the
Issues joined went out of Court to consult of their Verdict, and after
Some time returned into Court, and declared they could not
agree in their verdict by consent of the

parties and with the   (Pg. 111)   assent of the Court one
of the Jurors aforesaid was withdrawn and the rest of the Said Jurors
from rendering their Verdict discharged, and the cause is continued
'till the next Court for a new trial to be had thereon.

```
        '    UNITED STATES  .......  )
        '                            )
  2     '         vs         .       )    Charles Regan  prosecutor
  ──    '                            )
  84    '    JOSEPH NANCE   .......  )
```

On motion of the Prosecutor in this Suit by his Attorney,
It is ordered that he be not taxed with the attendance of any of
the Witnesses except the attendance of Joseph Johnston.

```
A. O.  '  MARY STEPHENSON & EDWARD STEPHENSON  Exor. of)
       '  ROBERT STEPHENSON  deceased  ...............).Plaintiffs)
88     '                                                          )
J. H.  '                vs                                        )  In
288    '                                                          )  Case
       '  BENJAMIN BLACKBURN  ........................ Defndt.   )
```

This day came the parties by their Attornies and by their
mutual consent and with the assent of the Court the trial of the
Issues is referred until next Court._____

```
A. O.  '  WILLIAM COX    ....... Plaintiff  )
96     '                                     )
A. R.  '             vs          .    .      )  In Case
Rhea   '                                     )
175    '  WILLIAM TRIMBLE  ....... Defendant )
```

This day came the parties by their Attornies and on Affidavit
of the Plaintiff the trial of the Issues is referred until next
Court.

Court adjourned 'till tomorrow 9 O'Clock

THURSDAY FEBRUARY 6th 1794

Thursday Morning November 6th 1794 Court met according to
adjournment present John Sawyers Thomas McCullough and Samuel
Newell esquires Justices & C. & C.

```
Rhea   '  THE UNITED STATES  ....... Plaintiff  )
17     '                                         )
Reese  '             vs                  .       )  Petit Larcemy
169    '                                         )
       '  JAMES McCOLLOCK    ....... Defendant   )
```

This day came as well the Solicitor for the County as the
Defendant by his Attorney, and the Said Defendant being charged
pleads not guilty and thereupon came a Jury to Wit Alexander
Caldwell, James Stockton, William Carmichael, William Cooper,
John McFarlan, William Cowan, William Colker, David Walker,
Samuel Flenniken, Joseph Brand, James Gibson, and John
Patterson who being elected tried and Sworn   (Pg. 112)
the truth of and upon the premises to Speak upon their Oath do
Say that the Defendant is not guilty as in pleading he hath alledged.

Therefore it is considered by the Court, that he be acquitted and
discharged of the Petit Larceny aforesaid, and go thereof without day;
Whereupon the Defendant by his Attorney moved the Court to Order the
prosecutor to pay the Costs of this prosecution, which was argued and
the motion discharged.

Rhea	:	THE UNITED STATES .... Plaintiff	)	
18	:		)	
203	:	vs	)	A B
	:		)	
	:	MICHAEL SWISHER .... Defendant	)	

This day came as well the Solicitor for the County as the
Defendant by his Attorney and the Said Defendant being charged
pleads not guilty and by their mutual consent and with the assent
of the Court the trial of the Issues is referred untill next Court.

Rhea	:	THE UNITED STATES .... Plaintiff	)	
21	:		)	
L. B.	:	vs	)	A B
204	:		)	
	:	MOSES STEGALL .... Defendant	)	

This day came as well the Solicitor for the County as the
Defendant by his Attorney and the Said Defendant being charged
pleads not guilty, and by their mutual consent and with the assent
of the Court the trial of the Issue is referred until next Court.

558	11	:	Ordered that process Issue against Zapher Tannery,
202	14	:	Christiana Amerine, James Bunch and Michael Foster
236	15	:	to cause them to appear at the next Court to answer
559	16	:	the Indictments found against them by the Grand
		:	Jury.

The Grand Jury appeared and having nothing further to
present were discharged.

Rhea	:	JOHN CHISOLM .... Plaintiff	)	
102	:		)	
176	:	vs	)	In Case
	:		)	
	:.	JOHN CHISOM .... Defendant	)	

This day came the Plaintiff by his Attorney and by his
consent and with the assent of the Court the enquiry of damages
is referred 'till next Court.

```
Rhea      '    DANIEL WILLSON    ....... Plaintiff  )
104       '                                         )
145       '              vs                         )   In Covenant
          '                                         )
          '    NICHOLAS HOLMES   .....:.. Defendant )
```

This day came the Plaintiff by his Attorney and thereupon
came a Jury to Wit, Paul Cunningham, John Liddy, Anderson Ashburn
(Pg. 113)   John Linney, William Lee, David Mitchell, William
Reed, James Anderson, Joseph Brooks, Moses Brooks, Benjamin
Pride and John Herran, who being elected tried and Sworn diligently
to enquire of damages in this Suit upon their Oath do Say that the
Plaintiff hath Sustained damages by occasion of the Defendants nonperformance of the Covenant in the Declaration mentioned to Amount
of Twenty three dollars, thirty three and one third Cents besides
his Costs; Therefore it is considered· by the Court that the Plaintiff recover against the Defendant his damages aforesaid in form
aforesaid assessed and his costs by him about his Suit in this
behalf expended, And the Said Defendant in Mercy & C.

```
Rhea      '    JOHN CHISOLM     ....... Plaintiff  )
113       '                                        )
A. O.     '              vs                        )   In Case
146       '                                        )
          '    JOSEPH SEVIER    ....... Defendant  )
```

The Defendant Joseph Sevier in his proper person appeared
and agrees to pay the costs of this Suit, and upon this the Plaintiff prays that his costs and charges by him about his Suit in this
behalf expended may be adjudged to him. Therefore It is considered
by the Court that the Plaintiff recover against the Said Defendant
his costs by him about his Suit in this behalf expended. And the
Said Defendant in Mercy & C. and the Plaintiff not farther prosecuting
It is ordered that this Suit be dismissed.

```
A. R.     '    ROBERT THOMPSON   ....... Plaintiff  )
115       '                                         )
Rhea      '              vs                         )   In Case
253       '                                         )
          '    JOHN McALLISTER   .....,. Defendant  )
```

This day came the parties by their Attornies and by their
mutual consent and with the assent of the Court the trial of the
Issue is referred untill next Court. ___

```
Rhea      '    ALEXANDER CARMICHAEL  ....... Plaintiff  )
118       '                                             )
A. O.     '              vs                             )   In Case
254       '                                             )
          '    JOSEPH SEVIER        ....... Defendant  )
```

This day came the parties by their Attornies and by their mutual consent and with the assent of the Court the Trial of the Issue is referred until next Court.

((Pg. 114)

```
Rhea   '   DAVID SMITH      ....... Plaintiff )
119    '                                      )
147    '        vs                            )  In Case
       ·'                                     )
       '   DAVID FORRESTER  ....... Defendant )
```

The Plaintiff not farther prosecuting It is ordered that this Suit be dismissed.

```
Rhea   '   JOHN WHITE       ....... Plaintiff )
122    '                                      )
148    '        vs                            )  · In Case
       '                                      )
       '   JOHN THOMAS      ....... Defendant )
```

This day came the Plaintiff by his Attorney and thereupon came a Jury to Wit, Paul Cunningham, John Liddy, Anderson Ashburn, Acquilla Johnston, John Linney, William Reed, James Anderson, Joseph Brooks, Moses Brooks, Benjamin Pride, John Herron, and David Mitchell who being elected tried and Sworn diligently to enquire of damages in this Suit upon their Oath do Say that the Plaintiff hath Sustained damages by occasion of the Defendants Nonperformance of the Assumption in the declaration mentioned to amount of One Cent; besides his Costs; Therefore it is considered by the Court that the Plaintiff recover against the Defendant his damages aforesaid in form aforesaid assessed and his Costs by him about his Suit in this behalf expended; And the Said Defendant in Mercy & C.

```
Rhea   '   SAMUEL COWAN &                            )
123    '   NATHANIEL COWAN  ....... Plaintiffs        )
H. L.  '                                              )  In Debt.
149    '        vs                                    )
       '                                              )
       '   JAMES CALLISON   ....... Defendant         )
```

This day came the parties by their Attornies and the Defendant acknowledges the Plaintiffs action of Thirty Dollars and twenty Cents besides their Costs; Therefore with the assent of the Plaintiffs It is considered by the Court that they recover against the Said Defendant the Said Thirty Dollars & twenty Cents and their Costs by them in this behalf expended; And the Said Defendant in Mercy & C.

```
J. H.    '    SOLOMON MARKS      ........ Plaintiff  )
124      '                                           )
150      '              vs                           )    In Debt.
         '                                           )
         '    WILLIAM ROSEBERRY   ........ Defendant )
```

The Plaintiff not farther prosecuting; It is ordered that this Suit be dismissed.

(Pg. 115)

```
A. O.    '    ANNE MILLS         ........ Plaintiff  )
132      '                                           )
J. H.    '              vs                           )    In Case.
177      '                                           )
         '    ANDREW PAUL  adm. of                   )
         '    JAMES PAUL  deceased  ........ Defendant )
```

This day came the parties by their Attornies and the Plaintiff having filed her declaration the Defendant by his Attorney demurs thereto, and the Plaintiff joins in the Said demurrer which being argued is overruled. Whereupon the Defendant by his Attorney filed his Plea to the Action and the Plaintiff by her Attorney demurs to the Said Plea and the Said Defendant joins in Demurrer which Demurrer being argued is adjudged good; Therefore it is considered by the Court that the Plaintiff recover against the Defendant Such damages as She hath Sustained by occasion of the Defendants Nonperformance of the Assumption in the declaration mentioned; which damages are to be enquired of by a Jury at the next Court.

```
A. O.    '    JOHN HUTCHISON     ........ Plaintiff  )
133      '                                           )
J. H.    '              vs            .              )    In Case
567      '                                           )
         '    ANDREW PAUL  adm. of )                 )
         '    JAMES PAUL  dec'd.    ) ........ Defdt. )
```

This day came the parties by their Attornies and the Plaintiff having filed his declaration, the Defendant filed his pleas and the Issues being joined the trial thereof is referred until next Court.'

```
J. H.    '    ANDREW PAUL  Adm. of
134      '    JAMES PAUL  dec'd.    ........ Plaintiff  )
J. L.    '                                             )
L. B.    '              vs                             )    In Case,
         '                                             )       Trover.
         '    JOSEPH WEAR                              )
                               ........ Defendant      )
```

This day came the parties by their Attornies and by their mutual consent and with the assent of the Court the trial of the Issue is referred until next Court; And on motion of the Defendant by his Attorney a Commission is awarded him to examine

and take the Deposition of John Irwin giving the Plaintiff legal
notice of the time and place of executing the Same.

S. M.	'	JAMES ALLISON	.... Plaintiff	)
135	'			)
J. H.	'	vs		) In Covenant
L. B.	'			)
356	'	ABRAHAM SWAGERTY	.... Defendant	)

This day came the Parties by their Attornies   (Pg. 116)
and by their mutual consent and with the assent of the Court the
trial of the Issues is referred until next Court. ____

137	'	JOHN FRYAR	.... Plaintiff	)
A. O.	'			)
151	'	vs		) Appeal
	'			)
.	'	WILLIAM SNEED	.... Defendant	)

This day came the Defendant by his Attorney and the Plaintiff
though Solmenly called came not but made default nor is his Suit
further prosecuted; Therefore on the prayer of the Said Defendant
It is considered by the Court that he recover against the Plaintiff
his costs by him about his defence in this behalf expended.

H. L.	'	JAMES GAILEY	.... Plaintiff	)
138	'			)
D. G.	'	vs		) In Case
152	'			)
	'	JOHN LINNEY &		)
		ROBERT CUSICK	.... Defendant	)

This day came the parties by their Attornies and thereupon
came a Jury to Wit, Paul Cunningham, John Liddy, Anderson
Ashburn, Acquilla Johnston, William Reed, James Anderson, Moses
Brooks, Joseph Brooks, Benjamin Pride, Henry Stirling, John Herron,
and David Mitchell, who being elected tried & Sworn the truth
to Speak upon the Issue joined upon their Oath do Say that the Defendants did not assume upon themselves as in pleading they have
alledged; Therefore It is considered by the Court that the Plaintiff take nothing by his Bill but for his false clamour be in Mercy
& C. and that the Defendants go thereof without day and recover
against the Said Plaintiff their Costs by them about their defence
in this behalf expended. ____

J. L.	'	WILLIAM LOWRY	.... Plaintiff	)
140	'			)
A. O	'	vs		) In Case
205	'			)
	'	GEORGE WOODS	.... Defendant	)

This day came the Parties by their Attornies and by their
mutual consent and with the assent of the Court the Trial of the
Issue is referred until next Court.

(Pg. 117)

```
A. R.    '    JOHN WALLACE  ....... Plaintiff  )
141      '                                     )
255      '            vs                       )  Crigl. Attachment,
         '                                     )       Case
         '    JAMES BRIANT  ....... Defendant  )
```

John Franklin Garnashee being first Sworn Saith he is indebted
to the Defendant Forty Shillings Virginia Currency and perhaps two
or three Shillings more, that he hath not, nor had he at the time
he was Summoned Garnashee any effects of the Defendants in his
hands that he knows of no other Debts due to or effects belonging
to the Defendant in the hands of any other person. And the cause
is continued 'till next Court.

Court adjourned 'till tomorrow 9 O'Clock.

FRIDAY FEBRUARY 7th 1794

Friday Morning February 7th 1794 Court met according
to Adjournment present James White, John Sawyers and John
Adair esquires Justices & C, & C.

```
Rhea     '    DAVID CRAIG  -  ........ Plaintiff  )
142      '                                        )
J. H.    '            vs                          )  Origl. Attachment
179      '                                        )
         '    SOLOMON MARKS  ........ Defendant    )
```

This day came the parties by their Attornies and thereupon
came a Jury to Wit Major Lea, Anderson Ashburn, John Cowan, Paul
Cunningham, John Liddy, Acquilla Johnston, James McElwee, John
Riddle, Henry Smith, John McCallister, John Heron and David Smith,
who being elected tried and Sworn the truth to Speak upon the
Issue joined upon their Oath do Say they find for the Plaintiff
Twenty one Dollars and twenty five Cents besides his Costs; Whereupon on the motion of the Defendant and for reasons appearing to
the Court, the Said verdict is Set aside; and it is ordered that
a new trial be had at the next Court, 'till which time the cause
is continued.

```
A. O.    '    JOHN EVANS    ........ Plaintiff  )
L. B.    '                                      )
145      '            vs                         )  In Case,
A. R.    '                                       )  Non Assumpsit,
153      '    HENRY MULVENEY  ....... Defendant  )
```

This day came the parties by their Attornies and thereupon
came a Jury to Wit, James Gibson, David Willson, William Cooper,
Alexander Brown, Martin Pruitt, James Thompson, Anderson Ashburn,
Paul   (Pg. 118)   Cunningham, Acquilla Johnston, John

McCallister, David Mitchell, and Fuller Pruitt who being elected
tried and Sworn the truth to Speak upon the issue joined upon their
Oath do Say that the Defendant did assume upon himself in manner
and form as the Plaintiff against him hath complained, and they do
assess the Plaintiffs damages by occasion of the Defendants Nonperformance of that assumption to Seventy four dollars, Sixteen and two
third Cents, besides his Costs; Whereupon the Defendant prayed an
Appeal & C. which was withdrawn; Therefore it is considered by the
Court that the Plaintiff recover against the Defendant his damages
aforesaid in form aforesaid assessed and his Costs by him about his
Suit in this behalf expended and the Said Defendant in Mercy & C.

Note, in this cause at this term the Plaintiff filed his
declaration, the Defendant his plea and the issue being joined
was tried by consent of the parties.

A. R.		JAMES BLAIR	.... Plaintiff	)
147				)
J. H.		vs		) In Case
180				)
		ANDREW THOMPSON &		)
		ROBERT THOMPSON	.... Defendants	)

This day came the parties by their Attornies and by their
mutual consent and with the assent of the Court the trial of the
Issues is referred until next Court.

Rhea		SAMUEL FLANNAGAN	.... Plaintiff	)
149				)
Reese		vs		) In
256				) Covenant
		ADAM MEEK and)		)
		JOHN SEVIER Exors. of)		)
		ISAAC TAYLOR deceased)	.... Defendants	)

This day came the parties by their Attornies and the
Plaintiff demurrs to the Defendants plea and the Defendant joins
in the Said demurrer and the argument thereof is referred 'till
next Court.

A. R.		JAMES FORGY Adm. of)		)`
150		JOHN FORGY deceased)	.... Plaintiff	)
J. H.				)
206		vs		) In Case
				)
		JOSEPH BEARD	.... Defendant	)

This day came the parties by their Attornies and by their
mutual consent and with the assent of the Court the Cause is
continued until the next Court.

(Pg. 119)

```
Rhea      '    STOCKLEY DONELSON  ....... Plaintiff )
151       '                                         )
A. R.     '              vs              -          )   In Case
181       '                                         )
          '    ELLIOTT GRILLS     ....... Defendant )
```

By consent of the Plaintiff It is ordered that the Judgment obtained against the Defendant at the last term be Set aside and thereupon the Defendant by his Attorney filed his plea and the Issue being joined the trial thereof is referred 'till next Court.

```
A. R.     '    THOMAS EMBREE      ....... Plaintiff )
152       '                                         )
J. H.     '              vs                         )   In Case
Rhea      '                                         )
257       '    JOHN CHISOLM       ....... Defendant )
```

This day came the parties by their Attornies and on affidavit of the Plaintiff the trial of the issues is referred 'till next Court; And on motion of the Plaintiff a Commission is awarded him to examine and take the depositions of his Witnesses giving the Defendant legal notice of the time and place of executing the Same.

```
D. G.     '    SAMUEL TATE        ....... Plaintiff )
153       '                                         )
Rhea      '              vs                         )   In Case
S. M.     '                                         )
207       '    JOHN CHISOLM       ....... Defendant )
```

This day came the parties by their Attornies and by their mutual consent and with the assent of the Court the trial of the Issue is referred until next Court.

```
A. R.     '    WILLIAM JOHNSTON   ....... Plaintiff )
W. C.     '                                         )
154       '              vs                         )   In Case
J. H.     '                                         )
A. O.     '    ANDERSON ASHBURN   ....... Defendant )
208       '
```

This day came the parties by their Attornies and the Plaintiff having filed his declaration the Defendant filed his plea and the Issue being joined the trial thereof is referred 'till next Court.

```
A. R.     '    AMOS BIRD          ....... Plaintiff )
155       '                                         )
154       '              vs                         )   In Case
          '                                         )
          '    DAVID WILLSON      ....... Defendant )
```

The Defendant David Willson in his proper person appeared
and agrees to pay the Costs of this Suit and upon this the
Plaintiff prays that his Costs and Charges by him about his Suit
in this behalf expended may be adjudged   (Pg. 120)   to him;
Therefore It is considered by the Court that the Plaintiff recover
against the Said Defendant his costs by him about his Suit in this
behalf expended. And the Said Defendant in Mercy & C. And the
Plaintiff not farther prosecuting; It is ordered that this Suit
be dismissed.

L. B.	JOHN FRAZER .... Plaintiff)	
156	)	
155	vs)	In Debt
	)	
	DAVID WILLSON ....))	
	&)	
	NATHANIEL LYONS.......) .... Defendant)	

The Defendant David Willson in his proper person appeared
and agrees to pay the costs of this Suit and upon this the Plaintiff
prays that his costs and charges by him about his Suit in this behalf
expended may be adjudged to him; Therefore It is considered by the
Court that the Plaintiff recover against the Defendants his costs
by him about his Suit the this behalf expended. And the Said Defendant in Mercy & C. And the Plaintiff not farther prosecuting
it is ordered that this Suit be dismissed.

Rhea	SAMUEL FINLEY .... Plaintiff)	
158	)	
J. Love	vs)	A B
258	)	
	JOHN BIRD .... Defendant)	

By consent of the parties the matter in dispute between
them is referred to the final determination of Joseph Perrian,
Joseph Robertson, James Hamilton, John Beard, William Hamilton
and Thomas Cox or a majority of them whose reward thereupon
is to be made the Judgment of the Court and the Same is ordered
accordingly.

Rhea	HUGH DUNLAP .... Plaintiff)	
159	)	
Reesse	vs)	In Debt
209	)	
	PETER McNAMEE .... Defendant)	

This day came the parties by their Attornies and by their
mutual consent and with the assent of the Court the trial of the
Issues is referred until the next Court.

(Pg. 121)

A. R.	'	JOHN McCAULEY .... Plaintiff	)
161	'		)
J. L.	'	vs	) In Case
210	'		)
	'	WILLIAM LOWRY .... Defendant	)

This day came the parties by their Attornies, and the Plaintiff having filed his declaration the Defendant filed his plea and the issue being joined the Trial thereof is referred 'till next Court.

J. L.	'	CHARLES REGAN .... Plaintiff	)
163	'		)
Rhea	'	vs	) In Case
L. B.	'		)
238	'	DANIEL CARMICHAEL .... Defendant	)

This day came the Plaintiff by his Attorney and the Sheriff having returned that the Defendant is not to be found in his County; On motion of the Plaintiff by his Attorney a Pluries Capias is awarded him against the Defendant returnable here at the next Court.

A. C.	'	JAMES McELWEE'S Lessee .... Plaintiff	)
165	'		)
Rhea	'	vs	) In
182	'		) Ejectment
	'	JAMES STIRLING .... Defendant	)

This day came the parties by their Attornies and by their mutual consent and with the assent of the Court the trial of the Issue is referred until the next Court.

166	'	HENRY WHITTENBERGER .... Plaintiff	)
L. B.	'		)
156	'	vs	) Original
	'		) Attachment
	'	JOHN BROWN .... Defendant	)

This day came the Defendant by his Attorney and filed a Plea in abatement, which was argued, and because it Seems to Court that the Said Plea and the matter therein contained is Sufficient in law to abate the Plaintiffs Writ, Therefore It is considered by the Court, that this Suit abate and that the Plaintiff pay to the Defendant his Costs.

J. H.	'	WILLIAM COBB .... Plaintiff	)
167	'		)
211	'	vs	) Original
	'		) Attachment
	'	WILLIAM COX .... Defendant	)

This day came the Plaintiff by his Attorney and the Defendant though Solemnly called not appearing It is ordered that a Writ of enquiry of damages be executed at the next Court. ___ Peter McNamee returned on our order of Sale of last Court, that he had exposed to Sale the property attached the amount of which Sale is Twenty two Dollars.___

(Pg. 122)

```
A. R.    '    SAMUEL BARTON  .........  Plaintiff  )
168      '                                         )
157      '         vs                              )  In Debt
         ' :                                       )
         '    JOHN COWAN &                         )
              JOSEPH BIRD   .........  Defendant   )
```

The Plaintiff not farther prosecuting; It is ordered that this Suit be dismissed.

```
H. L.    '    LANTY ARMSTRONG    .......  Plaintiff  )
169      '                                           )
158      '         vs                                )  In Case
         '                                           )
         '    BENJAMIN BLACKBURN  .......  Defendant  )
```

This day came the Plaintiff by his Attorney and the Defendant in his proper person, and the Defendant acknowledges the Plaintiffs action for Sixty-nine dollars, Sixty Six and two third Cents Therefore with the assent of the Plaintiff; It is considered by the Court that the Plaintiff recover against the Defendant the Said Sixty nine dollars Sixty Six and two third Cents and his Costs by him in this behalf expended; And the Said Defendant in Mercy; And the Plaintiff agrees to Stay the execution of this Judgment three Months.

```
Reese    '    WILLIAM DAVIDSON   .......  Plaintiff  )
171      '                                           )
J. L.    '         vs                                )  In Covenant
321      '                                           )
         '    WILLIAM LOWRY     .......  Defendant    )
```

This day came the parties by their Attornies and the Sheriff having returned the Writ of Capias executed; by their mutual consent a Commission is awarded to examine and take the deposition of William Young giving each other legal notice of the time and place of executing the Same.

```
Rhea     '    TITUS OGDEN      .......  Plaintiff  )
172      '                                         )
357      '         vs                              )  In Case
         '                                         )
         '    EZELIEL HENRY &                      )
              WILLIAM HENRY    .......  Defendant  )
```

Brian McCabe Administrator of Titus Ogden deceased by his

Attorney revives this Suit; and the Defendants having been
arrested and not appearing though Solemnly called; On Motion of
the Plaintiff by his Attorney It is considered by the Court that the
Plaintiff recover against the Defendants Such damages as he hath
Sustained by occasion of the Defendants Nonperformance of the Assumption in the declaration mentioned; which damages are to be enquired
of by a Jury at the next Court. ____

(Pg. 123)

Reese	'	LEWIS TINER .... Plaintiff	)	
173	'		)	
Rhea	'	vs	)	Appeal
212	'		)	
	'	HUGH DUNLAP .... Defendant	)	

This day came the parties by their Attornies and by their
mutual consent and with the assent of the Court the Cause is
continued until the next Court.____

1	'	JOHN COULTER	)	
78	'		)	
	'	vs	)	Scire Facias
	'		)	
	'	SAMUEL DOAK	)	

The Defendant having been duly warned and not appearing
though Solemnly called/ On motion of the Plaintiff by his Attorney
It is considered by the Court that the Plaintiff may have Execution
against the Said Defendant for Three Dollars, eighty one and one
half Cents, the Costs in the Writ aforesaid Specifyed, and also
 that the Plaintiff recover against the Said Defendant his costs
by him expended in Suing forth and prosecuting this Writ.

2	'	JOHN SHIRKY &	)	
92	'	JEAN SHIRKY	)	
	'		)	
	'	vs	)	Scire Facias
	'		)	
		JOHN THOMAS &	)	
		CORNELIUS ARCHER	)	

John Thomas one of the Defendants having been duly warned
and not appearing though Solemnly called; On Motion of the
Plaintiffs by their Attorney; It is considered by the Court that the
Plaintiffs may have execution against the Said Defendant for Eleven
dollars Seventy five Cents, the Costs in the Writ aforesaid
Specifyed, and also that the Plaintiffs recover against the Said
Defendant their costs by them expended in Suing forth and prosecuting
this Writ.

```
 3    '   SAMUEL ACKLIN &                )
59    '   SAMUEL NEWELL      ........    )
      '                                  )
      '           vs                     )      Soire Faoias
      '                                  )
          JOHN CHISOLM                   )
          DANIEL CARMICHAEL   ........   )
```

This day came the Plaintiff by his Attorney and the Defendant John Chisolm in his proper person and Saith he cannot gainsay the Plaintiffs having exooution against him, Therefore It is considered by the Court that the Plaintiff may have exeoution against him. for Seventeen Dollars and Sixty nine Cents the Costs in the Writ aforesaid Specifyed, and also that the Plaintiffs recover against the Said Defendant their costs by them expended in Suing forth and proseouting this Writ.

(Pg. 124)

```
 4    '   NICHOLAS HALE &  ........      )
73    '   SARAH HALE                     )
      '                                  )
      '           vs                     )      Soire Faoias
      '                                  )
          ANNANIAS McCOY    ........     )
```

This day came the Plaintiff by his Attorney, and the Defendant in his proper person, and Saith he cannot gainsay the Plaintiffs having execution against him; Therefore It is considered by the Court that the Plaintiff may have exeoution against the Defendant for Ten dollars and Seventy five Cents the costs in the Writ aforesaid Specified, and that the Plaintiffs recover against the Said Defendants their costs by them expended in Suing forth and proseouting this Writ.

```
A. R.   '   JOHN WALKER            )
175     '                          )
Rhea    '          vs             )        Appeal
213     '                          )
        '   JOHN SOMMERVILLE        )
```

This day came the parties by their Attornies and by their mutual consent and with the assent of the Court the Cause is . continued until next Court; On motion of the Defendant by his Attorney a Commission is awarded him to examine & take the Deposition of his Witnesses giving the Plaintiff legal notice of the time and place of exeouting the Same.

```
A. R.   '   ABRAHAM UTTER          )
176     '                          )
Rhea    '          vs             )        Appeal
183     '                          )
        '   ALEXANDER CARMICHAEL    )
```

This day came the parties by their Attornies and by their mutual consent and with the assent of the Court the Cause is continued until next Court;

Rhea	'	GEORGE HOULSTONE & CO	)
177	'		)
184	'	vs	) Original Attachment
	'		)
	.'	JOSEPH WEST	)

This day came the Plaintiff by his Attorney & having filed his declaration David Moor who was summoned to appear here to declare on Oath what he is indebted to the defendant or what effects he has or had in his hands at the time he was Summoned Garnashee and what debts he knows to be due to or effects belonging to the Defendant in the hands of any other person and who that person is; being Solemnly called came not; Therefore it is considered by the Court that the Plaintiffs recover against the Said David Moor the amount of the Plaintiffs demand against the Said Defendant and also his costs; unless he appears at our next Court and (Pg. 125) Shew Sufficient cause why this Judgment Should not be confirmed; and It is ordered a Scire Facias issue against him. And the Cause is continued 'till next Court.

A. R.	'	On the Petition of Adam Meek and John Sevier
212	'	Executors of Isaac Taylor deceased James Gibson
Rhea	'	on his motion is admitted Defendant and filed the
220	'	following Answer to Wit;
	'	

Answer of James Gibson to a Petition of Adam Meek and John Sevier Executors of the estate of Isaac Taylor deceased exhibited to the WorshipfulCourt of Knox County February Sessions 1794 James Gibson Answereth that before the making of the entry by which the Warrant in the Said Petition mentioned did issue, he this Respondent did give to Isaac Taylor their Testator the Sum of One hundred and twenty pounds Specie for the express purpose of entiring land to Wit Twelve hundred acres of which each of the parties were to have an equal half viz. This respondent Six hundred acres, (being the land on which this respondent had improved and now lives;) as his part for the Said Sum of money and Isaac Taylor Six hundred acres as a compensation for his trouble in going to, and entering the Same in the land Office and other requisites about that business; The Said land lying on the North Side of French Broad river, this Respondent further Sets forth that before the Said Isaac Taylor went to the land office to enter the Said quantity of land he and this Respondent James Gibson went upon Said Tract and made a conditional line by which at the Same time it was agreed that this Respondent Should have that part of the Said Tract of Twelve hundred acres which lay on one Side of the Said line and to contain Six hundred acres and his improvement; and the Said Isaac Taylor was to have his Six hundred acres on the other Side of the Said conditional line; the whole tract to contain Twelve hundred acres; this Respondent for a considerable time

expected that he was the true and only Owner of that whole part
(of the 1200 acre tract) which lay on his Side of the Said line
on which part he lived; as the Said Isaac had honestly made the
aforesaid conditional line, and afterwards was much Surprised to
hear how the Said business was conducted by the Said Isaac Taylor,
and that an entry by him was made only for Six hundred and forty
acres, being that part which this Respondent had on his Side of
the Said line, and on which he had largely improved; a grant for
which has issued in names of Isaac Taylor, and this Respondent;
this Respon-   (Pg. 126)   dent does not believe that Isaac Taylor
had any right to make the entry in manner he did as he had willingly
made the conditional line aforesaid; this Respondent thinks that
Sixty pounds Specie was full compensation for any trouble and Service
the Said Isaac Taylor and his executors might have in entering and
procuring a Grant for said land for the benefit Solely of this Respondent and that the heirs of Isaac Taylor or his executors have
no right to any part of Said land in equity or good conscience for
the reasons aforesaid that the Said Isaac Taylor might have paid
for his Six hundred acres of land lying elsewhere the Said Sixty pounds
Specie which this Respondent gave him with the other Sixty pounds,
this Respondent saith he has received no Satisfaction for the said
Sixty pounds hitherto from the Said executors or their testator
Isaac Taylor and thinks he has an equitable right to Six hundred
acres of the Said land in Said Grant mentioned all which circumstances
and other facts relative thereto not herein Stated this Respondent
prays this Worshipful Court to take cognizance of pursuant to the
Acts of Assembly of North Carolina in Such case made and provided,
that Subpoenas for witnesses to prove the facts aforesaid may issue
and that this Court will grant to him Such relief in the premises
as they Shall deem right.

                              James Gibson

        Ordered that Alexander Hanley an orphan, Sixteen
Years of age be bound to John Stone until he arrive to the age
of Twenty one Years, and agreeably to the Said order, Indentures
are signed and a counterpart filed in the Office.

            Court adjourned till tomorrow 8 O'Clock.

                SATURDAY FEBRUARY 8th 1794

        Saturday Morning February 8th 1794 Court met present
John Chisolm, George McNutt, James Cozby and John Hackett esquires
Justices & C. & C.____

J. H.	'	JAMES CARMICHAEL	)	
178	'		)	
Rhea	'	vs	)	In Covenant
L. B.	'		)	
214	'	ALEXANDER CARMICHAEL	)	

This day came the parties by their Attornies and the Plaintiff having filed his declaration the Defendant filed his plea and the issue being joined the trial thereof is referred 'till next Court.___

(Pg. 127)

J. L.	'	JOHN DUNCAN	)	
179	'		)	
A. R.	'	vs	)	In Covenant
412	'		)	
	'	JOHN McNUTT &	)	
		JAMES CALLISON	)	

This day came the parties by their Attornies & the Plaintiff having filed his declaration the Defendant filed his Plea and the Plaintiff demurrs thereto and the Defendant joins in Said Demurrer and the argument thereof is referred until next Court.

180	'	EDWARD FERGUSON	)	
160	'		)	
	'	vs	)	In Case
	'		)	
	'	JAMES ANDERSON	)	

The parties appeared and each agree to pay their own Costs & the Plaintiff not farther prosecuting; It is ordered that this Suit be dismissed.

H. L.	'	JOHN DAVIS	)	
181	'	.	)	
Rhea	'	vs	)	In Case
322	'		)	
	'	JOSEPH JANES	)	

This day came the parties by their Attornies and the Plaintiff having filed his declaration, the Defendant prays Oyer of the writing in the declaration mentioned; which is read to him in these words ... "Sir, you will please to pay John Davis, Twenty two pounds, three Shillings and three pence, lawfull money of Virginia which is the amount of Peter Tadivough Note due me and a Suit brought against him by Harry Innes, This with Said Davis's Receipt Shall be good against Yo Huml. Servt. ___

Joseph Janes

26th June 1790

Test

To W. Robert Forker

Sam'l South

Should not the Said Robert Forker discharge the above order that
then I stand indebted to the Said John Davis the above Sum of Twenty
two pounds, three Shillings and three pence lawfull money of Virginia
on demand as Witness my hand this 26th of June 1790.

Joseph Janes

Test

Saml. South

Whereupon the Defendant filed his pleas & the issues being joined
the Trial thereof is referred until next Court, And on Motion of
the Plaintiff a Commission is awarded him, to examine and take
the Deposition of his Witnesses giving the Defendant legal Notice
of the time and place of executing the Same.

(Pg. 128)

J. H.	'	ROBERT BLACKBURN	)	
182	'		)	
A. O.	'	vs	)	In Case, Trover
215	'		)	
	'	JOHN LOWRY esquire	)	

　　　This day came the parties by their Attornies and the plaintiff
having filed his declaration the Defendant filed his plea and the
issue being joined the trial thereof is referred until next Court.

183	'	REZIN HARLIN	)	
Rhea	'		)	
161	'	vs	)	In Case
	'		)	
	'	JAMES MILLER	)	

　　　The Plaintiff not farther prosecuting It is ordered that
this Suit be dismissed and that the Plaintiff pay to the Defendant his costs.

Rhea	'	JOHN CHISOLM	)	
A. O.	'		)	
184	'	vs	)	In Case
D. G.	'		)	
215	'	MARTIN ROLER	)	

The parties appeared and each agree to pay their own costs
and the Plaintiff not farther prosecuting It is ordered that
this Suit be dismissed.

J. L.	'	JEAN KERR by her	)
185	'	next friend	)
A. R.	'	JAMES KERR	)
W. C.	'		)
217	'	vs	)
			)
		JOHN CALDWELL	)

Malicious prosecution

This day came the parties by their Attornies and the Plaintiff
having filed her declaration, the Defendant filed his Plea and the
Issue being joined the trial thereof is referred 'till next Court.

H. L.	'	JAMES BRIGGAM	)
W. C. C.	'		)
D. G.	'	vs	)
186	'		)
A. R.	'	JOHN CHISOLM	)
A. O.	'		)
323	'		)

In Covenant

This day came the parties by their Attornies and the Plaintiff
having filed his declaration the Defendant filed his plea and the
Plaintiff his replication thereto and the issue being joined the trial
thereof is referred until next Court.

J. H.	'	PATRICK NINNEY	)
187	'		)
Rhea	'	vs	)
218	'		)
	'	SAMUEL HINDMAN	)

In Case

This day came the parties by their Attornies and the Plaintiff
having filed his declaration the Defendant filed his Pleas, and the
Issues being joined the trial thereof is referred 'till next Court.

(Pg. 129)

A. R.	'	FRANCIS BIRD	)
188	'		)
Rhea	'	vs	)
A. O.	'		)
259	'	JOHN CHISOLM &	)
		JOHN MILLER	)

In Case

This day came the parties by their Attornies and the Plaintiff
having filed his declaration the Defendants filed their pleas and the
Issues being joined the Trial thereof is referred 'till next Court.

A. R.	'	PEARSON BROCK	)	
189	'		)	
Rhea	'	vs	)	Case, words.
260	'		)	
	'	JAMES THOMPSON	)	

This day came the parties by their Attornies and the Plaintiff having filed his declaration the Defendant filed his pleas and the Issues being joined the trial thereof is referred 'till next Court.

Rhea	'	ROBERT·RHEA	)	
190	'		)	
219	'	vs	)	In Case
	'		)	
	'	DAVID MILLER	)	

This day came the Plaintiff by his Attorney and by his consent and with the assent of the Court the Cause is continued until. the next Court.

H.L.	'	DAVID WRIGHT	)	
192	'		)	
Rhea	'	vs	)	In Case
289	'		)	
	'	JAMES SPENCE	)	

This day came the parties by their Attornies and the Plaintiff having filed his declaration the Defendant filed his pleas and the issues being joined the trial thereof is referred until next Court; And on Motion of the Plaintiff a Commission is awarded him to examine and take the Deposition of his Witnesses giving the Defendant legal notice of the time and place of executing the Same.____

(Pg. 130)

S. M.	'	THOMAS KING	)	
Rhea	'		)	
193	'	vs	)	In Case
J. H.	'		)	
290	'	JOSEPH BEARD	)	
	'			

This day came the parties by their Attorneys and the Plaintiff having filed his declaration the Defendant filed his Pleas and the issues being joined the trial thereof is referred 'till next Court.

Rhea	'	AQUILLA JOHNSTON	)	
194	'		)	
J. H.	'	vs	)	In Case
261	'		)	
	'	MAJOR LEA	)	

This day came the parties by their Attornies and the Plaintiff having filed his declaration the Defendant filed his plea and the Plaintiff his replication thereto and the Issue being joined the trial thereof is referred 'till next Court.

195	'	STEHPEN DUNCAN & CO.	)	
163	'		)	
	'	vs	)	In Case
	'		)	
	'	JOHN TUNCRAY	)	

The Plaintiff not farther prosecuting It is ordered that this
Suit be dismissed.

J. L.	'	JAMES WEAR	)	
196	'		)	
Rhea	'	vs	)	In Case
262	'		)	
	'	DANIEL WILLSON	)	

This day came the parties by their Attornies, and the Plaintiff
having filed his declaration the Defendant filed his pleas and the
issues being joined the trial thereof is referred 'till next Court.

Rhea	'	JOHN SOMMERVILLE	)	
197	'		)	
185	'	vs '	)	In Case
	'		)	
	'	JAMES DYARAMONT	)	

This day came the Plaintiff by his Attorney and the Sheriff
having returned the Writ of Capias not executed by order of the
Plaintiff; On motion the cause is continued 'till next Court.

198	'	ANDREW MILLER	)	
164	'		)	
	'	vs	)	In Case
	'		)	
	'	DAVID CONLEY	)	

The Plaintiff not farther prosecuting; It is ordered that this
Suit be dismissed.

(Pg. 131)

	'	ROBERT COZBY	)	
199	'		)	
165	'	vs	)	In Case
	'		)	
	'	JOHN HERRAN	)	

The Plaintiff not farther prosecuting; It is ordered that this
Suit be dismissed.

J. L.   '   JAMES HAIL   )
200   '   )
166 .   '   vs   )   In Case
‾‾‾   '   )
        '   PETER DOSURE   )

The Defendant Peter Dosure in his proper person appeared
and agrees to pay the Costs of this Suit and upon this the Plaintiff
prays that his costs and Charges by him about his Suit in this behalf
expended may be adjudged to him; Therefore it is considered by the
Court that the Plaintiff recover against the Defendant his costs by
him about his Suit in this behalf expended. And the Said Defendant
in Mercy & C.

Rhea   '   BRIAN McCABE   )
201   '   Administrator of   )
703   '   TITUS OGDEN deceased   )
‾‾‾   '   )   In Case
        '   vs   )
        '   )
            WILLIAM TATHEM   )

This day came the Plaintiff by his Attorney and the Sheriff
having returned that the Defendant is not to be found in his County;
On motion of the Plaintiff by his Attorney a Judicial attachment is
awarded him against the estate of the Said Defendant returnable here
at the next Court.

H. L.   '   JOSEPH WEST   )
202   '   )
413   '   vs   )   In Debt
‾‾‾   '   )
        '   RICHARD FINDLESTON)

This day came the Plaintiff by his Attorney and filed his
declaration and the Defendant filed his Demurrer and the argument
thereof is referred 'till next Court.

Rhea   '   ANNANIAS McCOY   )
203   '   )
263   '   vs   )   Origl. Attachment, In Case
‾‾‾   '   )
        '   JOHN LUSK   )

This day came the Plaintiff by his Attorney & having filed his
Declaration And Jeremiah Jack Garnashee being first Sworn Saith
that he hath in his possession a Small Sorrel Mare the property of
John Lusk, that he oweth the Defendant nothing, that he hath not nor
(Pg. 132)   had he at the time he was summoned Garnashee any other
effects of the Defendants in his hands, that he knows of no debts due
to or effects belonging to the Defendant in the hands of any other person. Whereupon the Said John Lusk, not appearing to replevy the
Same although Solemnly called; It is considered by the Court that

the Plaintiff recover against the Defendant Such damages as he hath
Sustained by occasion of the Defendants Nonperformance of the assumption
in the declaration mentioned; which damages are to be enquired of by
a Jury at the next Court.

Rhea ' STEPHEN DUNCAN & CO)
204   '   )
739   '   vs   ) Original Attachment,
      '   )
      ' JOSEPH WEST   )   In Case

This day came the Plaintiff by his Attorney and having filed
his declaration, Hugh Dunlap who was Summoned to appear here to
declare on Oath, what he is indebted to the Defendant or what effects
he has or had in his hands at the time he was Summoned Garnashee, and
what debts he knows to be due or effects belonging to the Defendant in
the hands of any other person and who that person is; being Solemnly
called came not Therefore it is considered by the Court that the
Plaintiff recover against the Said Hugh Dunlap the amount of the Plaintiffs demand against the Said Defendant and also his costs; unless he
appear at our next Court and Shew Sufficient cause why this Judgment
Should not be confirmed; and. It is ordered a Scire Facias issue
against him And the Cause is continued until the next Court. ___

Rhea ' ROBERT FERGUSON   )
205   '   )
264   '   vs   ) Original Attachment, In Case
      '   )
      ' WILLIAM TATHOM   )

This day came the Plaintiff by his Attorney and the attachment
having been returned levied on three hundred acres of land, lying
in a Valley between third and fourth Creek adjoining Martin Pruitts
Survey. The Plaintiff filed his declaration and the proceedings
are Suspended for Six Months.

Rhea ' GEORGE PRESTON   )
206   '   )
448   '   vs   ) Original Attachment. In Case
      '   )
      ' JOSEPH ROBERTSON   )

This day came the Plaintiff by his Attorney & having filed
his Declaration, Charles Medlock Garnashee being first Sworn
Saith he owes the Defendant nothing that he hath not nor had he
at the time he was Summoned Garnashee any effects of the Defendants
in his hands that   (Pg. 133)   he knows of no debts due to or
effects of the Defendants in the hands of any other person. On
motion of the Plaintiff by his Attorney a Judicial Attachment is
awarded him against the estate of the Said Defendant returnable here
at the next Court. ___

```
A. R.    '    DAVID CALDWELL    )
207      '                      )
J. L.    '         vs           )    Appeal
291      '                      )
         '    WILLIAM LOWRY     )
```

This day came the parties by their Attornoys and by their mutual consent and with the assent of the Court the Cause is continued until next Court. ___

```
A. R.    '    SAMUEL BOGLE      )
208      '                      )
L. B.    '         vs           )    Original Attachment, in Covenant
167      '                      )
         '    JOHN BROWN        )
```

This day came the Plaintiff by his Attorney and the attachment having been returned levied on a Horse, Saddle and Bridle & the Same having been replevied, Thereupon came the Defendant by his Attorney and Demurs to the Attachment; The Plaintiff not farther prosecuting it is ordered that this Suit be dismissed, and that the Plaintiff pay to the Defendant his Costs.

```
A. O.    '    JONATHAN CUNNINGHAM  )
209      '                         )
J. L.    '         vs              )    Appeal
168      '                         )
         '    JOHN BRADLEY         )
```

This day came the parties by their Attornies and the Plaintiff not farther prosecuting It is ordered that this Suit be dismissed and that the Plaintiff pay to the Defendant his Costs.

```
L. B.    '    WILLIAM HENRY     )
210      '                      )
292      '         vs           )    Original Attachment
         '                      )
         '    JAMES DAVIS       )
```

This day came the Plaintiff by his Attorney and the attachment having been returned no property found; On motion of the Plaintiff by his Attorney a Judicial Attachment is awarded him against the estate of the Said Defendant returnable here at the next Court.

```
A. R.    '    JAMES WHITE       )
Rhea     '                      )
211      '         vs           )  Caveat.   James White withdrew
W. C.    '                      )                  from his Seat
186      '    JOHN WALKER       )
```

This day came the parties by their Attornies and   (Pg. 134)
James White having exhibited to the Court a Certificate under the hand
of the Honorable James Glassgow Secretary of the State of North Carolina,
bearing date the 14th day of November 1793 Certifying to the Justices
of this Court that his Excellency the Governor of the State of North
Carolina had Suspended the execution of a Grant to John Walker for a
tract of land in the County of Hawkins now called Knox, which land he
hath caused to be Surveyed under a Warrant No. 1040 Issuing from
John Armstrongs office, and which lands the Said James White claims
by purchase from Elisha Baker, and by title from the Said State to
himself in part and to himself & William Blount esquire and by
Possession and Occupation as in the Said Certificate of Suspension
mentioned, therefore in pursuance thereof it is ordered by this Court
that the Sheriff of this County do Summon a Jury of good and lawful men
to meet on the premises, to the end that the claim to the Said land
and the Controversy between the Said parties may be determined, and
return the proceedings which may be had thereon to our next Court to
be held for the Said County. _____

James White and George Roulstone come into Court and acknowledge
themselves indebted to John Walker in the Sum of Five hundred dollars,
to be void on condition that the Said James White doth with effect
prosecute a Suit brought by him this day against the Said John
Walker otherwise pay and Satisfy all costs and damages that may be
awarded against him for failure.

The Court proceeded to lay the County Tax for this Year which
is laid as follows:

               On each hundred Acres of land ----------------- 16 2/3 Cents
               On each Poll -------------------------------- 50   "

Ordered that the following Justices do take in and return to next
Court a list of the Taxables and Taxable property of the respective
Companies for which they are appointed._____

For Captain McGaugheys Company			John Evans
" "	Blacks	"	Samuel Newell
" "	Ervins	"	William Lowry
" "	Tedfords	"	Abraham Ghormly
" "	Singletons	"	William Hamilton
" "	Henrys	"	David Craig
" "	Flennekins	"	Thomas McCullough
" "	Cozby's	"	James Cozby
" "	Gillespies	"	Jeremiah Jack
" "	Cox's	"	John Kearns
" "	Beairds	"	John Sawyers
" "	Crawfords	"	James White
" "	Menifees	"	Luke Lea
" "	Campbells	"	John Hackett

(Pg. 135)

For Captain Samples Company			George McNutt
" "	Stones	"	John Chisolm

Ordered that the Sheriff do Summons the following persons to attend at the next Superior Court as Jurors to Wit.

Thomas McCullock,	John Evans,	David Craig	William Hamilton
Jeremiah Jack,	John Chisolm	James Houston	Abraham Ghormly
Samuel Newell	John Adair	Alexander Kelly	John Beard
Thomas Gillespie	John Menefee	David Campbell	John Kean
James Cozby, and	Paul Cunningham.		

Court adjourned 'till Court in Course.

MONDAY 5th MAY 1794

Monday May 5th 1794

At a Court of pleas and Quarter Sessions began and held for the County of Knox at the Court house in Knoxville on the first Monday of May 1794 present James White, John Chisolm, George McNutt, James Cozby, and Luke Lea esquires Justices &. C. & C.

Robert Houston esquire Sheriff & C. returned that he had executed our Writ of Venire Facias to him directed upon the following persons to Wit   William Regan, Warner Martin, John Kean, Moses Brooks, Joseph Evans, Andrew Evans, Senior, Nathaniel Evans, William Gillespie, Junior, Samuel Flennekin, John Thurman, John Gamble, William Bayles, George Stout, Hugh Forgey, Joseph Hinds, William Reed, Benjamin Gest, Senior, John McIntire, Robert Love, Andrew Martin, and Joseph Wear.

Out of which Venire the following persons were elected a Grand Inquest for the Body of this County to Wit, Joseph Hinds, foreman, William Regan, Warner Martin, John Kean, Moses Brooks, Andrew Evans, Senior, William Gillespie, Junior, John Gamble, William Bayles, George Stout, Hugh Forgey, Benjamin Gest, Senior, John McIntire, Andrew Martin, and Joseph Wear, who have been Sworn received their Charge and withdrew to enquire of their presentments.

Ordered that David Ogden, and Orphan, be bound to Thomas Woodward until he arrive to the age of Twenty one Years and agreeably to the Said order, Indentures are signed & a Counterpart filed in the Office. ____

(Pg. 136)

A. R.	'	JAMES WHITE	.... Plaintiff	)	
Rhea	'			)	
211	'	vs		)	Caveat. James White
W. C.	'			)	withdrew from his Seat.
186	'	JOHN WALKER	.... Defendant	)	

This day came the parties by their Attornies and the Sheriff
Robert Houston esquire now returned here the Panel and Verdict of
the Jury which he had caused to come upon the premises pursuant to
our Writ to him directed in these Words to Wit;   April 11th 1794
A Jury impanelled and Sworn,   Joseph Looney, Moses Looney, John
Patterson, James McElwee, John Cain, Major Lea, William Lea, Robert
Armstrong, George Hays, William Reed, Thomas Gillespie, George Brock
pursuant to act of Assembly in Such case made and provided, to try a
matter in controversy respecting a claim or title of land, Subsisting
in the Court of Knox formerly Hawkins County by an order of Said
Court, pursuant to a Certificate of Suspension by his Excellency the
Governor of North Carolina Signed the Honorable James Glassgow
Secretary.   wherein James White is Plaintiff and John Walker is
Defendant, We the Jury do Say we find for the Plaintiff;
Joseph Looney, John Patterson, James McElwee, John Cain, Major Lea,
William Lea, George Hays, William Reed, Thomas Gillespie, George Brock,
Robert Armstrong Whereupon on motion of the Defendant by his Attorney,
the plaintiff is put under a rule to Show cause why the Said Verdict
Should not be Set aside and a new trial Granted which was argued and
Overruled.   And on motion of the Plaintiff by his Attorney the
Said Verdict is confirmed and it is ordered that a transcript of the
Record properly authenticated be made and delivered to the Plaintiff
from which Judgment the Defendant prays an Appeal to the next Superior
Court to be holden for the District of Hamilton at the Court House
in Knoxville which was argued and Overruled.

             Court Adjourned 'till tomorrow 9 C'Clock.

                      TUESDAY MAY 6th 1794

        Tuesday Morning May 6th 1794 Court met according to
Adjournment present John Chisolm Samuel Newell, George McNutt
William Wallace, and John Adair esquires Justices & C. & C.____

        A Petition of James Harralson for liberty to keep a Public
Ferry at his own landing on Holston River was presented to Court and
William McBee on his Motion is admitted Defendant and the Parties
by their Attys. being fully heard; It is ordered that the Said
Petition be Granted.

(Pg. 137)

        The Petition of Abraham McCleary for liberty to keep a Public
Ferry at his own landing on French broad River was presented to
Court examined and Granted.

        Robert Kirkpatrick produced a Commission from Governor Blount,
by which it appears that he is appointed a Constable for this County
who entered into Bond with Hyram Geron and Benjamin Guest his
Securities in the Sum of Six hundred and twenty five dollars; with
condition for the faithful discharge of his duties; who hath been
Sworn as the law directs.____

Court adjourned 'till tomorrow 9 O'Clock.

Wednesday Morning May 7th 1794 Court met according to adjournment present James White, John Evans, Thomas McCullock Samuel Newell, Abraham Ghormly, George McNutt, John Adair, and David Campbell esquires Justices & C. & C.

558 11 ' Ordered that Process issue against Zapher Tannery,
236 15 ' Christiana Amerine and James Bunch, to cause them to
557 16 ' appear at the next Court to answer the Indictments
        ' found against them by the Grand Jury.
        '

Rhea   ' UNITED STATES   ....)
14   '   )
202   '   vs   ) Presentment
        '   )
        ' MICHAEL FOSTER ....)

The Sheriff having returned the Capias on Indictment executed. This day came John Rhea esquire Solicitor for the County, and he not farther prosecuting It is ordered that this prosecution be dismissed.

Phea   ' UNITED STATES   ....)
18   '   )
203   '   vs   ) T. A. B.
        '   )
        ' MICHAEL SWISHER ....)

This day came as well the Solicitor for the County as the Defendant by his Attorney and thereupon came a Jury to Wit, William Walker, Pearson Brock, Thomas Gillespie, John Kerr, Abraham McCleary, William Lea, George Wood, John Evans, James Ewing, Acquilla Johnston, Paul Cunningham, and Alexander Campbell who being elected tried and Sworn, the truth of and upon the premises to Speak upon their Oath do Say that the Said Michael Swisher is Guilty in manner and form as charged in the Bill of Indictment. Therefore it is considered by the Court that for Such his offence he be fined One Dollar and that he pay the Costs of this Prosecution._____

(Pg. 138)

Rhea   ' UNITED STATES   )
21   '   )
204   '   vs   )   A B
        '   )
        ' MOSES STEGALL   )

This day came as well the Solicitor for the County as the Defendant by his Attorney and thereupon came a Jury to Wit George Wood, John Evans, John Caldwell, John Tedford, William Davidson, John Benning, James Houston, Joseph Evans, Robert Wood, Sam'L McCullough, Samuel Paxton, and Abraham McCleary who being elected tried and Sworn, the truth of and upon the

Premises to Speak upon their Oath do Say that the Said Moses
Stegall is Guilty in manner and form as charged in the Bill of
Indictment. Therefore It is considered by the Court that for Such
his offence he be fined One Dollar and that he pay the Costs of this
prosecution. ____

The Grand Jury returned and presented an Indictment against
John Evans for an Assault and Battery a true Bill and also an
Indictment against William Evans, for an Assault and Battery a true
Bill and having nothing further to present were discharged.
Whereupon It is ordered that Process issue against the Said John
Evans & William Evans to cause them to appear at the next Court to
answer the Indictments this day found against them by the Grand Jury.___

237. 22.   235   23

J. H.	'	SOLOMAN MARKS	.... Plaintiff	)	
36	'			)	
Rhea	'	vs		)	In Case
252	'			)	
	'	ROBERT KING	.... Defendant	)	

This day came the parties by their Attornies and thereupon came a
Jury to Wit, Nathaniel Evans, David Walker, James Kerr, David Mitchell,
John Sterling, John McAlister, James McElwee, John Wear, James Stirling,
Henry Willson, William Reed and Abraham Utter who being elected tried
and Sworn the truth to Speak upon the Issues joined upon their Oath do
Say, the Defendant did not assume upon himself as in pleading he hath
alledged Whereupon on Motion of the Plaintiff and for reasons appearing
to the Court the Said Verdict is Set aside and It is ordered that the
Plaintiff pay all costs that have accrued in this Suit and that a New
trial be had at the next Court 'till which time the Cause is continued.___

William Evans produced a Commission from Governor Blount by which
it appears that he is appointed a Constable for this County who entered
into Bond with Nathaniel Evans and Joseph Alexander his Securities in
the Sum of Six hundred and twenty five dollars with Condition for the
faithful discharge of his duties; who hath been Sworn as the law directs.

(Pg. 139)

Rhea	'	JOHN CHISOLM	)	
49	'		)	
652	'	vs	)	In Case
	'		)	
	'	RICHARD HAMILTON	)	

This day came the Plaintiff by his Attorney and by his Consent
and with the assent of the Court, the enquiry of damages is referred
until the next Court. ____

```
J. H.   :   THOMAS BROWN          )
L. B.   :                         )
60      :         vs              )   A B
Rhea    :                         )
J. L.   :   LITTLE PAGE SIMS      )
172     :
```

The Defendant Little Page Sims in his proper person appeared and agrees to pay the Costs of this Suit and upon this the Plaintiff prays that his costs and charges by him about his Suit in this behalf expended may be adjudged to him. Therefore It is considered by the Court that the Plaintiff recover against the Said Defendant his costs by him about his Suit in this behalf expended. And the Said Defendant in Mercy & C. And the Plaintiff not farther prosecuting It is ordered that this Suit be dismissed. Whereupon the Plaintiff acknowledges that he has received Satisfaction for his Attornies fee, therefore as to So much the Said Defendant is acquitted & discharged.

```
A. R.   :   JOHN TODD    ....... Plaintiff  )
75      :                                   )
A. O.   :         vs                        )   In Case
173     :                                   )
        :   JOHN McAMY    ....... Defendant  )
```

This day came the parties by their Attornies and thereupon came a Jury to Wit, Nathaniel Evans, Paul Cunningham, Abraham McCleary, John McAlister, Robert Black, Henry Nelson, Abraham Utter, William Walker, Pearson Brock, Alexander Campbell, John Kerr, and William Lea, who being elected tried and Sworn the truth to Speak upon the Issue joined upon their Oath do Say that the Defendant did assume upon himself in manner and form as the Plaintiff against him hath complained and they do assess the Plaintiffs damages by occasion of the Defendants Nonperformance of that assumption to Thirty dollars besides his Costs; Therefore it is considered by the Court that the Plaintiff recover against the Defendant his damages aforesaid in form aforesaid, and his Costs by him about his Suit in this behalf expended, and the Said Defendant in Mercy & C.

```
Rhea    :   JOHN FEE          ..... Plaintiff  )
82      :                                      )
J. H.   :         vs                           )   In Case
A. R.   :                                      )
174     :   ANDREW PAUL  Admr. of              )
            JAMES PAUL  dec'd.  ..... Defdt.    )
```

This day came the parties by their Attornies and   (Pg. 140) thereupon came a Jury to Wit, Archibald Cowan, David Walker, Daniel Willson, Robert Williams, Burton Pride, John Sommerville, Stephen Duncan, Raleigh Hogan, William McNutt, Martin Armstrong, Junior,

Samuel Hindman, and Anderson Ashburn who being elected tried and
Sworn the truth to Speak upon the issues joined upon their Oath do
Say the Defendant did not assume upon himself as in pleading he hath
alledged. Whereupon on Motion of the Plaintiff the Defendant is put
under a rule to Shew cause why the Said Verdict Should not be Set
aside and a New trial Granted which was argued and Overruled.

```
A. O.    '    MARY STEPHENSON &)              )
88       '    EDWARD STEPHENSON)              )
J. H.    '                     )              )
288      '       Exor. of      )              )
         '                     )              )
              ROBERT STEPHENSON)              )
              deceased         ) ....... Plaintiffs )
                                              )          In Case
                   vs                         )
                                              )
              BENJAMIN BLACKBURN ....... Defendant )
```

This day came the parties by their Attornies and by their
Mutual consent and with the assent of the Court the trial of the
Issues is referred until next Court.

```
A. O.    '    WILLIAM COX        )
96       '                       )
A. R.    '         vs            )    In Case
Rhea     '                       )
175      '    WILLIAM TRIMBLE     )
```

The Plaintiff not farther prosecuting It is ordered that
this Suit be dismissed. ___   Note: Francis A. Ramsey assumes
payment of Costs.

Court adjourned 'till tomorrow 9 O'Clock.

THURSDAY MAY 8th 1794

Thursday Morning May 8th 1794 Court met according to
Adjournment present James White, Samuel Newell, Jeremiah Jack,
and David Craig esquires Justices & C. & C.

```
Rhea     ' '    JOHN CHISOLM  ....... Plaintiff )
102      '                                      )
176      '                                      )    In Case
         '         vs                           )
         '    JOHN CHISOM   ....... Defendant )
```

This day came the Plaintiff by his Attorney and thereupon came
Jury to Wit, Robert Thompson, John McAlister, David Dermond,
Aquilla Johnston, Abraham McCleary, James McElwee, David Mitchell,
Charles Regan, James Thompson, John Evans, James Kerr, and John

Fryar, who being elected tried and Sworn, diligently to enquire
of damages in this Suit upon their Oath do Say that the Plaintiff hath
Sustained damages by occasion of the Defendants Nonperformance of the
assumption in the declaration mentioned to Thirty dollars besides his
costs; Therefore It is considered by the Court that the Plaintiff
recover against the Defendant his damages aforesaid in form aforesaid
assessed and his Costs by him about his Suit in this behalf expended.
And the Said Defendant in Mercy & C. & C. _____

(Pg. 141)

A. R.	'	ROBERT THOMPSON .... Plaintiff	)	
115	'		)	
Rhea	'	vs	)	In Case
253	'		)	
	'	JOHN McALISTER .... Defendant	)	

This day came the parties by their Attornies and thereupon
came a Jury to Wit, William Roberts, John Dyer, Acquilla Johnston,
Abraham McCleary, James McElwee, David Mitchell, Charles Ragan,
John Evans, James Kerr, Andrew Paul, James Briggam, and James
Cochran who being elected tried and Sworn the truth to Speak upon
the issue joined upon their Oath do Say that the Defendant did assume
upon himself in manner and form as the Plaintiff against him hath
complained and they do assess the Plaintiff damages by occasion thereof to Forty dollars besides his Costs. Whereupon on Motion of the
Defendant, the Plaintiff is put under a rule to Shew cause why the
Said Verdict Should not be Set aside and a new trial Granted, which
was argued and Granted.

The propriety of allowing Mileage to Witnesses who attend
County Courts being Submitted to this Court, It is their opinion
that the law does allow witnesses One Dollar for every thirty Miles
travelled in coming to and returning from a Court.

Rhea	'	ALEXANDER CARMICHAEL	)	
118	'		)	
A. O.	'	vs	)	In Case
254	'		)	
	'	JOSEPH SEVEIR	)	

This day came the parties by their Attornies and by their
mutual consent and with the assent of the Court the trial of the
Issue is referred until next Court. ____

A. O.	'	ANNE MILLS .... Plaintiff	)	
132	'		)	
J. H.	'	vs	)	In Case
177	'		)	
	'	ANDREW PAUL admr. of	)	
		JAMES PAUL dec'd. .... Defendant	)	

This day came the parties by their Attornies and thereupon came
a Jury to Wit, Robert Rhea, Paul Cunningham, George Woods, Pearson

Brock, David Walker, James Millikin, Anderson Ashburn, Obadiah Bounds, William Doak, James Harralson, William Reed, & Aquilla Low who being elected tried and Sworn diligently to enquire of damages in this Suit upon their Oath do Say the Plaintiff hath Sustained damages by occasion of the Defendants Nonperformance (Pg. 142) of the Assumption in the Declaration mentioned to Sixty Six dollars and fifty Cents besides her costs; Therefore it is considered by the Court that the Plaintiff recover against the Defendant her Damages aforesaid in form aforesaid assessed and her Costs by her Suit in this behalf expended.

A. O.	'	JOHN HUTCHINSON	.......)	
133	'		)	
J. H.	'	vs	)	In Case.
567	'		)	
	'	ANDREW PAUL admr. of	)	
		JAMES PAUL dec'd.	.......)	

. This day came the parties by their Attornies and by their Mutual consent, and with the assent of the Court the trial of the issues is referred until the next Court. ____

J. H.	'	ANDREW PAUL admr. of		)	
134	'	JAMES PAUL dec'd.	.... Plaintiff	)	
J. L.	'			)	In Case
L. B.	'	vs	.	)	Trover
178	'			)	
		JOSEPH WEAR	.... Defdt.	)	

This day came the parties by their Attornies and thereupon came a Jury to Wit, William Murphy, Robert Blackburn, James Brook, Archibald Cowan, Samuel Acklin, John Brown; Thomas Gillespie, Samuel Flennikin, Robert Williams, Joseph Hart, John Walker, and William Robertson who being elected tried and Sworn the truth to Speak upon the issue joined upon their Oath do Say that the Defendant doth detain two Red Cows, with white faces, One Black and White Cow, and one Silver Watch in the Declaration mentioned in manner and form as the Plaintiff against him hath complained and that the Said Cows and Watch are of the price of thirty Nine dollars, and they do assess the Plaintiffs damages by occasion of the detention aforesaid to One Cent, besides his Costs; Whereupon the Plaintiff was put under a rule to Shew cause why the Said Verdict Should not be Set aside and a new trial Granted, which was argued and Overruled. ____

Therefore it is considered by the Court that the Plaintiff recover against the Said Defendant the Cows and Watch aforesaid if they may be had but if not then the price aforesaid of them together with his damages aforesaid in form aforesaid assessed, and his Costs by him about his Suit in this behalf expended. And the Said Defendant in Mercy & C. & C.

Note, In this Cause a Motion was made for an Appeal, and reasons filed but bond and Security not being given the Same was discharged. ____

(Pg. 143)

```
S. M.   '    JAMES ALLISON        )
135     '                         )
J. H.   '         vs              )    In Covenant
L. B.   '                         )
356     '    ABRAHAM SWAGERTY      )
```

This day came the parties by their Attornies and by their
Mutual consent, and with the assent of the Court the trial of the
issues is referred until next Court. _____

```
J. L.   '    WILLIAM LOWRY        )
140     '                         )
A. O.   '         vs              )    In Case
205     '                         )
        '    GEORGE WOODS          )
```

This day came the parties by their Attornies and by their
Mutual consent and with the assent of the Court the trial of the
Issue is referred until next Cour. _____

```
A. R.   '    JOHN WALLACE         )
141     '                         )
255     '         vs              )    Original Attachment,  In Case
        '                         )
        '    JAMES BRIANT          )
```

This day came the Plaintiff by his Attorney and by his consent
and with the assent of the Court the Cause is continued until next
Court. _____

```
Rhea    '    DAVID CRAIG   ....... Plaintiff )
142     '                                    )   Original Attachment
J. H.   '         vs                         )   David Craig withdrew
179     '    SOLOMAN MARKS  ....... Defendant )   from his Seat.
        '                                    )
```

This day came the parties by their Attornies and thereupon came a
Jury to Wit, Robert Rhea, George Woods, Pearson Brock, David Walker,
James Millikin, Anderson Ashburn, Obadian Bounds, William Doak, James
Harralson, William Reed, Andrew McCampbell and James Millikin, Junior,
who being elected tried and Sworn the truth to Speak upon the issues
joined upon their Oath do Say they find for the Plaintiff twenty one
Dollars and twenty five Cents, besides his Costs. Therefore it is con-
sidered by the Court that the Plaintiff recover against the Defendant
the Said Twenty one Dollars and twenty five Cents and his Costs by him
about his Suit in this behalf expended. And the Said Defendant in
Mercy & C. _____ Note In this Cause a Motion was made for an Appeal,
Bond with Security entered into the reasons filed but the Tax on the
Appeal not being paid the Same was discharged. _____

(Pg. 144)

```
A. R.    '    JAMES BLAIR                )
147      '                                ) ·
J. H.    '         vs                     )        In Case
180      '                                )
         '    ANDREW THOMPSON &           )
              ROBERT THOMPSON             )
```

The Plaintiff not farther prosecuting It is ordered that this Suit be dismissed and that the Plaintiff pay to the Defendants their Costs.

```
Rhea     '    SAMUEL FLANNAGAN      ....... )
149      '              .                   )
Reesse   '         vs                       )        In Covenant
256      '                                  )
         '    JOHN SEVEIR &       )         )
              ADAM MEEK Exrs. of  )         )
              ISAAC TAYLOR deceased )  ....... )
```

This day came the parties by their Attornies and by their mutual consent, and with the assent of the Court the argument of the Demurrer is referred 'till next Court. ___

```
A. R.    '    JAMES FORGEY adm. of          )
150      '    JOHN FORGEY dec'd.  ....... )
J. H.    '                                  )
206      '         vs     .                  )        In Case
         '                                  )
              JOSEPH BEARD       ....... )
```

This day came the parties by their Attornies and by their Mutual consent and with the assent of the Court the trial of the issue is referred until the next Court. ___

```
Rhea     '    STOCKLEY DONELSON  ........... )
151      '                                   )
A. R.    '         vs                        )        In Case
181      '                                   )
         '    ELLIOT GRILLS  .............. )
```

This day came the parties by their Attornies and each agree to pay one half of the Costs except the Plaintiffs Attorneys fee which the Defendant agrees to pay. The Plaintiff not farther prosecuting It is ordered that the Suit be dismissed.

```
A. R.    '    THOMAS EMBREE              )
152      '                              )
S. M.    '         vs                   )        In Case
Rhea     '                              )
257      '    JOHN CHISOLM              )
```

This day came the parties by their Attornies and by their Mutual consent and with the assent of the Court the trial of the Issue is referred until next Court. ___

(Pg. 145)

D. G.	'	SAMUEL TATE	)	
153	'		)	
Rhea	'	vs	)	In Case
S. M.	'		)	
207	'	JOHN CHISOLM	)	

    This day came the parties by their Attornies and by their Mutual consent and with the assent of the Court the trial of the Issue is referred 'till next Court.

A. R. W. C.	'	WILLIAM JOHNSTON	)	
154	'		)	
J. H.	'	vs	)	In Case
A. O.	'		)	
208	'	ANDERSON ASHBURN	)	

    This day came the parties by their Attornies and by their Mutual consent and with the assent of the Court the trial of the Issue is referred 'till next Court.

Rhea	'	SAMUEL FINLEY	)	
158	'		)	
T. Love	'	vs	)	A B
258	'		)	
	'	JOHN BIRD	)	

    This day came the parties by their Attornies and the Cause is continued for the award of the Arbitrators 'till next Court.

Rhea	'	HUGH DUNLAP	)	
159	'		)	
Reesse	'	vs	)	In Debt
209	'		)	
	'	PETER McNAMEE	)	

    This day came the parties by their Attornies and by their Mutual Consent and with the assent of the Court the trial of the issues is referred 'till next Court.

A. R.	'	JOHN McCAULEY	)	
161	'		)	
J. L.	'	vs	)	In Case
210	'		)	
	'	WILLIAM LOWRY	)	

    This day came the parties by their Attornies and by their Mutual Consent and with the assent of the Court the trial of the issue is referred 'till next Court.

J. L.	'	CHARLES REGAN	)
163	'		)
Rhea	'	vs	) In Case
L. B.	'		)
238	'	DANIEL CARMICHAEL	)

This day came the Plaintiff by his Attorney and the Sheriff
having returned that the Defendant is not be found in his County;
On motion of the Plaintiff by his Attorney a Judicial Attachment is
awarded him against the estate of the Said Defendant returnable here
at the next Court.

Ordered that George Pharo, an Orphan Child now of the Age
of Six weeks be bound apprentice to John Dyer, until he arrive to
the Age of Twenty one years; And that Elizabeth Pharo an Orphan
child now of the Age of Five years be bound Apprentice to the Said
John Dyer until She arrive to the age of Eighteen Years.

                Court Adjourned 'till tomorrow 9 O'Clock.

(Pg. 146)

                        FRIDAY MAY 9th 1794

        Friday Morning May 9th 1794 Court met according to
Adjournment present James White, David Campbell, William
Hamilton and George McNutt esquires Justices & C. & C.

        Agreeably to an order of Court made Yesterday for binding
George Pharo and Elizabeth Pharo orphan Children to John Dyer;
Indentures have been executed by James White Chairman, on behalf
of himself and his Successors; and by John Dyer on behalf of himself,
and a Counterpart executed by the parties and filed in the Office.
And the Said John Dyer with William Cocke his Security entered into
and acknowledged their Bond in the Sum of Five hundred dollars, with
condition for the Said John Dyer's faithful performance of his Covenant
in the Said Indentures, mentioned.

A. O.	' ·	JAMES McELWEE'S Lessee .... Plaintiff	)	
165	'		)	
Rhea	'	vs	)	In
182	'		)	Ejectment.
	'	JAMES STERLING .... Defendant	)	

        This day came the parties by their Attornies and thereupon
came a Jury to Wit, John McDowell, Andrew Paul, Hugh Forgey,
William Brazelton, Major Lea, Martin Armstrong, Junior, Robert
Wood, Samuel Cowan, George Greer, Stephen Duncan, John Evans and
James Harralson who being elected tried and Sworn the truth to
Speak upon the issue joined upon their Oath do Say that the defendant
is not guilty of the Tresspass and Ejectment in the declaration

Supposed, as in pleading he hath alledged; Therefore It is considered by the Court that the Plaintiff take nothing by his Bill but for his false clamour be in Mercy & C. and the defendant go thereof without day and recover against the lessor of the Plaintiff his Costs by him about his defence in this behalf expended. _____

J. H.	'	WILLIAM COBB	)	
167	'		)	
211	'	vs	)	Original Attachment
	'		)	
	'	WILLIAM COX	)	

This day came the Plaintiff by his Attorney and by his consent and with the assent of the Court the enquiry of damages is referred 'till next Court. _____

Reese	'	WILLIAM DAVIDSON	)	
171	'		)	
J. L.	'	vs	)	In Covenant
321	'		)	
	'	WILLIAM LOWRY	)	

This day came the parties by their Attornies and by their Mutual consent and with the assent of the Court the Cause is continued until the next Court. _____

(Pg. 147)

Rhea	'	BRIAN McCABE adm. of	)	
172	'	TITUS OGDEN dec'd.	)	
357	'		)	
	'	vs	)	In Case
	'		)	
		EZEKIEL HENRY &	)	
		WILLIAM HENRY	)	

This day came the Plaintiff by his Attorney and by his Consent and with the Assent of the Court, the enquiry of damages is referred 'till next Court. _____

Reese	'	LEWIS TINER	)	
173	'		)	
Rhea	'	vs	)	Appeal
212	'		)	
	'	HUGH DUNLAP	)	

This day came the parties by their Attornies and by their Mutual consent, and with the assent of the Court the Cause is continued until the next Court. _____

```
A. R.    '      JOHN WALKER          )
175      '                           )
Rhea     '         vs               )        Appeal
213      '                           )
  '      '      JOHN SOMMERVILLE     )
```

This day came the parties by their Attornies and by their mutual Consent and with the assent of the Court the Cause is continued 'till next Court.

```
A. R.    '      ABRAHAM UTTER        )
176      '                           )
Rhea     '         vs               )        Appeal
183      '                           )
         '      ALEXANDER CARMICHAEL )
```

This day came as well the Plaintiff by his Attorney as the Defendant in his proper person and the Said Defendant Saith he cannot gainsay the Plaintiffs action for One Dollar and forty Cents; Therefore by consent of the parties, It is considered by the Court that the Plaintiff recover against the Said Defendant the Said One Dollar and forty Cents agreed as aforesaid; And also his Costs by him about his Suit in this behalf expended. And the Said Defendant in Mercy &c. & C.

```
Rhea     '      GEORGE ROULSTONE & CO.  ..... Plaintiff )
177      '                                             )
184      '              vs                            )  Origl.
         '                                             )     Attachment
         '      JOSEPH WEST             ..... Defendant )
```

This day came the Plaintiffs by their Attorney and David Moor the Garnashee appearing ON Motion It is ordered that the Judgment obtained at the last Court, against him be Set aside; The Plaintiffs not farther prosecuting It is ordered that this Suit be dismissed.

```
J. H.    '      JAMES CARMICHAEL     )
178      '                           )
Rhea     '         vs               )     In Covenant
L. B.    '                           )
214      '      ALEXANDER CARMICHAEL )
```

This day came the Parties by their Attornies and by their Mutual consent and with the assent of the Court the trial of the Issue is referred 'till next Court.

(Pg. 148)

```
J. L.    '      JOHN DUNCAN          )
179      '                           )
412      '         vs               )     In Covenant
A. R.    '                           )
         '      JOHN McNUTT  &       )
              JAMES CALLISON         )
```

This day came the parties by their Attornies and by their
mutual consent and with the assent of the Court the argument of
the Plaintiffs Demurrer to the Defendants plea is referred 'till
next Court. ____

H. L.	'	JOHN DAVIS	)	
181	'		)	
Rhea	'	vs	)	In Case
322	'		)	
	'	JOSEPH JANES	)	

This day came the parties by their Attornies and by their
mutual consent and with the assent of the Court the trial of the
issues is referred 'till next Court.

J. H.	'	ROBERT BLACKBURN	)	
182	'		)	
A. O.	'	vs	)	In Case Trover
215	'		)	
	'	JOHN LOWRY esquire	)	

This day came the parties by their Attornies and by their
mutual consent and with the assent of the Court the trial of the
Issue is referred until next Court. ____

J. L.	'	JEAN KERR	)	
185	'	by	)	
A. R.	'	her next friend	)	
W. C.	'	JAMES KERR	)	
217	'		)	
		vs	)	Malicious prosecution
			)	
		JOHN CALDWELL	)	

This day came the parties by their Attornies and by their
mutual Consent and with the assent of the Court the trial of the
Issue is referred 'till next Court. ____

H. L.	'	JAMES BRIGGAM	)	
D. G.	'		)	
W. C.	'	vs	)	In Covenant
C. C.	'		)	
186	'	JOHN CHISOLM	)	
A. R.	'			
A. O.	'			
323	'			

This day came the parties by their Attornies and by their
mutual consent and with the assent of the Court the trial of the
Issue is referred until next Court; And on motion of the Defendant
a Commission is awarded him to examine and take the deposition of
his Witnesses giving the Plaintiff legal notice of the time and
place of executing the Same. ____

```
J. H.      :    PATRICK HENNEY        )
187        :                          )
Rhea       :          vs             )      In Case
218        :                          )
           :    SAMUEL HINDMAN        )
```

This day came the parties by their Attornies and by their mutual Consent and with the assent of the Court the trial of the issues is referred until the next Court. _____

(Pg. 149)

```
A. R.      :    FRANCIS BIRD          )
168        :                          )
Rhea       :          vs             )      In Case
A. O.      :                          )
259        :    JOHN CHISOLM &        )
                JOHN MILLER
```

This day came the parties by their Attornies and by their mutual consent and with the assent of the Court the trial of the issues is referred until the next Court. _____

```
A. R.      :    PEARSON BROCK         )
189        :                          )
Rhea       :          vs             )      In Case   Words
260        :                          )
           :    JAMES THOMPSON        )
```

This day came the parties by their Attornies and by their Mutual Consent and with the assent of the Court the trial of the issues is referred 'till next Court. _____

```
Rhea       :    ROBERT RHEA        ·  )
190        :                          )
219        :          vs          ·  )      In Case
           :                          )
           :    DAVID MILLER          )
```

This day came the Plaintiff by his Attorney and having filed his Declaration, and the Defendant having been arrested and not appearing though Solemnly called, On motion of the Plaintiff by his Attorney; It is considered by the Court that the Plaintiff recover against the Defendant Such damages as he hath Sustained by occasion of the Defendants Nonperformance of the Assumption in the declaration mentioned; which damages are to be enquired of by a Jury at the next Court. _____

```
H. L.      :    DAVID WRIGHT          )
192        :                          )
Rhea       :          vs             )      In Case
289        :                          )
           :    JAMES SPENCE          )
```

This day came the parties by their Attornies and on affidavit
of the Defendant the trial of the issues is referred till next Court.
And on Motion a Commission is awarded the parties to examine and take
the deposition of James Austin, and Joseph Richardson giving each other
notice of the time and place of executing the Same. ____

```
S. M.    '    THOMAS KING          )
Rhea     '                         )
193      '         vs·             )        In Case
J. H.    '                         )
290      '    JOSEPH BEARD         )
```

This day came the parties by their Attornies and by their
Mutual Consent and with the assent of the Court, the trial of the
Issues is referred 'till next Court.

```
Rhea     '    ACQUILLA JOHNSTON    )
194      '                         )
J. H.    '         vs             )        In Case
261      '                         )
         '    MAJOR LEA            )
```

This day came the parties by their Attornies and by their
mutual Consent and with the assent of the Court the trial of the
Issue is referred 'till next. Court.

(Pg. 150)

```
J. L.    '    JAMES WEAR           )
196      '                         )
Rhea     '         vs             )        In Case
262      '                         )
         '    DANIEL WILLSON       )
```

This day came the parties by their Attornies and by their
mutual Consent and with the assent of the Court the trial of the
issue is referred 'till next Court. ____

```
Rhea     '    JOHN SOMMERVILLE     )
197      '                         )
185      '         vs             )        In Case·
         '                         )
         '    JAMES DYARMONT       )
```

This day came the plaintiff by his Attorney and by his Consent
and with the assent of the Court the Cause is continued 'till next
Court.   The plaintiff not farther prosecuting It is ordered that
this Suit be dismissed.   Note, This dismission was at the request
of the Plaintiff ____

Rhea '   BRIAN McCABE admr. of   )
201 '   TITUS OCDEN deceased   )
703 '   )
     '   vs   )   In Case
     '   )
              WILLIAM TATHAM   )

  This day came the Plaintiff by his Attorney and by his consent
& with the assent of the Court the Cause is continued 'till next
Court.____

H. L. '   JOSEPH WEST   )
202 '   )
413 '   vs   )   In Debt
     '   )
     '   RICHARD FINDLESTON   )

  This day came the Plaintiff by his Attorney and by the consent
of the parties and with the assent of the Court the argument of the
Demurrer is referred 'till next Court.

Rhea '   ANNANIAS McCOY   )
203 '   ). Original Attachment
263 '   vs   )   In Case
     '   )
     '   JOHN LUSK   )

  This day came the Plaintiff by his Attorney and by his Consent
and with the assent of the Court, the enquiry of damages is referred
'till next Court.

Rhea '   STEPHEN DUNCAN & CO.   )
204 '   )
739 '   vs   )   Original Attachment
     '   )   In Case
     '   JOSEPH WEST   )

  This day came the Plaintiff by their Attorney and Hugh Dunlap
Garnashee being first Sworn Saith that Captn McGauhey, Joseph Janes,
David Moor, and Richard Findleston all owe the Defendant and that he
had at the time of being Served with the Scire Facias the Books of
the Said Joseph West in his possession, but that there was at the
time of the ScireFacias being Served on him receipts from Joseph
West to George Greer certifying the payment by the   '(Pg. 151)
Said Greer to the Defendant Joseph West, in full of the Debt due on
the Said Books and a power of Attorney from the Said West to him
the Said Dunlap to collect and that Since the return of Joseph West
the Defendant to this Country he took the aforesaid Books without the
Consent of him the Said Hugh Dunlap. Whereupon on motion of the Said
Hugh Dunlap It is ordered that the Judgment obtained at the last Court
against him be Set aside.____ The Defendant not appearing to replevy
the property attached although Solemnly called On motion of the Plaintiffs
It is considered by the Court, that the Plaintiffs recover against the
Defendant Such damages as they have Sustained by occasion of the Defendants
Nonperformance of the assumption in the declaration mentioned; which
damages are to be enquired of by a Jury at the next Court.____

```
Rhea        '     GEORGE PRESTON        )
206         '                           )
448         '          VS               )        Original Attachment
            '                           )
            '     JOSEPH ROBINSON       )            In Case
```

This day came the Plaintiff by his Attorney and Charles
Medlock Garnashee, being first Sworn Saith, that he oweth the
Defendant nothing, that he hath not, nor had he at the time he was
Summoned Garnashee any of the effects of the Defendants in his hands,
that he knows of no debts due to the Defendant, but that he hath
understood there is property belonging to the Defendant in the hands
of Samuel McBee therefore on motion of the Plaintiff by his Attorney
a Judicial attachment is awarded him against the estate of the Said
Defendant returnable here at the next Court. ____

```
A. R.       '     DAVID CALDWELL        )
207         '                           )
J. L.       '          vs               )        Appeal
291         '                           )
            '     WILLIAM LOWRY         )
```

This day came the parties by their Attornies and by their
mutual consent and with the assent of the Court the Cause is continued 'till next Court.

```
L. B.       '     WILLIAM HENRY         )
210         '                           )
292         '          vs               )        Original Attachment
            '                           )
            '     JAMES DAVIS           )
```

This day came the Plaintiff by his Attorney and the attachment
having been returned no property found; On Motion of the Plaintiff
by his Attorney the Cause is continued 'till the next Court. ____

(Pg. 152)

```
A. R.       '     ADAM MEEK &           )
212         '     JOHN SEVEIR  Exers. of )
Rhea        '     ISAAC TAYLOR  deceased )
220         '                           )
            '          vs               )        Petition for Partition
            '     JAMES GIBSON .......... )
```

This day came the parties by their Attornies and by their
Mutual consent, and with the assent of the Court the Argument is
refferred 'till next Court. ____

            Court Adjourned 'till tomorrow 9 O'Clock.

                    SATURDAY MAY 10th 1794

Saturday Morning May 10th 1794 Court met according to Adjournment present James White, John Chisolm, George McNutt, Jeremiah Jack and William Hamilton esquires Justices & C. & C.

5	'	JOHN THOMAS	)	
124	'		)	
	'	vs	)	Scire Facias
	'		)	
	'	JOHN BURDIN &	)	
		BENJAMIN BURDIN	)	

Benjamin Burdin one of the Defendants having been duly warned, and not appearing though Solemnly called; On Motion of the Plaintiff by his Attorney; It is considered by the Court that the Plaintiff may have execution against the Said Defendants for Eleven Dollars and Eighty eight Cents the Costs in the Writ aforesaid Specified And also that the Plaintiff recover against the Said Defendants his Costs by him expended in Suing forth and prosecuting this Writ.

6	'	JOHN THOMAS	)	
44	'		)	
	'	vs	)	Scire Facias
	'		)	
	'	JOHN BURDIN, JOHN HERRON &	)	
		NICODEMUS KEITH.	)	

John Herron and Nicodemus Keith two of the Defendants, having been duly warned, and not appearing though Solemnly called; On Motion of the Plaintiff by his Attorney; It is considered by the Court that the Plaintiff may have Execution against the Said Defendants for Nine dollars Seventy Six and One half Cents the Costs in the Writ aforesaid Specifyed, And also that the Plaintiff recover against the Said Defendants his Costs by him expended in Suing forth and prosecuting this Writ.

(Pg. 153)

7	'	JAMES KEARNS	)	
91	'		)	
	'	vs	)	Scire Facias
	'		)	
	'	WILLIAM REED	)	

The Defendant having been duly warned and not appearing though Solemnly called; On Motion of the Plaintiff by his Attorney; It is considered by the Court that the Plaintiff may have Execution against the Said Defendant for Twelve dollars and Ninety four Cents, the Costs in the Writ aforesaid Specifyed, And also that the Plaintiff recover against the Said Defendant his Costs by him expended in Suing forth and prosecuting this Writ.

| 8
132 | '<br>'<br>'<br>'<br>' | DAVID WALKER

vs

ALEXANDER CARMICHAEL &
JOHN CHISOLM |)
)
)
)
)
) | Scire Facias |

The Defendants having been duly warned and not appearing though Solemnly called; On Motion of the Plaintiff by his Attorney; It is considered by the Court that the Plaintiff may have execution against the Said Defendants for Ten Dollars Seventy eight and one half Cents, the Costs in the Writ aforesaid Specifyed and also that the Plaintiff recover against the Said Defendants his Costs by him expended in Suing forth and prosecuting this Writ.____

| 9
81 | '<br>'<br>'<br>'<br>' | HUGH L. WHITE

vs

THOMAS TAYLOR and
JOHN CHISOLM |)
)
)
)
)
) | Scire Facias |

The Defendants having been duly warned, and not appearing though Solemnly called; On Motion of the Plaintiff by his Attorney; It is considered by the Court that the Plaintiff may have execution against the Said Defendants for Fourteen Dollars and thirty five Cents the Debt and Costs in the Writ aforesaid Specifyed And also that the Plaintiff recover against the Said Defendants his Costs by him expended in Suing forth and prosecuting this Writ.____

| 213
187 | '<br>'<br>'<br>'<br>' | ABRAHAM McCLEARY

vs

WILLIAM HAYS &
HENRY MULVENY |)
)
)
)
)
) | Origl. Attachment |

The Plaintiff not farther prosecuting; It is ordered that this Suit be dismissed. ____

(Pg. 154)

| 214
188 | '<br>'<br>'<br>' | MORDECAI MENDINGHALL

vs

RICHARD GRILLS |)
)
)
)
) | Original Attachment. |

The Plaintiff not farther prosecuting; It is Ordered that this Suit be dismissed

A. O.	'	JOHN BROWN	)	
215	'		)	
L. B.	'	vs	)	In Case
265	'		)	
	'	ABRAHAM SWAGGERTY	)	

This day came the parties by their Attornies and the Plaintiff having filed his Declaration the Defendant filed his Plea and the Issue being joined the trial thereof is referred until next Court.___

L. B.	'	JOHN BROWN	)	
J. H.	'		)	
216	'	vs	)	In Debt
A. R.	'		)	
189	'	SAMUEL BOGLE	)	

The Plaintiff not farther prosecuting It is ordered that this Suit be dismissed And that the Plaintiff pay to the Defendant his Costs.

L. B.	'	JOHN BROWN	)	
J. H.	'		)	
217	'	vs	)	In Case
A. R.	'		)	
190	'	HENRY WHITTENBERGER	)	

The Plaintiff not farther prosecuting It is ordered that this Suit be dismissed and that the Plaintiff pay to the Defendant his Costs.___

J. L.	'	GAWIN BLACK	)	
218	'		)	
Rhea	'	vs	)	False Imprisonment.
191	'		)	
	'	JAMES BLAIR	)	

The parties appeared and each agree to pay one half of the Costs, And the Plaintiff not farther prosecuting It is order that this Suit be dismissed.___

A. R.	'	SAMUEL BOGLE	)	
219	'		)	
L. B.	'	vs	)	In Covenant
J. H.	'		)	
266	'	JOHN BROWN	)	

This day came the parties by their Attornies and the Plaintiff having filed his Declaration the Defendant filed his pleas and the issues being joined the trial thereof is referred 'till next Court.

(Pg. 155)

L. B.	'	ISAAC BULLARD	)	
A. O.	'		)	
220	'	vs	)	In Case
A. R.	'		)	
Rhea	'	HUGH BODKIN Jr.	)	
414	'			

This day came the Plaintiff by his Attorney and filed his declaration, and the Defendant filed his pleas and the issues being joined the trial thereof is referred 'till next Court. ____

Rhea	'	WILLIAM BLOUNT GOVERNOR	)	
221	'		)	
192	'	vs	)	In Debt
	'		)	
	'	WILLIAM WALLACE ESQUIRE	)	

.   The Plaintiff not farther prosecuting It is ordered that this Suit be dismissed. ____   Note The Clerk, Sheriff and Attorney relinquish their fees except the Government tax. ____

A. R.	'	AMOS BIRD	)	
222	'		)	
A. O.	'	vs	)	In Covenant
293	'		)	
	'	JACOB VANHOOVER	)	

This day came the parties by their Attornies and the Plaintiff having filed his declaration the Defendant filed his plea and the issue being joined the trial thereof is referred 'till next Court.

H. L.	'	BENJAMIN BLACKBURN	)	
223	'		)	
Rhea	'	vs	)	Original Attachment
415	'		)	
	'	ROBERT BLACKBURN	)	

This day came the Plaintiff by his Attorney And Stockley Donelson who was Summoned to appear here and declare on Oath what he is indebted to the Defendant or what effects he has or had in his hands at the time he was Summoned Garnashee and what debt he knows to be due to or effects belonging to the Defendant in the hands of any other person and who that person is, being Solemnly called came not; On Motion of the Plaintiff by his Attorney It is Considered by the Court that the Plaintiff recover against the Said Stockley Donelson the amount of the Plaintiffs demand against the Said Defendant and also his Costs; unless he appear at our next Court and Shew Sufficient cause why this Judgment Should not be Confirmed: and It is ordered a Scire Facias Issue against him, And the Cause is continued till next Court.

(Pg. 156)

| Rhea
224
Roesse
358 | ' | NATHANIEL & SAMUEL COWAN
vs
PETER McNAMEE |)
)
)
)
) | In Covenant |

This day came the parties by their Attornies and the Plaintiff having filed his declaration the Defendant filed his Plea, and the Plaintiff his replication thereto and the Issue being joined the trial thereof is referred 'till next Court.____

| Rhea
225
L. B.
239 | ' | JOHN COWAN
vs
ANDREW MILLER |)
)
)
)
) | In trover |

This day came the parties by their Attornies and the Plaintiff having filed his declaration the Defendant filed his plea and the issue being joined the trial thereof is referred 'till next Court.____

| Rhea
226
A. R.
324 | ' | JOHN CASHALY
vs
OBADIAH BOUNDS |)
)
)
)
) | In Case |

This day came the parties by their Attornies and the Plaintiff having filed his declaration the Defendant filed his plea and the issue being joined the trial of the issues is referred until next Court.____

| W. C.
227
Rhea
267 | ' | WILLIAM DAVIDSON
vs
JAMES CAREY |)
)
)
)
) | In Case |

This day came the Plaintiff by his Attorney and the Sheriff having returned that the Defendant is not to be found in his County On Motion of the Plaintiff by his Attorney an Alias Capias is awarded him against the Defendant returnable here at the next Court.

| 228
Rhea
A. O.
221 | ' | JONATHAN DOUGLASS
vs
ROBERT KING |)
)
)
)
) | In Covenant |

This day came the Plaintiff in his proper person and the Sheriff having returned that the Defendant is not to be found in his County On Motion of the Plaintiff an Alias Capias is awarded him against the Defendant returnable here at the next Court.____

(Pg. 157)

| J. H.
A. O.
229
193 | ' | STOCKLEY DONELSON

vs

JAMES DIXON |)
)
)
)
) | In Case |

The Defendant assumes payment of Costs. The Plaintiff nor farther prosecuting It is ordered that that this Suit be dismissed.

| Rhea
230
W. C.
194 | ' | CHRISTIAN RHODES Lessee

vs

FEN |)
)
)
)
) | In Ejectment |

John Dyer the tenant in possession comes into Court by William Cocke his Attorney and disclaims all right and title of the premises in the declaration mentioned; And the parties appeared and each agree to pay their own Costs and the Plaintiff not farther prosecuting It is ordered that this Suit be dismissed._____

| L. B.
231
195 | ' | JOHN DYER

vs

HENRY THOMAS |)
)
)
)
) | In Case |

The Defendant Henry Thomas in his proper person appeared and agrees to pay the Costs of this Suit and upon this the Plaintiff prays that his Costs and charges by him about his Suit in this behalf expended may be adjudged to him. Therefore it is considered by the Court that the Plaintiff recover against the Said Defendant his Costs by him about his Suit in this behalf expended, And the Said Defendant in Mercy & C. and the Plaintiff not farther prosecuting It is ordered that this Suit be dismissed._____

Whereupon the Plaintiffs Attorney acknowledges that he has received Satisfaction of the Defendant for his fee _____ therefore as to So much the Said Defendant is acquitted and discharged.

| Rhea
232
196 | ' | HUGH DUNLAP

vs

ROBERT THOMPSON |)
)
)
)
) | Original Attachment |

The Plaintiff not farther prosecuting It is ordered that this Suit be dismissed._____

Rhea   ' JOHN EVANS esquire,   )
L. B. - A. O.   ' a Justice of the Peace .....)
233   '   )
A. R.   ' vs   )   A   B
240   '   )
                MICHAEL SWISHER ....)

     This day came the parties by their Attornies and the Plaintiff having filed his declaration the Defendant filed his Pleas and the issues being Joined the trial thereof is referred 'till next Court.

(Pg. 158)

D. G.   ' ROBERT EVANS   )
234   ' by his next friend)
Rhea   '   )
A. O.   ' vs   )   In Case Trover.
L. B.   '   )
294   ' JOHN EVANS   )

     This day came the parties by their Attornies and the Plaintiff having filed his Declaration the Defendant filed his pleas and the issue being joined the trial thereof is referred 'till next Court. And on Motion of the Defendant a Commission is awarded him to examine and take the deposition of Darky Holms giving the Plaintiff legal notice of the time and place of executing the Same.

Rhea   ' ROBERT FERGUSON)
235   '   )
197   ' vs   )   In Case, Trover.
         '   )
         ' THOMAS JACKSON   )

     The Plaintiff not farther proseouting, It is ordered that this Suit be dismissed and that the Plaintiff pay to the Defendant his Costs.

A. O.   ' JESTER HUFACRE   )
236   '   )
232   ' vs   )   In Case.
         '   )
         ' ANDREW EVANS   )

     This day came the Plaintiff by his Attorney and having filed his declaration and the Defendant having been arrested and not appearing though Solemnly called On Motion of the Plaintiff by his Attorney; It is considered by the Court that the Plaintiff recover against the Defendant Such damages as he hath Sustained by occasion of the Defendants Nonperformance of the assumption in the declaration mentioned; which damages are to be enquired of by a Jury at the next Court.

A. R.	'	JOHN HILL	)	
237	'		)	
Rhea	'	vs	)	In Case
325	'		)	
	'	JAMES MILLIKEN and JAMES MILLIKEN Junior	)	

This day came the parties by their Attornies and the Plaintiff having filed his declaration, the Defendant filed his plea and the Issue being joined the trial thereof is referred 'till next Court._____

A. R.	'	ALEXANDER KELLY	)	
238	'		)	
L. B.	'	vs	)	In Debt.
J. H.	'		)	
295	'	ABRAHAM SWAGERTY	)	

This day came the Plaintiff by his Attorney and the Sheriff having returned that the Defendant is not to be found in his County; On Motion of the Plaintiff by his Attorney; An Alias Capais is awarded him returnable here at the next Court. _____

(Pg. 159)

Rhea	'	NICHOLAS MANSFIELD	)	
239	'		)	
A. O.	'	vs	)	In Covenant
248	'		)	
	'	JOSEPH SEVIER	)	

This day came the Plaintiff by his Attorney and the Sheriff having returned that the Defendant is not to be found in his County On Motion of the Plaintiff by his Attorney an Alias Capias is awarded him against the Said Defendant returnable here at the next Court.

Rhea	'	JAMES MILLIKEN	)	
A. O.	'		)	
240	'	vs	)	In Covenant.
L. B.	'		)	
326	'	ABRAHAM SWAGERTY	)	

This day came the Plaintiff by his Attorney and the Sheriff having returned that the Defendant is not to be found in his County On Motion of the Plaintiff by his Attorney An Alias Capias is awarded him against the Said Defendant returnable here at the next Court._____

Rhea	'	JOHN McFARLAND	)	
241	'		)	
296	'	vs	)	In Case
	'		)	
	'	JOHN LINNEY	)	

This day came the Plaintiff by his Attorney and the Sheriff having returned that the Defendant is not to be found in his County On Motion of the Plaintiff by his Attorney An Alias Capias is awarded him against the Said Defendant returnable here at the next Court.

L. B.	DAVID MILLER	)	
242		)	
198	vs	)	In Debt
		)	
	BENJAMIN BLACKBURN	)	

The Defendant Benjamin Blackburn in his proper person appeared and agrees to pay the Costs of this Suit and upon this the Plaintiff prays that his Costs and Charges by him about his Suit in this behalf expended may be adjudged to him; Therefore It is considered by the Court that the Plaintiff recover against the Said Defendant his Costs by him about his Suit in this behalf expended. And the Said Defendant in Mercy & C. And the Plaintiff not farther prosecuting It is ordered that this Suit be dismissed.

A. O.	JAMES McELWEE	)	
243		)	
Rhea	vs	)	In Case
223		)	
	JAMES ANDERSON	)	

This day came the parties by their Attornies & the Plaintiff having filed his Declaration the Defendant filed his Plea, And the Plaintiff his Demurrer thereto and the Argument thereof is referred 'till next Court.

(Pg. 160)

Rhea	JAMES MILLER	)	
244		)	
L. B.	vs	)	In Case
A. R.		)	
269	ALEXANDER CARMICHAEL & JOSEPH JANES	)	

This day came the parties by their Attornies and the Plaintiff having filed his declaration the Defendant filed his Plea and the issue being joined the trial thereof is referred 'till next Court.

A. R.	JAMES McOLLOCK	)	
245		)	
Reessee	vs	)	Original Attachment.
224	ANDREW LACKY	)	

This day came the parties by their Attornies and the Defendant replevys the property attached. Whereupon Peter McNamee of this County comes into Court and undertakes for the Defendant that in case he Should be cast in this Suit he Shall Satisfy and pay the Condemnation or render his body to prison in execution for the Same or that he the Said Peter McNamee will do it for him. & the cause is continued 'till next Court._____

A. R.	'	NICHOLAS NEAL	)	
246	'		)	
Rhea	'	vs	)	In Case
297	'		)	
	'	WILLIAM TRIMBLE	)	

This day came the parties by their Attornies and the Plaintiff having filed his declaration the Defendant filed his pleas and the Issues being Joined the Trial thereof is referred 'till next Court._____

A. R.	'	JOHN PATTERSON	)	
247·	'		)	
Rhea	·'	vs	)	In Case
225	'	JOHN BEATY	)	

This day came the parties by their Attornies and with the Consent of the Defendant time is given the Plaintiff 'till next Court to file his Declaration._____

L. B.	'	JOHN RIDDLE	)	
248	'		)	
J. H.	'	vs	)	In Case
A. O.	'		)	
327	'	JESSE ELDRIDGE	)	

This day came the parties by their Attornies and the Plaintiff having filed his declaration the Defendant filed his plea and the Issue being Joined the trial thereof is referred 'till next Court._____

Rhea	'	ROBERT RHEA	)	
249	'		)	
J. H.	'	vs	)	In Case
328	'		)	
	'	ROBERT THOMPSON	)	

This day came the parties by their attornies and with the Consent of the Defendant time is given the Plaintiff 'till the next Court to file his Declaration.

(Pg. 161)

A. R.	'	MICHAEL SWISHER	)	
250	'		)	
A. O.	'	vs	)	T. A.
L. B.	'		)	
Rhea	'	JOHN EVANS	)	
241	'			

This day came the parties by their Attornies and the Plaintiff having filed his Declaration the Defendant filed his pleas and the issues being joined the trial thereof is referred 'till next Court.____

W. C.	'	ABRAHAM SWAGERTY	)	
251			)	
A. R.	'	vs	)	In Case
287	'		)	
	'	JAMES WHITE	)	

This day came the parties by their Attornies and the Plaintiff having filed his declaration the Defendant filed his plea and the issue being Joined the Trial thereof is referred 'till next Court.____

W. C.	'	JOSEPH SEVIER	)	
A. O.	'		)	
252		vs	)	In Case, Trover
Rhea	'		)	
329	'	HUGH DUNLAP	)	

This day came the parties by their Attornies and the Plaintiff having filed his declaration the Defendant filed his plea and the Issue being Joined the trial thereof is referred 'till next Court.____

L. B.	'	JAMES TEMPLETON.	)	
253	'		)	
Rhea	'	vs	)	In Case
270	'		)	
	'	SAMUEL GIBSON	)	

This day came the Plaintiff by his Attorney & having filed his declaration the Defendant by his next friend filed his plea and the Plaintiff his replication thereto and the issue being Joined the Trial thereof is referred 'till next Court.____

D. G.	'	ARCHIBALD TRIMBLE	)	
254	'		)	
Rhea	'	vs	)	In Case
298	'		)	
	'	ROBERT BLACKBURN	)	

This day came the parties by their Attornies, and with the Consent of the Defendant time is given the Plaintiff 'till next Court to file his Declaration.____

A. R.	'	BENJAMIN TIPTON	)	
255	'		)	
J. L.	'	vs	)	A B
242	'		)	
	'	JOHN BRADLEY	)	

This day came the parties by their Attornies and the Plaintiff having filed his Declaration the Defendant filed his plea and the Issue being Joined the trial thereof is referred 'till next Court.

(Pg. 162)

W. C. '	JACOB VANHOOSER	)	
C. C. '		)	
W. C. '	vs	)	In Covenant
A. O. '		)	
256 '	AMOS BIRD	)	
A. R. '			
Rhea . '			
330 '			

This day came the parties by their Attornies and the Plaintiff having filed his declaration the Defendant filed his pleas and the Cause is continued 'till next Court._____

257 '	DAVID WALKER	)	
199 '		)	
'	vs	)	In Case
'		)	
'	JOHN CHISM	)	

The Defendant John Chism in his proper person appeared and agrees to pay the Costs of this Suit, and upon this the Plaintiff prays that his Costs and Charges by him about his Suit in this behalf expended may be adjudged to him. Therefore it is considered by the Court that the Plaintiff recover against the Said Defendant his Costs by him about his Suit in this behalf expended. And the Said Defendant in Mercy & C. And the Plaintiff not further prosecuting; It is ordered that this Suit be dismissed. ____

A. R. '	JOHN WOOD	)	
258 '		)	
L. B. '	vs	)	In Covenant
226 '		)	
'	WILLIAM HENRY	)	

This day came the parties by their Attornies and the Plaintiff having filed his declaration the Defendant filed his plea and the Issue being Joined the trial thereof is referred 'till next Court._____

J. L. '	SAMUEL WEAR	)	
259 '		)	
A. O. '	vs	)	In Case
W. C. '		)	
Rhea '	MATTHEW WALLACE	)	
331			

This day came the parties by their Attornies and the Plaintiff having filed his Declaration the Defendant filed his plea and the issue being Joined the trial thereof is referred 'till next Court.

H. L.	:	THOMAS WILLIAMS	)
260	:		)
299	:	vs	) In Case
	:		)
	:	JOEL MORRISON	)

This day came the Plaintiff by his Attorney & having filed his declaration & the Defendant having been arrested & not appearing though Solemnly called, on Motion of the Plaintiff by his Attorney, It is considered by the Court that the Plaintiff recover against the Said Defendant Such damages as he hath Sustained by occasion of the Defendants Nonperformance of the assumption in the declaration mentioned; which damages are to be enquired of by a Jury at the next Court.____

(Pg. 163)

261	:	WILLIAM McBEE	)
W. C.	:		)
200	:	vs	) Appeal
	:		)
	:	JAMES HARRALSON	)

This day came the Plaintiff in his proper person and the Defendant by his Attorney and the parties being fully heard, and Sundry Witnesses examined. It is considered by the Court that the Judgment of the Justices be Set aside, and that the Defendant go hence without day, and recover against the Plaintiff his Costs by him about his defence in this behalf expended.

Reess	:	SAMUEL PAXTON	)
A. R.	:		)
262	:	vs	) Appeal
J. H.	:		)
227	:	JOHN TEDFORD	)

This day came the parties by their Attornies and by their Mutual consent and with the assent of the Court the Cause is continued 'till next Court.____

263	:	WILLIAM McBEE	)
W. C.	:		)
201	:	vs	) Appeal
	:		)
	:	JAMES HARRALSON	)

The Plaintiff not farther prosecuting It is ordered that this Suit be dismissed, And that the Plaintiff pay to the Defendant his Costs.

Robert Houston produced a Commission appointing him Sheriff for this County, who entered into Bond with James White and John Chisolm his Securities in the Sum of Twelve thousand five hundred dollars with condition for the faithful execution of the duties of his office as Sheriff And also entered into Bond with James White and John Chisolm his Securities in the Sum of One thousand dollars with condition for the faithful Collection of the County Tax for the present Year, and for the payment thereof as the law directs and was qualifyed accordingly.

Henry Breazeal is by Robert Houston Sheriff of this County appointed his deputy Sheriff during pleasure and thereupon the Said Henry Breazeale was qualifyed accordingly.

Willie Blound appeared and produced a license from Governor Blount, authorizing him to practice as an Attorney in the Several Courts of Pleas and Quarter Sessions within the Territory who took an Oath to Support the Constitution of the United States and also took the Oath prescribed by law for Attornies, he is therefore admitted. ____

(Pg. 164)

:
:
James White withdrew from his Seat: :   Ordered that there be paid to John Rhea Solicitor for this County out of the County Tax Twenty four dollars per Year for the time he has acted as Solicitor.

Ordered that there be paid to James White out of the County Tax, Thirty dollars per Year for the use of the Court house from the time it was used until this Court.

Ordered that there be paid to Charles McClung Clerk of this Court, out of the County Tax for his exofficio Services Seventy Seven dollars and fifty Cents for the past Year.

Ordered that the Sheriff retain out of the County Tax for his exofficio Services for the past Year Fifty two dollars and fifty Cents.

COURT ADJOURNED 'TILL COURT IN COURSE.

(Pg. 164)

MONDAY AUGUST 4th 1794

At a Court of Pleas and Quarter Sessions began and held for the County of Knox at the Court House in Knoxville on the first Monday of August 1794.____

Present James White, Abraham Ghormly George McNutt, Thomas McCullough, William Lowry, William Hamilton, and John Kearnes esquires Justices & C. & C. _____

Robert Houston   esquire Sheriff & C.   returned that he had
executed our Writ of Venire Facias to him directed upon the following
persons to Wit, Moses Looney, George Preston, Thomas Ritchey, Major
Lea, James Mill, Thomas Ingles, David Adair, Henry Roberts, Nicholas
Roberson, William Doak, Jesse Bounds, James Swan, Samuel Samples,
Thomas Woodward, William Walker, Alexander Campbell, James Brock,
John Brown, John Dermond, Thomas Ray, William Colker, John Singleton,
Nicholas T. Perkins, Jesse Green, and Levi Hinds. _____

Out of which Venire the following persons were elected a
Grand Inquest for the Body of this County to Wit Samuel Samples,
Foreman, Thomas Ray, John Brown, William Colker, Thomas
(Pg. 165) Ingles, Jesse Green, Moses Looney, Thomas Ritchey,
David Adair, Thomas Woodward, James Brock, Major Lea, Henry Roberts,
Alexander Campbell, and William Walker who have been Sworn received
their Charge and withdrew to enquire of their presentments.

John Cooke appeared and produced a license from Governor Blount
authorizing him to practice as an Attorney in the Several Courts of
Pleas and Quarter Sessions within this Territory, who took an Oath
to Support the Constitution of the United States, and also took the
Oath prescribed by law for Attornies he is therefore admitted.

William Cooke, and William Charles Cole Claiborne, appeared
in Court, and Severally took the Oath prescribed by law for Attornies
they are therefore admitted.

Court Adjourned 'till tomorrow 9 O'Clock.

TUESDAY AUGUST 5th 1794

Tuesday Morning August 5th 1794 Court met according to
Adjournment present James White, George McNutt and William
Lowry esquires Justice & C & C.

J. H.	:	SOLOMON MARKS	)	
36	:		)	
Rhea	:	vs	)	In Case
252	:		)	
	:	ROBERT KING	)	

This day came the parties by their Attornies and thereupon
came a Jury to Wit, James Swan, Nicholas T. Perkins, John Bradley,
William Davidson, James Williams, Gawen Black, Samuel Bogle
Warner Martin, Joseph Black, William McBroom, John Millar & Henry
Buchannon, who being elected tried and Sworn the truth to Speak
upon the Issues Joined. ((Samuel Acklin, David Craig, and Joel Dyer
who were Summoned to appear here this day as Witnesses for the
Plaintiff were Solemnly called but came not, Therefore on the
motion of the Plaintiff, It is considered by the Court that he
recover against the Said Samuel Acklin, David Craig, and Joel Dyer,
Severally One hundred and twenty five dollars unless they Severally

appear at the next Court after notice of this Judgment - and
Show Sufficient cause why this Judgment Should not be confirmed:
And it is ordered that Soire Facias issue against them.)) The
Plaintiff being Solemnly called came not, Therefore It is considered
by the Court that the Jurors aforesaid from rendering their Verdict
be discharged And that the Plaintiff be Nonsuited, Whereupon on
Motion of the Plaintiff and for reasons appearing to the Court; the
Said Non Suit is Set aside And it is ordered that the Plaintiff pay
all costs that have accrued Since the last term, and the Trial of
the Issues is referred till next Court.

(Pg. 166)

Rhea	:	JOHN CHISOLM	)	
49	:		)	
662	:	vs	)	In Case
	:		)	
	:	RICHARD HAMILTON	)	

This day came the Plaintiff by his Attorney and by his
Consent and with the assent of the Court the enquiry of damages is
referred till next Court. _____

A. O.	:	ROBERT STEPHENSON Exor.	)	
88	:		)	
J. H.	:	vs	)	In Case
288	:		)	
	:	BENJAMIN BLACKBURN	)	

This day came the parties by their Attornies and by their
Mutual consent, and with the assent of the Court the trial of the
issues is referred till next Court. _____

A. R.	:	ROBERT THOMPSON	)	
115	:		)	
Rhea	:	vs	)	In Case
253	:		)	
	:	JOHN McALLISTER	)	

This day came the parties by their Attornies and by their
Mutual consent and with the assent of the Court the trial of the
issue is referred 'till next Court._____

Rhea	:	ALEXANDER CARMICHAEL	)	
118	:		)	
A. O.	:	vs	)	In Case
254	:		)	
	:	JOSEPH SEVIER	)	

This day came the parties by their Attornies and on Affidavit of the Plaintiff the trial of the issue is referred till
next Court.

```
A. O.    :    JOHN HUTCHINSON              )
133      :                                 )
J. H.    :         vs                      )          In Case
567      :                                 )
         :    ANDREW PAUL  Admr. of        )
              JAMES PAUL  dec'd.           )
```

This day came the parties by their Attornies and by their
Mutual consent and with the assent of the Court the trial of the
issues is referred 'till next Court._____

```
S. M.    :    JAMES ALLISON        )
135      :                         )
J. H.    :         vs             )          In Covenant
L. B.    :                         )
356      :    ABRAHAM SWAGERTY     )
```

This day came the parties by their Attornies and thereupon
came a Jury to Wit, James Swan, Nicholas T. Perkins, Devereaux
Gillam, William Davidson, James Williams, Gawen Black, Samuel
Bogle, Warner Martin, Joseph Black, William McBroom, John Millar
and Henry Bachannon, who being elected tried and Sworn the truth to
(Pg. 167) Speak upon the issues Joined. The Plaintiff was Solemnly
called but came not, Therefore on Motion of the Defendant It is considered by the Court that the Jurors aforesaid from rendering their
Verdict be discharged and that the Plaintiff be Nonsuited; Whereupon on Motion of the Plaintiff by his Attorney and for reasons appearing to the Court, the Said Non Suit is Set aside; and the trial of the
issues is referred 'till next Court.

Henry Rowan, who was Summoned to appear here this day as a
Witness for the Plaintiff in this Suit was Solemnly called but came
not; Therefore on Motion of the Plaintiff by his Attorney It is considered by the Court that the Plaintiff James Allison recover
against the Said Henry Rowan One hundred and twenty five Dollars,
unless he appear at the next Court after notice of this Judgment
and Shew Sufficient cause why the Same Should not be Confirmed,
And it is ordered that a Scire Facias issue against him. _____

```
J. L.    :    WILLIAM LOWRY        )
140      :                         )
A. O.    :         vs             )          In Case
205      :                         )
         :    GEORGE WOODS         )
```

This day came the parties by their Attornies and thereupon
came a Jury to Wit; James Swan, Nicholas T. Perkins, Devereaux
Gilliam, William Davidson, James Williams, Gauin Black, Samuel
Bogle, Warner Martin, Joseph Black, William McBroom, John Millar
and Henry Buchannon, who being elected tried and Sworn the truth
to Speak upon the issue Joined upon their Oath do Say that the Defendant did not assume upon himself in manner and form as the Plaintiff against him hath complained as in pleading he hath alledged;

Therefore it is considered by the Court that the Plaintiff take nothing by his bill, but for his false clamour be in Mercy & C. and the Defendant go hence without day and recover against the Plaintiff his Costs by him about his Suit in this behalf expanded.___ Note, In this Cause the Plaintiff was put under a rule to Shew cause why a new trial Should not be granted, which was argued and overruled._____

A. R.   JOHN WALLACE   )
141   )
255   vs   )   Original Attachment, In Case
)
          JAMES BRIANT   )

This day came the Plaintiff by his Attorney And the Defendant not appearing to replevy the property attached though Solemnly called, On motion of the Plaintiff by his Attorney It is considered by the Court that the Plaintiff recover against the Said Defendant Such damages as he hath Sustained by occasion of the Defendants Nonperformance of the assumption in the Declaration mentioned, which damages are to be enquired of by a Jury at the next Court. _____

(Pg. 168)

Rhea   : SAMUEL FLANNAGAN   )
149   :   )
Reesse   :   vs   )   In Covenant
256   :   )
            JOHN SEVIER &   )
            ADAM MEEK Exors. of   )'
            ISAAC TAYLOR deceased)

This day came the parties by their Attornies, and the matters of law arising upon the Plaintiffs Demurrer to the Defendants plea being argued, and adjudged good; It is considered by the Court that the Plaintiff recover against the Defendant Such damages as he hath Sustained by occasion of the Defendants Nonperformance of the Covenant in the declaration mentioned, which damages are to be enquired of by a Jury at next Court.

A. R.   : THOMAS EMBREE   )
152   :   )
S. M.   :   vs   )   In Case
Rhea   :   )
257   : JOHN CHISOLM   )

This day came the parties by their Attornies and by their mutual Consent and with the assent of the Court the trial of the issue is referred until the next Court._____

```
A. R.     :    WILLIAM JOHNSTON      )
W. C.     :                          )
154       :         vs              )          In Case
J. H.     :                          )
A. O.     :    ANDERSON ASHBURN      )
208       :
```

This day came the parties by their Attornies and thereupon came a Jury to Wit, George Preston, John Rider, Jesse Eldridge, James Dail, Edward Freel, Daniel McDonald, Stephen Bishop, James Cochran, James Gibson, Crain Brush, Benjamin Pride, and Paul Cunningham, who being elected tried and Sworn the truth to Speak upon the issue Joined upon their Oath do Say that the Defendant did assume upon himself in manner and form as the Plaintiff against him hath complained and they do assess the Plaintiffs damages by occasion of the Defendants Nonperformance of that Assumption to Eighty three dollars and ten Cents besides his Costs. Therefore it is considered by the Court that the Plaintiff recover against the Defendant his damages aforesaid in form aforesaid assessed and his Costs by him about his Suit in this behalf expended. And the Said Defendant in Mercy & C.___

```
Rhea      :    SAMUEL FINLEY         )
158       :                          )
J. Love   :         vs              )          A B
258       :                          )
          :    JOHN BIRD             )
```

This day came the parties by their Attornies and the Cause is Continued for the award of the Arbitrators 'till next Court.

(Pg. 169)

```
Rhea      :    HUGH DUNLAP           )
159       :                          )
Reesse    :         vs              )          In Debt
209       :                          )
          :    PETER McNAMEE         )
```

This day came the parties by their Attornies and thereupon came a Jury to Wit, James Swan, Nicholas T. Perkins, William Davidson, James Williams, Gavin Black, Warner Martin, Joseph Black, Wm. McBroom, John Miller, Henry Bucharnon, John Bradley, and John Kerr, who being elected tried and Sworn the truth to Speak upon the issues Joined upon their Oath do Say the writing obligatory declared on is the Deed of the Defendant, in manner and form as the Plaintiff against him hath complained and that the Said Defendant hath paid Twenty five pounds and two pence part of the Debt in the Declaration Mentioned, and that Eleven pound, ten Shillings and ten pence Virginia Currency other part of the Said Debt remains unpaid equal in value to Thirty eight dollars and forty Six Cents and they do assess the Plaintiffs damages by occasion of the detention thereof to Forty four Cents besides his Costs. Therefore it is considered by the Court that the Plaintiff recover against the Said Defendant,

Thirty eight dollars and forty Six Cents, the residue of the Debt in the Declaration mentioned together with his damages aforesaid in form aforesaid assessed and his Costs by him about his Suit in this behalf expended. And the Said Defendant in Mercy & C. & C. _____

In the prosecutions on behalf of the United States against Thomas Hardin, Warner Martin, and Samuel McCulloh, It is ordered that a Noli Prosequi be entered, and that James Kerr the prosecutor pay the Costs thereof. _____

Court adjourned 'till tomorrow 9 O'Clock.

WEDNESDAY AUGUST 6th 1794

Wednesday Morning August 6th 1794 Court met according to Adjournment present James White, Samuel Nowell, Jeremiah Jack and William Lowry esquires Justices & C. & C.

A. R.	:	JAMES FORGEY Admr. of	)	
150	:	JOHN FORGEY deceased	)	
J. H.	:		)	
206	:	vs	)	In Case
	:		)	
		JOSEPH BEARD	)	

This day came the parties by their Attornies and thereupon came a Jury to Wit, John Burden, James Thompson, Daniel McDonald, Jesse Eldridge, John Evans, Michael Foster, James Johnston, James Campbell, John Liddy, George Amerine, Michael Swisher, and James Gibson who being elected tried and Sworn the truth to Speak upon the issue Joined upon their Oath do Say that the Defendant did assume upon himself in manner and form as the Plaintiff against him hath complained, and they do assess the Plaintiffs damages by occasion of the Defendants Nonperformance of that assumption to Sixty Seven Dollars besides his Costs. Therefore it is considered by the Court that the Plaintiff recover against the Defendant his damages aforesaid in form aforesaid assessed and his Costs by him about his Suit in this behalf expended, And the Said Defendant in Mercy & C._____ From which Judgment the Defendant prays an Appeal to the next Superior Court of law to be holden for the district of Hamilton at the Court House in Knoxville hath filed his reasons and entered into Bond with Security with condition for the prosecution of the Said Appeal with effect, which appeal is allowed._____

A. R.	:	JOHN McCAULEY	)	
161	:		)	
J. L.	:	vs	)	In Case
210	:		)	
	:	WILLIAM LOWRY	)	

This day came the parties by their Attornies and thereupon came a Jury to Wit, William Hazlet, Henry Regan, Pearson Brook, Andrew McCampbell, James Gealey, John Cowan, Junior, John Cowan, James Adair, William Lea, James Millikin, Benjamin Blackburn and John Cochran, who being elected tried and Sworn the truth to Speak upon the issue joined upon their Oath do Say that the Defendant did assume upon himself in manner and form as the plaintiff against him hath complained and they do assess the Plaintiffs damages by occasion of the Defendants Nonperformance of the assumption in the declaration mentioned, to Forty three dollars and twenty Cents besides his Costs, Therefore it is considered by the Court, that the Plaintiff recover against the Defendant his Damages aforesaid in form aforesaid assessed and his Costs by him about his Suit in this behalf expended And the Said Defendant in Mercy & C. _____ Note, in this Cause a motion was made for an Appeal, and reasons filed, but bond and Security not being given the Same was discharged. _____

Ordered that it be entered of Record, that it is the opinion of this Court, that one Attorney only Shall be admitted to plead for either Plaintiff or Defendant in any Suit in this Court.

(Pg. 171)

558.	11	:	Ordered that Process issue against Zapher Tannery
559.	16	:	and James Bunch to cause them to appear at the next
		:	Court to answer the Indictments found against them
			by the Grand Jury.

Rhea	:	UNITED STATES	)	
15	:		)	
L. B.	:	vs	)	Assault
236	:		)	
	:	CHRISTIANA AMERINE	)	

This day came as well the Solicitor of the County as the Defendant by her Attorney and the Said Defendant being charged pleads not guilty and thereupon came a Jury to Wit, James Thompson, Daniel McDonald, Jesse Eldridge, John Evans, Michael Foster, Nicodemus Keith, William Hazlet, Junior, James Gibson, Michael Swisher, John Liddy, James Johnston, and Thomas Hamilton who being elected tried and Sworn the truth of and upon the premises to Speak upon their Oath do Say that the Said Christiana Amerine is guilty in manner and form as charged in the Bill of Indictment Therefore it is considered by the Court that for Such her offence She be fined four Dollars and that She pay the costs of this prosecution.

Rhea	:	UNITED STATES	)	
22	:		)	
W. C.	:	vs	)	A B
237	:		)	
	:	JOHN EVANS	)	

This day came as well the Solicitor for the County as the Defendant by his Attorney, and the Said Defendant demurs to to the Indictment which being argued was overruled and the Defendant being charged pleads not Guilty and thereupon came a Jury to Wit, Pearson Brock, Henry Regan, John Caldwell, James McNair, John Ewing, Paul Cunningham, James Williams, Joseph Alexander, Joseph Caldwell, Thomas Gillespie, John Cowan and John Evans who being elected tried and Sworn, the truth of and upon the premises to Speak upon their Oath do Say the Defendant is not Guilty as in pleading he hath alledged, Whereupon the Solicitor for the County prays an appeal to the next Superior Court of law to be holden for the district of Hamilton at the Court House in Knoxville: Whereupon on Motion of the Defendant and with the assent of the Solicitor for the County the Motion for an appeal is discharged and the aforesaid Verdict Set aside and the Said John Evans because he will not contend Saith that he is guilty in Manner and form as in the Indictment against him is alledged, & putteth himself upon the Grace & Mercy (Pg. 172) of the Court; Therefore it is considered by this Court that for Such his offence he be fined One dollar, and that he pay the Costs of this prosecution._____ On Petition of the Defendant the fine aforesaid is remitted.

Rhea	:	UNITED STATES	)	
23	:		)	
W. C.	:	vs	)	A B
235	:		)	
	:	WILLIAM EVANS	)	

This day came as well the Solicitor for the County as the Defendant by his Attorney and the Said William Evans because he will not contend Saith that he is guilty in manner and form as in the Indictment against him is alledged and putteth himself upon the Grace and Mercy of the Court. Therefore it is considered by the Court that for Such his offence he be fined four dollars and pay the Costs of this prosecution. On Petition of the Defendant the fine aforesaid is remitted.

Court adjourned 'till tomorrow 9 O'Clock.

THURSDAY AUGUST 7TH 1794

Thursday August 7th 1794 Court met according to Adjournment present James White, George McNutt and William Hamilton esquires Justices & C.

J. L.	:	CHARLES REGAN	)	
163	:		)	
Rhea	:	vs	)	In Case
L. B.	:		)	
238	:	DANIEL CARMICHAEL	)	

This day came the Plaintiff by his Attorney Samuel Hindman, and Alexander Carmichael 'Garnashees being first Sworn Saith they owe the Defendant nothing, that they have not nor had they at the time they were Summoned Garnashees any effects of the Defendants in their hands, that they know of no debts due to, or effects belonging to the Defendant in the hands of any other person. And the Cause is continued till next Court.

J. H.	:	WILLIAM COBB	)	
165	:		)	
211	:	vs	)	Original Attachment.
	:		)	
	:	WILLIAM COX	)	

This day came the Plaintiff by his Attorney and thereupon came a Jury to Wit, George Stout, Hugh Bodkin, James White, Nathan Evans, James Gibson, James Ewing, William Ewing, John Sloan, Thomas Hamilton, James Johnston, James Millikin and William Hazlet who being elected tried and Sworn diligently (Pg. 173) to enquire of damages in this Suit upon their Oath do Say they assess the Plaintiffs damages to One Cent besides his Costs: Therefore it is considered by the Court that the Plaintiff recover against the Defendant his Damages aforesaid in form aforesaid assessed and his Costs by him about his Suit in this behalf expended and the Said Defendant in Mercy.

Reesse	:	WILLIAM DAVIDSON	)	
171	:		)	
J. L.	:	vs	)	In Covenant
321	:		)	
	:	WILLIAM LOWRY	)	

This day came the parties by their Attornies and by their Mutual consent, and with the assent of the Court the Cause is continued until next Court._____

Rhea	:	BRIAN McCABE admr. of	)	
172	:	TITUS OGDEN dec'd.	)	
357	:		)	
	:	vs	)	In Case
	:		)	
	:	EZEKIEL HENRY and	)	
	:	WILLIAM HENRY	)	

This day came the plaintiff by his Attorney and by his Consent and with the assent of the Court the enquiry of damages is referred 'till the next Court._____

Reesse	:	LEWIS TINER	)	
173	:		)	
Rhea	:	vs	)	Appeal
212	:		)	
	:	HUGH DUNLAP	)	

This day came the parties by their Attornies and thereupon
came a Jury to Wit, George Stout, Hugh Bodkin, James White,
Nathan Evans, James Gibson, James Ewing, William Ewing, John Sloan,
Thomas Hamilton, James Johnston, James Milliken, and William Hazlet
who being elected tried and Sworn well and truly to try the matter
of controversy between the parties upon their Oath do Say they find
for the Defendant.   Therefore It is considered by the Court, that
the Defendant go hence without day and recover against the Plaintiff
his Costs by him about his defence in this behalf expended.

Court adjourned till tomorrow 6 O'Clock.

FRIDAY AUGUST 8th 1794

Friday Morning August 8th   Court met according to Adjournment
present James White, James Cozby, William Lowry, Jeremiah Jack,
George McNutt, and Luke Lea esquires Justices & C &C &C &C.

(Pg. 174)

Robert Love came into Court and made Oath that Benjamin
Blackburn who then stood present was the Same Man who was Wounded
in an Action commonly called the Battle of Point Pleasant.

A. R.	:	JOHN WALKER	)	
175	:		)	
Rhea	:	vs	)	Appeal
213	:		)	
	:	JOHN SOMMERVILLE	)	

This day came the parties by their Attornies who being fully
heard and Sundry Witnesses examined, It is considered by the Court
that the Plaintiff recover against the Defendant four dollars and
Sixty four Cents and his Costs by him about his Suit in this behalf
expended And the Said defendant in Mercy & C.

J. H.	:	JAMES CARMICHAEL	)	
178	:		)	
Rhea	:	vs	)	In Covenant
L. B.	:		)	
214	:	ALEXANDER CARMICHAEL	)	

This day came the parties by their Attornies and the Defendant
filed an Affidavit and moved for a Continuance to which the Plaintiff
did object which being argued the Defendant was ruled to trial;
From which opinion the Defendant prayed an Appeal to the next
Superior Court of law to be holden for the district of Hamilton at the
Court House in Knoxville, to which the Plaintiff did object and on
Argument It is ordered that the Said motion be discharged and there-
upon came a Jury to Wit, Pearson Brock, John Cowan, Joseph Rovely,
James Evans, John Evans, Michael Swisher, Joseph Looney, Alexander
Milliken, Joseph Caldwell, William Ewing, John Caldwell and James
King, who being elected, tried and Sworn the truth to Speak upon the

issue joined upon their Oath do Say that the Defendant did not tender
as in pleading he hath alledged and they do assess the Plaintiffs
damages by occasion of the Defendants Nonperformance of the Covenant
in the Declaration mentioned to Sixty dollars and Sixty one Cents besides his Costs; Therefore it is considered by the Court that the
Plaintiff recover against the Defendant his damages aforesaid in form
aforesaid assessed and his Costs by him about his Suit in this behalf
expended And the Said Defendant in Mercy & C._____

(Pg. 175)

J. L.	:	JOHN DUNCAN	)	
179	:		)	
A. R.	:	vs	)	In Covenant
412	:		)	
	:	JOHN McNUTT &	)	
		JAMES CALLISON	)	

This day came the parties by their Attornies and by their
Mutual consent and with the assent of the Court the Argument of the
Demurrer is referred 'till next Court._____

H. L.	:	JOHN DAVIS	)	
181	:		)	
Rhea	:	vs	)	In Case
322	:		)	
	:	JOSEPH JANES	)	

This day came the parties by their Attornies and on motion of
the Plaintiff and at his Costs the trial of the issues is referred
'till next Court.

J. H.	:	ROBERT BLACKBURN	)	
182	:		)	
A. O.	:	vs	)	In Case Trover
215	:		)	
	:	JOHN LOWRY esquire	)	

This day came the parties by their Attornies and thereupon
came a Jury to Wit, Josias Gamble, William Doak, George Caldwell,
Amos Bird, William Lea, Willoughby Robinson, William Kerr, Paul
Cunningham, Robert Williams, William Hazlet, Joseph Alexander,
and Henry Regan, who being elected tried and Sworn the truth to
Speak upon the Issue Joined upon their Oath do Say the Defendant is
guilty of the trover and conversion in manner and form as the Plaintiff against him hath complained and they do assess the Plaintiffs
damages by occasion thereof to Thirty Seven dollars besides his Costs:
Therefore it is considered by the Court, that the Plaintiff recover
against the Defendant his damages aforesaid in form aforesaid assessed
and his Costs by him about his Suit in this behalf expended; And the
Said Defendant in Mercy & C. From which Judgment the Defendant
prays an Appeal to the next Superior Court to be holden for the District of Hamilton at the Court House in Knoxville hath filed his

reasons and entered into Bond with Security with Condition for the prosecution of the Said appeal with effect, which Appeal is allowed.

J. L.	:	JEAN KERR by her next friend	)	
185	:	JAMES KERR	)	
A. R.	:		)	
W. C.	:	vs	)	Malicious
	:		)	prosecution
		JOHN CALDWELL	)	

This day came the parties by their Attornies and thereupon came a Jury to Wit, Richard Reynolds, Pearson Brock, George McEwn, James Thompson, James Gibson, Thomas Dodson, Leonard Dodson, James Mitchell, Joseph Kearns, Thomas Taylor, John Thomas (Pg. 176) and John Cowan who being elected tried and Sworn the truth to Speak upon the Issue Joined upon their Oath do Say, the Defendant is guilty in manner and form as the Plaintiff against him hath complained; and they do assess the Plaintiffs damages by occasion thereof to Fifty dollars besides her Costs, therefore it is considered by the Court that the Plaintiff recover against the Said Defendant her damages aforesaid in form aforesaid assessed and her Costs by her about her Suit in this behalf expended. And the Said Defendant in Mercy & C.____ Note in this cause a motion was made for an appeal, and bond filed, but reasons not being filed nor tax paid, the Same was discharged.____ On Motion of the Defendant, It is ordered that the Costs of but four witnesses be taxed to him._____

D. G.	:	SAMUEL TATE	)	
153	:		)	
Rhea	:	vs	)	In Case
S. M.	:		)	
207	:	JOHN CHISOLM	)	

This day came the parties by their Attornies and thereupon came a Jury to Wit, Martin Armstrong, Drewry W. Breazeale, John Payne, George McEwen, John Caldwell, David Laird, Joseph Sevier, John McNeill, Jesse Howard, Joseph West, Joseph Brooks, and Stephen Duncan, to part of which the Defendant did object, but the Court ordered that they Should be Sworn, Whereupon the Defendant tendered a Bill of exceptions which were Signed, and Sealed, and the Jury aforesaid being Sworn the truth to Speak upon the Issue joined upon their Oath do Say the Defendant did assume upon himself in manner and form as the Plaintiff against him hath complained and they do assess the Plaintiffs damages by occasion of the Nonperformance of that assumption to One hundred Sixty one Dollars and twenty five Cents besides his Costs. Whereupon the Said Defendant Saith that the Court ought not to proceed to Judgment upon the Verdict aforesaid for the reasons following to Wit, " that Drury W. Breazeale, George McEwen, John Caldwell, David Laird, Joseph Sevier, Jesse Howard, Joseph West, and Joseph Brooks, Jurors Sworn in this Cause and who passed thereon are not Free holders or good and lawful men to Set on Such trial," and prayed that the argument thereof might be referred 'till the next Court. But on Motion of the Plaintiff, the parties were directed to proceed, upon the

argument, to do which the Defendants attorney did refuse and thereupon on Motion of the Plaintiff the Plea of the Defendant in Arrest
of Judgment was Overruled. Therefore it is Considered by the Court,
that the Plaintiff recover against the Defendant his damages aforesaid in form aforesaid assessed & his Costs by him about his Suit in
this behalf expended. And the Said Defendant in Mercy & C. & C.____

(Pg. 177)

H. L.	:			
D. G.	:	JAMES BRIGGAM	)	
W. C.	:		)	
C. C.	:	vs	)	In Covenant
186	:		)	
A. R.	:	JOHN CHISOLM	)	
A. O.	:			
323	:			

    This day came the parties by their Attornies and by their
Mutual Consent and with the assent of the Court the trial of the
issue is referred 'till next Court.____

J. H.	:	PATRICK NINNEY	)	
187	:		)	
Rhea	:	vs	)	In Case
218	:		)	
	:	SAMUEL HINDMAN	)	

    This day came the parties by their Attornies and thereupon
came a Jury to Wit, Martin Armstrong, Drury W. Breazeale, John
Payne, George McEun, John Caldwell, David Laird, Joseph Sevier,
John McNeill, Jesse Howard, John Evans, Joseph West & Joseph Brooks
who being elected tried and Sworn the truth to Speak upon the issues
joined upon their Oath do Say that the Defendant hath paid and hath
a Sett off of Eighty two dollars Seventy five and one third Cents
against the assumption in the Declaration mentioned and that there is
Fifty nine dollars and fifty eight Cents part of the Said Assumption
remains unpaid, Therefore it is considered by the Court that the
Plaintiff recover against the Defendant the Said Fifty nine dollars
and fifty eight Cents and his Costs by him about his Suit in this
behalf expended, 'And the Said Defendant in Mercy & C. _____.

A. R.	:	FRANCIS BIRD	)	
188	:		)	
Rhea	:	vs	)	In Case
A. O.	:		)	
259	:	JOHN CHISOLM and	)	
		JOHN MILLAR	)	

    This day came the parties by their Attornies and by their
mutual consent and with the assent of the Court the trial of the
issues is referred till next Court.____

```
A. R.      :    PEARSON BROCK        )
189        :                         )
Rhea       :         vs             )        In Case Words
260        :                         )
           :    JAMES THOMPSON       )
```

This day came the parties by their attornies and by their
Mutual Consent and with the assent of the Court the Trial of the
Issues is referred 'till Thursday of the next Court._____

```
Rhea       :    ROBERT RHEA         )
190        :                         )
219        :         vs             )        In Case
           :                         )
           :    DAVID MILLER         )
```

The Defendant David Miller in his proper person appeared
and agrees to pay the Costs of this Suit. The Plaintiff not farther
prosecuting It is ordered that this Suit be dismissed.____

(Pg. 178)

```
H. L.      :    DAVID WRIGHT         )
192        :                         )
Rhea       :         vs             )        In Case
289        :                         )
           :    JAMES SPENCE         )
```

This day came the parties by their Attornies and on Motion of
the Plaintiff and at his Costs the trial of the issues is referred
till next Court.

```
S. M.      :    THOMAS KING          )
Rhea       :                         )
193        :         vs             )        In Case
J. H.      :                         )
290        :    JOSEPH BEARD         )
```

This day came the parties by their Attornies and by their
Mutual consent, and with the assent of the Court the trial of the
issues is referred 'till next Court._____

```
Rhea       :    ACQUILLA JOHNSTON    )
194        :                         )
J. H.      :         vs             )        In Case
261        :                         )
           :    MAJOR LEA            )
```

This day came the parties by their Attornies and by their
Mutual Consent, and with the assent of the Court the trial of the
issue is referred till next Court. _____

```
J. L.        :    JAMES WEAR            )
196          :                          )
Rhea         :         vs              )    In Case
262          :                          )
             :    DANIEL WILLSON        )
```

This day came the parties by their Attornies, and by their mutual consent, and with the assent of the Court, the trial of the issues is referred till next Court.

```
Rhea         :    BRIAN McCABE  admr. of )
201          :    TITUS OGDEN  deceased  )
703          :                           )
             :         vs                )    In Case
             :                           )
             :    WILLIAM TATHOM         )
```

This day came the plaintiff by his Attorney and Samuel Cowan Garnashee being first Sworn Saith he oweth the Defendant nothing, but on the Contrary the Defendant is in his Debt fifteen dollars that there was left in his possession by the Defendant; Two decanters with a Cooler for the Same, 1 Small Candle box of tin, Six Wine Glasses, 1 Sett Cups and Saucers, 2 Sugar dishes, 2 Small Cream pots, Queens Ware; 1 Common flowered looking Glass, 1 plain pine Table, 1 pair Blankets, 3 Small law Books, Some Small Instruments for drawing drafts, a Quantity of Maps, an Instrument for measuring Roads, a large Walnut Square, & a few Sheets of White paper, and that he knows of no debts to or effects belonging to the Defendant in the hands of any other person. And the Cause is Continued until the next Court. _____

(Pg. 179)

```
H. L.        :    JOSEPH WEST           )
202          :                          )
413          :         vs              )    In Debt
             :                          )
             :    RICHARD FINDLESTON     )
```

This day came the Plaintiff by his Attorney and by Consent of the parties and with the assent of the Court the argument of the demurrer is referred till next Court. _____

```
Rhea         :    ANNANIAS McCOY        )
203          :                          )
263          :         vs              )    Original Attachment  In Case
             :                          )
             :    JOHN LUSK             )
```

This day came the Plaintiff by his Attorney and by his consent and with the assent of the Court the enquiry of damages is referred 'till next Court.

Rhea	:	STEPHEN DUNCAN & CO.	)	
204	:		)	
739	:	vs	)	ORIGINAL ATTACHMENT,
	:		)	IN CASE
	:	JOSEPH WEST	)	

This day came the Plaintiff by his Attorney and by his consent and with the assent of the Court the Enquiry of damages is referred until next Court. And on Motion of the Plaintiff by his Attorney a Judicial attachment is awarded him against the estate of the Said Defendant returnable here at the next Court. ____

Rhea	:	ROBERT FERGUSON	)	
205	:		)	
264	:	vs	)	Original Attachment, In Case
	:		)	
	:	WILLIAM TATHOM	)	

This day came the Plaintiff by his attorney, and the Defendant not appearing to replevy the property attached though Solemnly called, On motion of the Plaintiff by his Attorney It is considered by the Court, that the Plaintiff recover against the Said Defendant Such damages as he hath Sustained by occasion of the Defendants Nonperformance of the assumption in the declaration mentioned; which damages are to be enquired of by a Jury at next Court. ____

Rhea	:	GEORGE PRESTON	)	
206	:		)	
448	:	vs	)	Original Attachment In Case
	:		)	
	:	JOSEPH ROBINSON	)	

This day came the Plaintiff by his Attorney and Samuel McBee having been duly Summoned to appear here at this term as Garnashee; being Solemnly called but came not. Therefore on Motion of the Plaintiff by his Attorney, It is considered by the Court, that the Plaintiff recover against the Said Samuel McBee the amount of the Plaintiffs demand against the Said Defendant, and also his Costs unless he appear at the next Court after notice of this Judgment and Shew Sufficient cause why the Same Should not be confirmed; And It is ordered that a Scire Facias issue against him and the Cause is continued till next Court. ____

(Pg. 180)

A. R.	:	DAVID CALDWELL	)	
207	:		)	
J. L.	:	vs	)	Appeal
291	:		)	
	:	WILLIAM LOWRY	)	

This day came the parties by their Attornies and by their Mutual consent and with the assent of the Court the Cause is continued until the next Court. ____

```
L. B.      :    WILLIAM HENRY              )
210        :                               )
292        :           vs                  )    Original Attachment.
           :                               )
           :    JAMES DAVIS                )
```

This day came the Plaintiff by his Attorney and on his motion the Cause is continued 'till next Court.____

```
A. R.      :    ADAM PEEK    and           )
212        :    JOHN SEVEIR  Excrs. of     )
Rhea       :    ISAAC TAYLOR  deceased ... )
220        :                               )
           :           vs                  )    Petition for Partition
           :                               )
           :    JAMES GIBSON ............  )
```

This day came the parties by their Attornies and having been fully heard, and Sundry Witnesses examined: It is considered by the Court that Partition be made of the tract of land in the Petition mentioned by laying off for the Testator of the Petitioners three hundred Acres off the lower end of the Said tract of land, by a line parrallel to the upper and lower lines of the Said tract and that Francis A. Ramsey, Samuel Samples, Thomas Gillespie, John Patterson and George McNutt be Commissioners for that purpose, who are to make Report thereof to next Court; ____ From which Judgment the Defendant prayed an appeal to the next Superior Court of law to be holden for the District of Hamilton at the Court House in Knoxville and entered into Bond with Security, with condition for the prosecution of the Said Appeal with effect which Appeal is allowed. ____

Court Adjourned 'till tomorrow 8 O'Clock.

SATURDAY AUGUST 9th 1794

Saturday Morning August 9th 1794 Court met according to Adjournment present James White, George McNutt, James Cozby, William Lowry and John Evans esquires Justices & C. & C. ____

```
A. O.      :    JOHN BROWN                 )
215        :                               )
L. B.      :           vs                  )    In Case
265        :                               )
           :    ABRAHAM SWAGERTY           )
```

This day came the parties by their Attornies and by their Mutual consent & with the assent of the Court the trial of the Issue is referred 'till next Court. ____

(Fg. 181)

A. R.	:	SAMUEL BOGLE	)	
219	:		)	
L. B.	:	vs	)	In Covenant.
J. H.	:		)	
266	:	JOHN BROWN	)	

This day came the parties by their Attornies and by their Mutual Consent and with the assent of the Court the trial of the Issues is referred 'till next Court.

L. B.	:	ISAAC BULLARD	)	
A. O.	:		)	
220	:	vs	)	In Case
J. R.	:		)	
Rhea	:	HUGH BODKIN, Junior	)	
414	:			

This day came the parties by their Attornies and by their Mutual Consent and with the assent of the Court, the trial of the Issues is referred 'till next Court.

A. R.	:	AMOS BIRD	)	
222	:		)	
A. O.	:	vs	)	In Covenant
293	:		)	
	:	JACOB VANHOOSER	)	

This day came the Parties by their Attornies and by their Mutual Consent and with the assent of the Court the trial of the Issue is referred 'till next Court.

H. L.	:	BENJAMIN BLACKBURN	)	
223	:		)	
Rhea	:	vs	)	Original Attachment
415	:		)	
	:	ROBERT BLACKBURN	)	

This day came the Plaintiff by his Attorney, and Stockley Donelson Garnashee being first Sworn Saith he has received a Deed of conveyance from the Defendant for a tract of land the title of which is disputed, if the title Should prove not to be a good one he owes the Defendant nothing, if it Should prove to be a good one he owes the Defendant; that he hath not, nor had he at the time he was Summoned Garnashee any effects of the Defendants in his hands, that he knows of no debts due to or effects of the Defendants in the hands of any other person. Whereupon on Motion of the Said Stockley Donelson. It is ordered that the Judgment obtained against him at the last Court be Set aside, And the Cause is continued till the next Court. ____

Rhea   :   NATHANIEL and SAMUEL COWAN)
224   :   )
Reese   :   vs   )   In Covenant
358   :   )
          :   PETER McNAMEE   )

This day came the parties by their Attornies and by their Mutual consent and with the assent of the Court the trial of the Issue is referred 'till the next Court.____

(Pg. 182)

Rhea 225 :   JOHN COWAN   )
L. B. 239 :   )
          :   vs   )   In Case Trover
          :   )
          :   ANDREW MILLER   )

This day came the parties by their Attornies and by their Mutual Consent and with the assent of the Court the trial of the Issues is referred till next Court. ____

Rhea   :   JOHN CASHALLY   )
226   :   )
A. R.   :   vs   )   In Case
324   :   )
          :   OBADIAH BOUNDS   )

This day came the parties by their Attornies and by their Mutual consent, and with the assent of the Court the trial of the issue is referred 'till next Court.

W. C.   :   WILLIAM DAVIDSON   )
227   :   )
Rhea   :   vs   )   In Case
267   :   )
          :   JAMES CAREY   )

This day came the parties by their Attornies & by their Mutual consent and with the assent of the Court, the Cause is continued till next Court. ____

228   :   JONATHAN DOUGLASS   )
Rhea   :   )
A. O.   :   vs   )   In Covenant
221   :   )
          :   ROBERT KING   )

The parties appeared and each agree to pay half the Costs & the Plaintiff not farther prosecuting It is ordered that this Suit be dismissed.

```
Rhea        :   JOHN EVANS  esquire         )
L. B.       :   a Justice of the Peace      )
A. O.       :                               )
233         :           Vs                  )        A  B
A. R.       :                               )
240         :   MICHAEL SWISHER             )
```

This day came the parties by their Attornies and by their Mututal consent, and with the assent of the Court the trial of the issues is referred 'till the next Court.

```
D. G.       :   ROBERT EVANS         .      )
234         :   by his next friend          )
A. O.       :                               )
Rhea        :           vs                  )        In Case, Trover
L. B.       :                               )
294         :   JOHN EVANS                  )
```

This day came the parties by their attornies and by their Mutual Consent and with the assent of the Court the trial of the issue is referred till the next Court. _____

```
A. O.       :   JESTER HUFACRE              )
236         :                               )
222         :           vs                  )        In Case
            :                               )
            :   ANDREW EVANS                )
```

This day came as well the Plaintiff by his Attorney as the Defendant in his proper person; And the parties agree that the Plaintiff hath Sustained forty dollars damages by occasion of the Defendants Nonperformance of the Assumption in the declaration mentioned; Therefore It is considered by the Court that the Plaintiff recover against the Defendant the Damages agreed as Aforesaid And his Costs by him about his Suit (Pg. 183)   in this behalf expended. And the Said Defendant in Mercy & C.

```
A. R.       :   JOHN HILL                   )
237         :                               )
Rhea        :           vs                  ).       In Case
325         :                               )
            :   JAMES MILLIKEN &            )
            :   JAMES MILLIKIN JUNIOR )
```

This day came the parties by their Attornies, and by their Mutual Consent and with the assent of the Court the Trial of the Issues is referred 'till next Court.

```
A. R.       :   ALEXANDER KELLY             )
238         :                               )
L. B.       :           vs                  )        In Debt
J. H.       :                               )
295         :   ABRAHAM SWAGERTY            )
```

This day came the parties by their Attornies and the Plaintiff having filed his declaration the Defendant filed plea and the issue being joined the trial thereof is referred till next Court. ____

Rhea	:	NICHOLAS MANSFEILD	)	
239	:		)	
L. O.	:	vs	)	In Covenant
248	:		)	
	:	JOSEPH SEVIER	)	

This day came the parties by their Attornies and the Plaintiff having filed his declaration the Defendant filed his plea and the issues being joined the trial thereof is referred 'till next Court. ____

Rhea	:	JAMES MILLIKIN	)	
A. O.	:		)	
240	:	vs	)	In Covenant
L. B.	:		)	
326	:	ABRAHAM SWAGERTY	)	

This day came the Plaintiff by his Attorney and having filed his Declaration and the Defendant having been arrested and not appearing though Solemnly called, on Motion of the Plaintiff by his Attorney It is Considered by the Court that the Plaintiff recover against the Defendant Such damages as he hath Sustained by occasion of the Defendants Nonperformance of the Covenant in the Declaration mentioned which damages are to be enquired of by a Jury at the next Court. ____

Rhea	:	JOHN McFARLAND	)	
241	:		)	
296	:	vs	)	In Case
	:		)	
	:	JOHN LINNEY	)	

This day came the plaintiff by his Attorney and the Sheriff having returned that the Defendant is not to be found in his County On motion of the Plaintiff by his Attorney a Judicial attachment is awarded him against the estate of the Said Defendant returnable here at the next Court.

A. O.	:	JAMES McELWEE	)	
243	:		)	
Rhea	:	vs	)	In Case.
223	:		)	
	:	JAMES ANDERSON	)	

This day came as well the Plaintiff by his Attorney as the Defendant in his proper person, And the parties agree that the Plaintiff hath Sustained (Pg. 184) Three Dollars, thirty three and One third Cents damages by occasion of the Defendants Nonperformance of the Assumption in the declaration mentioned. Therefore it is considered by the Court that the Plaintiff recover against the Defendant the Damages agreed as aforesaid and his Costs by him about his Suit in this behalf expended. And the Said Defendant in Mercy & C. And the Plaintiff agrees to Stay the execution of this Judgment and Attornies fee for three Months. ____

Rhea	:	JAMES MILLAR	)
244	:		)
L. B.	:	vs.	) In Case
A. R.	:		)
269	:	ALEXANDER CARMICHAEL &	)
		JOSEPH JANES	)

This day came the parties by their Attornies and by their Mutual Consent and with the assent of the Court the trial of the Issue is referred 'till next Court.

A. R.	:	JAMES McCULLOCK	)
245	:		)
Roscoe	:	vs	) Original Attachment
224	:		)
	:	ANDREW LUCKEY	)

The Plaintiff not further prosecuting It is ordered that this Suit be dismissed and that the Plaintiff pay to the Defendant his Costs._

A. R.	:	NICHOLAS NEAL	)
246	:		)
Rhea	:	vs	) In Case
297	:		)
	:	WILLIAM TRIMBLE	)

This day came the parties by their Attornies and by their mutual Consent and with the assent of the Court, the trial of the issues is referred 'till next Court.

A. R.	:	JOHN PATTERSON	)
247	:		)
Rhea	:	vs	) In Case
225	:		)
	:	JOHN BEATTY	)

The Plaintiff not further prosecuting, It is ordered that this Suit be dismissed and that the Plaintiff pay to the Defendant his Costs._

L. B.	:	JOHN RIDDLE	)
248	:		)
J. H.	:	vs	) In Case
A. O.	:		)
327	:	JESSE ELDRIDGE	)

This day came the parties by their Attornies and by their Mutual Consent and with the assent of the Court the trial of the Issue is referred 'till next Court. ____

Rhea	:	ROBERT RHEA	)	
249	:		)	
J. H.	:	vs	)	In Case
328	:		)	
	:	ROBERT THOMPSON	)	

This day came the parties by their Attornies, and the Plaintiff having filed his Declaration the Defendant filed his plea and the issue being Joined the trial thereof is referred till next Court. ___

(Pg. 185)

A. R.	:	MICHAEL SWISHER	)	
250	:		)	
A. O.	:	vs	)	T A
L. B.	:		)	
Rhea	:	JOHN EVANS	)	
241	:			

This day came the parties by their Attornies and by their Mutual Consent, and with the assent of the Court the Trial of the Issues is referred 'till next Court._____

W. C.	:	ABRAHAM SWAGERTY	)	
251	:		)	
A. O.	:	vs	)	In Case
287	:		)	
	:	JAMES WHITE	)	

This day came the parties by their Attornies and by their Mutual Consent and with the assent of the Court the trial of the Issue is referred 'till neot Court, And on Motion of the Plaintiff by his Attorney a Commission is awarded him to examine and take the deposition of his Witnesses giving the Defendant legal notice of the time and place of executing the Same. ___

W. C.	:	JOSEPH SEVIER	)	
A. O.	:		)	
252	:	vs	)	In Case Trover
Rhea	:		)	
329	:	HUGH DUNLAP	)	

This day came the parties by their Attornies and by their Mutual Consent and with the assent of the Court the trial of the Issue is referred till next Court.

L. B.	:	JAMES TEMPLETON	)	
253	:		)	
Rhea	:	vs	)	In Case
270	:		)	
	:	SAMUEL GIBSON	)	

This day came the Plaintiff by his Attorney and the Defendant
by his next friend and by their Mutual Consent, and with the assent
of the Court the trial of the issue is referred till next Court. ___

D. G.	:	ARCHIBALD TRIMBLE	)	
254	:		)	
Rhea	:	vs	)	In Case
298	:		)	
	:	ROBERT BLACKBURN	)	

This day came the parties by their Attornies and by their
Mutual consent, and with the assent of the Court the trial of the
issues is referred till next Court. ____

(Pg. 186)

A. R.	:	BENJAMIN TIPTON	)	
255	:		)	
J. L.	:	vs	)	A B
242	:		)	
	:	JOHN BRADLEY	)	

This day came the parties by their Attornies and by their
mutual consent and with the assent of the Court the trial of the
issue is referred till next Court. ____

W. C.	:	JACOB VANHOOSER	)	
C. C.	:		)	
W. C.	:		)	
A. O.	:	vs	)	In Covenant
256	:		)	
A. R.	:	AMOS BIRD	)	
Rhea	:		)	
330	:			

This day came the parties by their Attornies and by their
mutual Consent and with the assent of the Court, the trial of the
issue is referred 'till next Court. ____

A. R.	:	JOHN WOOD	)	
258	:		)	
L. B.	:	vs	)	In Covenant
226	:		)	.
	:	WILLIAM HENRY	)	

The Defendant William Henry in his proper person appeared
and agrees to pay the Costs of this Suit, and upon this the Plaintiff
prays that his Costs and Charges by him about his Suit in this behalf
expended may be adjudged to him. Therefore it is considered by the
Court, that the Plaintiff recover against the Defendant his Costs by him
about his Suit in this behalf expended. And the Said Defendant in
Mercy & C. And the Plaintiff not farther prosecuting It is ordered
that this Suit be dismissed. _____

```
J. L.    :    SAMUEL WEAR          `)
259      :                          )
Rhea     :         vs              )    In Case
A. O.    :                          )
W. C.    :    MATTHEW WALLACE       )
331
```

This day came the parties by their Attornies and by their mutual consent and with the assent of the Court the trial of the issue is referred 'till next Court. _____

```
H. L.    :    THOMAS WILLIAMS       )
260      :                          )
299      :         vs              )    In Case
         :                          )
         :    JOEL MORRISON         )
```

This day came the Plaintiff by his Attorney and by his Consent and with the assent of the Court, the enquiry of damages is referred 'till next Court. _____

(Pg. 187)

```
Roesse   :    SAMUEL PAXTON         )
A. R.    :                          )
262      :         vs              )    Appeal
J. H. 227 :                         )
         :    JOHN TEDFORD          )
```

The Defendant John Tedford in his proper person appeared and agrees to pay the Costs of this Suit, and upon this the Plaintiff prays that his costs and charges by him about his Suit in this behalf expended may be adjudged to him, Therefore It is considered by the Court that the Plaintiff recover against the Defendant his Costs by him about his Suit in this behalf expended. And the Defendant in Mercy & C. And the Plaintiff not farther prosecuting It is ordered that this Suit be dismissed Whereupon the Plaintiff acknowledges Satisfaction for his Attorneys fee therefore as to So much the Said Defendant is acquitted and discharged.

```
10       :    WILLIAM ROSEBERRY     )
150      :                          )
         :         vs              )    Soire Facias
         :                          )
         :    SAMUEL ACKLIN         )
```

The Defendant having been duly warned and not appearing though Solemnly called, On Motion of the Plaintiff by his Attorney, It is considered by the Court that the Plaintiff may have Execution against the Said Defendant for Nine Dollars and Seventy eight Cents, the Costs in the Writ aforesaid Specifyed, And also that the Plaintiff recover against the Said Defendant his costs by him expended in Suing forth and prosecuting this Writ. _____

Note, This Judgment was of October Term 1794 but by mistake in Transcribing was entered here.

11	:	NATHANIEL COWAN &	)
149	:	SAMUEL COWAN	)
	:		) Soire Facias
	:	vs	)
	:		)
		STOCKLEY DONELSON	

The Defendant having been duly warned and not appearing though Solemnly called, On Motion of the Plaintiff by his Attorney It is considered by the Court, that the Plaintiff may have Execution against The Said Defendant for Forty one Dollars, eighty Seven and one half Cents for Debt, Damage, and Costs, in the Writ aforesaid Specifyed, And also that the Plaintiff recover against the Said Defendant his Costs by him expended in Suing forth and prosecuting this Writ. ___

Note, This Judgment was of October Term 1794 but by mistake in Transcribing was entered here.

(Pg. 188)

W. B.	:	DAVID ALLISON	)
264	:		)
Rhea	:	vs	) In Case
416	:		)
	:	JOHN McDOWELL Execr. of	
		JOSIAH LOVE deceased	)

This day came the Parties by their Attornies and the Plaintiff having filed his Declaration the Defendant filed his plea and the issue being Joined the trial thereof is referred 'till next Court. ___

W. C.	:	JOHN KEARNS	)
265	:		)
J. H.	:	vs	) In Case
359	:		)
	:	JAMES DALE	)

This day came the parties by their Attornies and the Plaintiff having filed his declaration the Defendant filed his pleas and the Issues being Joined the trial thereof is referred 'till next Court. ___

W. C.	:	JOHN KEARNS	)
266	:		)
J. H.	:	vs	) In Case
260	:		)
	:	JAMES DALE	)

This day came the parties by their Attornies and the Plaintiff having filed his declaration the Defendant filed his pleas and the Issues being Joined the trial thereof is referred 'till next Court.___

```
J. L.      :     JAMES CAMRAN       )
267        :  by his next friend    )
D. G.      :                        )
247        :         vs            )   A B
           :                        )
                 JOSIAS GAMBLE       )
```

This day came the parties by their Attornies and the Plaintiff having filed his Declaration the Defendant filed his pleas and the issues being Joined the trial thereof is referred 'till next Court. ___

```
268        :     JESSE CLAYWELL     )
228        :                        )
           :         vs             )   Trovor and Conversion
           :                        )
           :     HUGH DUNLAP        )
```

The Plaintiff not farther prosecuting It is ordered that this Suit be dismissed And that the Plaintiff pay to the Defendant his Costs. ___

```
Rhea       :     JAMES GILLESPIE    )
269        :                        )
W. C.      :         vs             )   In Case
J. H.      :                        )
332        :  WILLIAM McBROOM  admr. of )
              WILLIAM ROSEBERRY dec'd.  )
```

This day came the parties by their Attornies, and the Plaintiff having filed his declaration the Defendant filed his pleas and the issues being Joined the trial thereof is referred till next Court. ___

(Pg. 189)

```
W. B.      :     JACOB HARMER       )
Rhea       :                        )
270        :         vs             )   In Debt
A. R.      :                        )
271        :     JOHN ISH           )
```

This day came the Plaintiff by his Attorney and having filed his Declaration, the Death of the Defendant is Suggested in abatement And on Motion it is Ordered that a Notice issue to Elizabeth Ish Administratrix of John Ish deceased, to appear at next Court and defend this Suit.

```
Rhea       :     THOMAS HARDIN and SARAH  his Wife )
271        :                                       )
229        :              vs                       )   In Case
           :                                       )
           :     JAMES KERR .....................  )
```

The Defendant James Kerr in his proper person appeared and agrees to pay the Costs of this Suit, and upon this the Plaintiff prays that his Costs and Charges by him about his Suit in this behalf expended may be adjudged to him. Therefore it is considered by the Court that the Plaintiff recover against the Said Defendant his Costs by him about his Suit in this behalf expended. And the Said Defendant in Mercy. And the Plaintiff not farther prosecuting, it is ordered that this Suit be dismissed.

L. B.	:	WILLIAM HENRY	)	
272	:		)	
230	:	vs	)	In Debt
	:		)	
	:	CRANE BRUSH	)	

The Defendant Crane Brush in his proper person appeared and agrees to pay the Costs of this Suit, and upon this the Plaintiff prays that his Costs and Charges by him about his Suit in this behalf expended, may be adjudged to him. Therefore it is considered by the Court that the Plaintiff recover against the Said Defendant his Costs by him about his Suit in this behalf expended. And the Said Defendant in Mercy & C. And the Plaintiff not farther prosecuting, It is ordered that this Suit be dismissed.

W. B.	:	ANDREW JACKSON	)	
273	:		)	
333	:	vs	)	Original
	:		)	Attachment
	:	ROBERT BELL, WILLIAM WALLACE & CO.	)	

This day came the Plaintiff by his Attorney and Robert Love Garnashee being first Sworn Said that he hath in his possession the property of the Defendants, Fifteen Shillings Virginia Currency, a Note of hand on James Neeley for Five pound, Sixteen Shillings and nine pence, a Note of hand on William Sneed for Three pound, Six Shillings and Six pence, a Note of hand on Andrew Edger for One pound two Shillings & two pence a Note of hand on David Forrester for One pound Sixteen Shillings (Pg. 190) and Nine pence, A Note of hand on James Scot for One pound fourteen Shillings and two Books of Accounts which he here delivers to Court, that he knows of no debts due to or effects belonging to the Defendants in the hands of any other person, except Such as appear in the Book aforesaid, And on motion of the Plaintiff by his Attorney a Judicial Attachment is awarded him against the Estate of the Defendants returnable here at the next Court. The Defendants not appearing to replevy the property attached though Solemnly called, It is ordered that a Writ of enquiry of damages be executed at the next Court.

Reesse	:	NATHANIEL LYON	)	
J. H.	:		)	
274	:	vs	)	In Case
Rhea	:		)	
300	:	JAMES MITCHELL	)	

This day came the parties by their`Attornies and the Plaintiff having filed his declaration the Defendant filed his pleas and the issues being joined the trial thereof is referred 'till next Court.____

W. C. :	:	GERSHAM MOORE	)	
275	:		)	
$\overline{449}$	:	vs	)	In Case
	:		)	
	:	MATTHEW BISHOP	)	

This day came the Plaintiff by his Attorney and the Sheriff having returned ordered by Plaintiff not to be executed, On Motion of the Plaintiff by his Attorney an Alias Capias is awarded him against the ~~estate of~~ the Said Defendant returnable here at the next Court.____

276	:	JAMES MILLIKIN	)	
$\overline{231}$	:		)	
	:	vs	)	In Covenant
	:		)	
	:	SAMUEL BEARD &	)	
		JOHN BEARD	)	

The Defendants Samuel Beard and John Beard in their proper persons appeared and agrees to pay the Costs of this Suit, and upon this the Plaintiff prays that his Costs and Charges by him about his Suit in this behalf expended may be adjudged to him. Therefore It is considered by the Court that the Plaintiff recover against the Said Defendant his Costs by him about his Suit in this behalf expended And the Said Defendant in Mercy & C. And the Plaintiff not farther prosecuting It is ordered that this Suit be dismissed. _____

Reesse	:	MORDECAI MENDENHALL	)	
J. H.	:		)	
277	:	vs	)	In Case
Rhea	:		)	
L. B.	:	ALEXANDER CARMICHAEL &	)	
450	:	JOSEPH JANES	)	

This day came the parties by their Attornies and the Plaintiff having filed his Declaration the Defendants filed their pleas and the Cause is continued 'till next Court. ____

(Pg. 191)

Rhea	:	JOHN McAMEY	)	
278	:		)	
J. L.	:	vs	)	In Case
301	:		)	
	:	JAMES COCHRAN	)	

This day came the parties by their Attornies and the Plaintiff having filed his declaration, the Defendant filed his pleas and the Issues being joined the trial thereof is referred 'till next Court. ____

Rhea : JOHN MORGAN)
279 :)
L. B. : vs) Trover & Conversion.
248 :)
: MOSES STEGALL)

This day came the Plaintiff by his Attorney and the Sheriff having returned too. late came to hand On Motion of the Plaintiff by his Attorney an Alias Capias is awarded him against the Said Defendant returnable here at the next Court.

Rhea : ALEXANDER MONTGOMERY)
280 :)
J. H. : vs) In Case
534 :)
: ROBERT THOMPSON)

This day came the Plaintiff by his Attorney and the Sheriff having returned not exeucted by reason of his Swiftness in running On Motion of the Plaintiff by his Attorney An Alias Capias is awarded him against the Said Defendant returnable here at the next Court. _____

Rhea : JAMES McCOLLOCK)
281 :)
335 : vs) In Case
:)
: ANDREW LUCKY)

This day came the Plaintiff by his Attorney and having filed his Declaration and the Defendant having been arrested & not appearing though Solemnly called On motion of the Plaintiff by his Attorney It is considered by the Court that the Plaintiff recover against the Defendant Such damages as he hath Sustained by occasion of the Defendants Nonperformance of the assumption in the Declaration mentioned, which damages are to be enquired of by a Jury at the next Court. _____

W. B. : BRIAN McCABE admr. of)
A. R. : TITUS OGDEN dec'd.)
282 :)
L. B. : vs) Origl. Atta.
355 :)
: ALEXANDER CARMICHAEL)

This day came the parties by their Attornies and by their Mutual Consent and with the assent of the Court the Cause is continued until the next Court. _____

(Pg. 192)

W. B. : WILLIAM ROBERSON)
283 :)
272 : vs) Trover and Conversion
:)
: JAMES DERMAND)

This day came the Plaintiff by his Attorney and having filed his declaration the Defendant in his proper person filed his plea & the issue being Joined the trial thereof is referred 'till next Court.

	:	CHARLES REGAN	)	
284	:		)	
232	:	vs	)	In Case
	:		)	
	:	JESSE SMITH	)	

The Plaintiff not farther prosecuting It is ordered that this Suit be dismissed.

Rhea	:	JOHN STONE	)	
285	:		)	
H. L.	:	vs	)	In Debt
451	:		)	
	:	JOSEPH WEST	)	

This day came the parties by their Attornies and the Plaintiff having filed his declaration the Defendant filed his plea and the issue being Joined the trial thereof is referred 'till next Court.

Rhea	:	JOHN SOMMERVILLE & CO.	)	
286	:		)	
W. C.	:	vs	)	In Case
536	:		)	
	:	WILLIAM McBROOM admr. of	)	
		WILLIAM ROSEBERRY dec'd.	)	

This day came the parties by their Attornies and the Plaintiff having filed his declaration, the Defendant filed his pleas and the issues being Joined the trial thereof is referred 'till next Court.

J. H.	:	JAMES STINSON	)	
287	:		)	
Rhea	:	vs	)	In Case
L. B.	:		)	
338	:	WILLIAM HENRY	)	

This day came the parties by their Attornies and the Plaintiff having filed his Declaration the Defendant filed his plea and the issue being joined the trial thereof is referred until next Court.

J. L.	:	SAMUEL WEAR and	)	
288	:	WILLIAM LOWRY	)	
J. H.	:		)	
233	:	vs	)	In Covenant
	:		)	
	:	JAMES CUNNINGHAM	)	

The Plaintiffs not farther prosecuting It is ordered that this Suit be dismissed and that Plaintiffs pay to the Defendant his Costs.

(Pg. 193)

J. L.   :   SAMUEL WEAR &   )
289   :   WILLIAM LOWRY Exors. of   )
490   :   JAMES WALKER deceased.   )
A. R.   :   )
        :   vs   )   In Debt
        :   )
        :   JOHN COWAN & GEORGE TEDFORD   )

    This day came the parties by their Attornies and the plaintiff having filed their Declaration the Defendants filed their plea and the issue being joined the trial thereof is referred 'till next Court.___

J. L.   :   SAMUEL WEAR &   )
290   :   WILLIAM LOWRY Exors & Co.   )
J. H.   :   of   )
337   :   JAMES WALKER deceased.   )
        :   )
        :   vs   )   In Debt
        :   )
        :   JAMES CUNNINGHAM and George TEDFORD   )

    This day came the parties by their Attornies and the Plaintiffs having filed their Declaration the Defendants filed their Pleas and the issues being Joined the Tryal thereof is referred till next Court.__

J. L.   :   JOHN COWAN   )
291   :   )
302   :   vs   )   Original Attachment
        :   )
        :   ROBERT LIGGIT   )

    This day came the Plaintiff by his Attorney and John Lowry Garnashee being first Sworn, Saith he owes the Defendant Forty one pound Some Shillings Virginia Currency, that he hath not nor had he at the time he was summoned Garnashee any effects belonging to the Defendant in his hands, that he knows of no debts due to or effects belonging to the Defendant in the hands of any other person. The Defendant not appearing to replevy the property attached, though Solemnly called It is ordered that a Writ of enquiry of damages be executed at the next Court.

A. R.   :   ROBERT WILLSON   )
292   :   )
339   :   vs   )   Original Attachment.
        :   )
        :   SOLOMON MARKS   )

    This day came the plaintiff by his Attorney, and Samuel Newell Garnashee being first Sworn Saith he owes the Defendant forty Nine pounds and perhaps Some Shillings and pence payable in discharges and Powers of Attorney for which Sum he gave the Defendant his Note

of hand, that he also owes the Defendant Thirty Dollars payable in
Beef Cattle at Abingdon, which has provided payment for and lodged
in the hands of Samuel Vance Junior near that place, and that he
hath not nor had he at the time he was Summoned Garnashee any other
effects of the Defendants in his hands, that he knows of no debts
due to or effects belonging (Pg. 194) to the Defendant in the hands
of any other person. The Defendant not appearing to replevy the property attached though Solemnly called. It is ordered that a Writ of
enquiry of damages be executed ~~at the next Court~~ unless the Said Defendant Shall appear replevy the property attached and plead at next
Court. _____

Rhea	:	DAVID OGDEN	)	
293	:		)	
W. C.	:	vs	)	Appeal
234	:		)	
	:	SAMUEL REED	)	

This day came the parties by their Attornies and being fully
heard and Sundry witnesses examined, It is considered by the Court
that the Judgment of the Justices be Set aside, and that the Defendant
go hence without day, and recover against the Plaintiff his Costs by
him about his Suit in this behalf expended.

JOSEPH WALKER, being appointed Deputy Surveyor by Stockley
Donelson ~~Deputy~~ Surveyor of the Eastern district appeared and
took the Oath to Support the Constitution of the United States and also
the Oath of office. _____

Ordered that the Sheriff do Summon the following persons to
attend at the next Superior Court as Grand Jurors to Wit. _____
John Adair, George McNutt, Luke Lea, John Hackett, Major Lea,
Jeremiah Jack, Thomas Gillespie, John Sawyers, John Manifee, William
Lea, John Crawford, Thomas McCullough, William Wallace, William Lowry,
Samuel Newell, William Hamilton, James Cozby, John Evans, William
Walker, and Robert Armstrong.

Ordered that John Stone, Stephen Duncan, and Alexander Carmichael
be patrolers for the District of Captn Stones Company.

Charles McClung is appointed Trustee for this County who
entered into Bond with Robert Houston and James White his Securities
in the Sum of Four thousand dollars with Condition for the faithful
discharge of his duties as Trustee.

To all whom it may concern, Know ye that on the 13th of June
1794 Andrew Paul and Joseph Wear, both of the County of Knox S. W.
Territory have agreed to Submit all and every of our disputes
relative to James Paul deceased's Estate, all Actions and Causes of
Actions to the verdict of James White, Samuel Newell, William Hamilton,
William Lowry, William Wallace, James Houston, and (Pg. 195)
Alexander Kelly, or a majority of them, when given; to be determined
by law and evidence on friday the 20th Instant, to meet at the house
of James Beard, and if any of the above named persons Shall not attend

then the party Shall appoint another in his or their place to the performance of which we bind ourselves to each other in the full Sum of
five hundred dollars as Witness our hands and Seals this 13th June
1794, in presence of

Thos. McCullock   Andrew Paul admr. (Seal)
Thos. Hardin   Joseph Wear   (Seal)

     We the under Subscribers being chosen to Settle a matter of
Controversy between Andrew Paul and Joseph Wear agreeable to the
Contents of the within Bond, after hearing and duly considering the
Evidence on both Sides, do Say that Joseph Wear, Shall pay Andrew
Paul fourteen dollars and Sixteen and one third Cents, given under
our hands this 20th day of June 1794.

N. B.   The Arbitrators consider that each of the parties pays
their own Costs in all Suits heretofore commenced relative to the
estate of James Paul deceased.   Alexander Kelly, Samuel Newell
William Hamilton, James White, William Wallace James Houston
William Lowry. _____

             COURT ADJOURNED 'TILL COURT IN COURSE.

                  MONDAY OCTOBER 27th 1794

     At a Court of Pleas and Quarter Sessions began and held
for the County of Knox at the Court House in Knoxville on the
last Monday of October 1794.

     Present James White George McNutt, John Chisolm, and
David Craig esquires Justices & C. & C. & C. _____

   Robert Houston esquire Sheriff & C. returned that he
had executed our Writ of Venire Facias to him directed upon the
following persons to Wit William Haslet Senior, Robert Gamble,
Senior, Amos Byrd, Junior, Samuel Sterling, Jacob Pruit, George
Hays, Alexander Cole, Elliott Grills, Nathan Evans, James Gillespie,
Joseph Wear, John Tedford, Samuel Thompson, Little Page Sims, Anderson
Ashburn, James Gealey, John Allison, Joseph Woods, Samuel Hogg,
William Rhea, James Davis, James Millikin, Alexander McMillin, James
Blakely, John Ingram, Charles Gillam, Martin Fryley & Matthew Kerr
(Pg. 196)   Out of which Venire the following persons were elected
a Grand Inquest for the Body of this County to Wit, Amos Byrd foreman,
Robert Gamble, James Gealey, William Lea, Major Lea, Acquilla Johnston,
Andrew Paul, Stephen Duncan, George Stout, Henry Neill, William Roberts,
William Harralson, John Cowan, Samuel Doak, and John Payne who have
been Sworn received their Charge and withdrew to enquire of their
presentments.

```
J. H.    :    SOLOMON MARKS           )
36       :                            )
Rhea     :          vs                )          In Case
252      :                            )
         :    ROBERT KING             )
```

This day came the parties by their Attornies and by their mutual consent and with the assent of the Court the trial of the issues is referred until next Court. For reasons appearing to the Court the Judgment of the last Court against Samuel Acklin, David Craig and Joel Dyer, for not appearing as Witnesses for Solomon Marks against Robert King is Set aside.

```
Rhea     :    JOHN CHISOLM            )
49       :                            )
662      :          vs                )          In Case
         :                            )
         :    RICHARD HAMILTON        )
```

This day came the Plaintiff by his Attorney and by his Consent and with the assent of the Court the enquiry of damages is referred 'till next Court. __

```
A. O.    :    MARY STEPHENSON &                 )
88       :    EDWARD STEPHENSON  Excrs. of       )
J. H.    :    ROBERT STEPHENSON  deceased        )
288      :                                       )
         :              vs                       )      In Case
         :                                       )
         :    BENJAMIN BLACKBURN                 )
```

This day came the parties by their Attornies and by their Mutual Consent and with the assent of the Court the trial of the issues is referred till next Court.

```
A. R.    :    ROBERT THOMPSON         )
115      :                            )
Rhea     :          vs                )          In Case
253      :                            )
         :    JOHN McALLISTER         )
```

This day came the parties by their Attornies and by their Mutual Consent and with the assent of the Court the trial of the issue is referred 'till next Court. _____

```
Rhea     :    ALEXANDER CARMICHAEL    )
118      :                            )
A. O.    :          vs                )          In Case
254      :                            )
         :    JOSEPH SEVEIR           )
```

This day came the Parties by their Attornies and on Affidavit
of the Plaintiff the trial of the issue is referred 'till next Court.

(Pg. 197)

A. O.	:	JOHN HUTCHINSON	)
133	:		)
J. H.	:	vs	) In Case
567	:		)
	:	ANDREW PAUL admr. of	)
	:	JAMES PAUL dec'd.	)

This day came the parties by their Attornies and by their Mutual
consent and with the assent of the Court the trial of the issues is
referred 'till next Court. _____

S. M.	:	JAMES ALLISON	)
135	:		)
J. H.	:	vs	) In Covenant
L. B.	:		)
356	:	ABRAHAM SWAGERTY	)

This day came the parties by their Attornies and by their Mutual
Consent and with the assent of the Court, the trial of the issues
is referred till next Court.

A. R.	:	JOHN WALLACE	)
141	:		)
255	:	vs	) Original Attachment, In Case
	:		)
	:	JAMES BRIANT	)

This day came the Plaintiff by his Attorney and by his Consent
and with the assent of the Court the enquiry of damages is referred
'till next Court.

Rhea	:	SAMUEL FLANNAGAN	)
149	:		)
Reese	:	vs	) In Covenant
256	:		)
	:	JOHN SEVIER & ADAM MEED, Excrs. of	)
	:	ISAAC TAYLOR deceased	)

This day came the parties by their Attornies and by their
Mutual consent and with the assent of the Court the enquiry of
damages is referred 'till next Court.

A. R.	:	THOMAS EMBREE	)
152	:		)
S. M.	:	vs	) In Case
Rhea	:		)
257	:	JOHN CHISOLM	)

This day came the parties by their Attornies and by their Mutual consent and with the assent of the Court the trial of the issue is referred until next Court. _____

Rhea	:	SAMUEL FINLEY	)
158	:		)
J. Love	:	vs	) A B
258	:		)
	:	JOHN BIRD	)

This day came the parties by their Attornies and the cause is continued for the award of the Arbitrators till next Court. _____

J. L.	:	CHARLES REGAN	)
165	:		)
Rhea	:	vs	) In Case
L. B.	:		)
238	:	DANIEL CARMICHAEL	)

The Plaintiff not farther prosecuting, It is ordered that this Suit be dismissed.

Reese	:	WILLIAM DAVIDSON	)
171	:		)
J. L.	:	vs	) In Covenant
321	:		)
	:	WILLIAM LOWRY	)

This day came the parties by their Attornies and by their Mutual Consent & with the assent of the Court the Cause is continued till next Court. _____

(Pg. 198)

Rhea	:	BRIAN McCABE admr. of	)
172	:	TITUS OGDIN dec'd.	)
357	:		)
	:	vs	) In Case
	:		)
	:	EZEKIEL HENRY &	)
	:	WILLIAM HENRY	)

This day came the Plaintiff by his Attorney and by his Consent and with the assent of the Court the enquiry of damages is referred 'till next Court. _____

J. L.	:	JOHN DUNCAN	)
179	:		)
A. R.	:	vs	) In Covenant
412	:		)
	:	JOHN McNUTT and	)
	:	JAMES CALLISON	)

This day came the parties by their Attornies and by their Mutual consent and with the assent of the Court, the Argument of the Demurrer is referred 'till next Court. _____

H. L.	:	JOHN DAVIS	)	
181	:		)	
Rhea	:	vs	)	In Case
322	:		)	
	:	JOSEPH JANES	)	

This day came the parties by their Attornies and by their mutual Consent, and with the assent of the Court the trial of the issues is referred till next Court. _____

H. L.	:	JAMES BRIGGAM	)	
D. G.	:		)	
W. C.	:	vs	)	In Covenant
C. C.	:		)	
186	:	JOHN CHISOLM	)	
A. R.	:			
A. O.	:			
323	:			

This day came the parties by their Attornies and by their mutual Consent and with the assent of the Court, the trial of the issue is referred 'till next Court.

A. R.	:	FRANCIS BIRD	)	
188	:		)	
Rhea	:	vs	)	In Case
A. O.	:		)	
259	:	JOHN CHISOLM and	)	
		JOHN MILLER	)	

This day came the parties by their attornies and by their mutual Consent and with the assent of the Court the trial of the issues is referred 'till next Court. _____

A. R.	:	PEARSON BROCK	)	
189	:		)	
Rhea	:	vs	)	In Case Words
260	:		)	
	:	JAMES THOMPSON	)	

By Consent of the parties the matters in difference between them in this Suit are referred to the final determination of Francis A. Ramsey Devéreaux Gilliam, James Davis, Andrew McCampbell, John Patterson, Robert Black and James White, whose award thereupon or the award of a Majority of them is to made the Judgment of the Court, and the Same is ordered Accordingly. _____

H. L.	:	DAVID WRIGHT	)	
192	:		)	
Rhea	:	vs	)	In Case
289	:		)	
	:	JAMES SPENCE	)	

This day came the parties by their Attornies and by their
(Pg. 199)   mutual consent, and with the assent of the Court, the
trial of the issues is referred till next Court. And on Motion of
the Defendant a Commission is awarded him to Examine and take the
Deposition of his Witnesses giving the Plaintiff legal notice of the
time and place of executing the Same. _____

S. M.	:	THOMAS KING	)	
Rhea	:		)	
193	:	vs	)	In Case
J. H.	:		)	
290	:	JOSEPH BEARD	)	

This day came the parties by their Attornies and by their Mutual
Consent and with the assent of the Court the trial of the issues is
referred 'till next Court. _____

Rhea	:	ACQUILLA JOHNSTON	)	
194	:		)	
J. H.	:	vs	)	In Case
261	:		)	
	:	MAJOR LEA	)	

This day came the parties by their Attornies and by their Mutual
Consent and with the assent of the Court the trial of the issue is
referred till next Court.

J. L.	:	JAMES WEAR	)	
196	:		)	
Rhea	:	vs	)	In Case
262	:		)	
	:	DANIEL WILLSON	)	

This day came the parties by their Attornies and by their Mutual
Consent and with the assent of the Court the trial of the issue is
referred till next Court.

Rhea	:	BRIAN McCABE admr. of	)	
201	:	TITUS OGDEN deceased	)	
703	:		)	
	:	vs	)	In Case
	:		)	
	:	WILLIAM TATHOM	)	

This day came the Plaintiff by his Attorney and by his Consent
and with the assent of the Court the Cause is continued till next Court.

H. L. : JOSEPH WEST)
202 :)
413 : vs) In Debt
:)
: RICHARD FINDLESTON)

    This day came the Plaintiff by his Attorney and the Defendant
in his proper person and by their Mutual Consent and with the assent
of the Court the Argument of the Demurrer is referred 'till next Court. —

Rhea : ANNANIAS McCOY)
203 :)
263 : vs) Origl. Attachmt. In Case
:)
: JOHN LUSK)

    This day came the Plaintiff by his Attorney and by his Consent
and with the assent of the Court the enquiry of damages is referred
'till next Court. _____

(Pg. 200)

Rhea : STEPHEN DUNCAN & COMPANY)
204 :)
739 : vs) Origl. Atta.
:) In Case
: JOSEPH WEST)

    James Anderson having been duly Summoned to appear here at this
term as Garnashee, being Solemnly called came not, Therefore On Motion
of the Plaintiff by his Attorney It is considered by the Court that
the Plaintiff recover against the Said James Anderson the amount of the
Plaintiffs demand against the Said Defendant and also his Costs unless
he appear at the next Court after notice of this Judgment and Shew
Sufficient cause why this Judgment Should not be confirmed And it is
ordered a Scire Facias issue against him, Whereupon by consent of the
Plaintiff and with the assent of the Court the enquiry of damages is
referred 'till next Court.

Rhea ROBERT FERGUSON)
, 205)
264 vs) Original Attachment, In Case
)
WILLIAM TATHAM)

    This day came the Plaintiff by his Attorney and by his Consent
and with the assent of the Court the enquiry of damages is referred
'till next Court. ____

Rhea : GEORGE PRESTON)
206 :)
448 : vs) Original Attachment
:) In Case
: JOSEPH ROBINSON)

This day came the Plaintiff by his Attorney And the Sheriff having returned Samuel McBee, not to be found in his County On Motion of the Plaintiff by his Attorney An Alias Scire Facias is awarded him against the said Samuel McBee returnable here at the next Court.

```
A. R.    :    DAVID CALDWELL          )
207      :                            )
J. L.    :         vs                 )        Appeal
291      :                            )
         :    WILLIAM LOWRY           )
```

This day came the parties by their Attornies and by their Consent and with the assent of the Court, the Cause is Continued 'till next Court. _____

(Pg. 201)

```
L. B.    :    WILLIAM HENRY           )
210      :                            )
292      :         vs                 )        Original Attachment.
         :                            )
         :    JAMES DAVIS             )
```

This day came the Plaintiff by his Attorney and by his Consent and with the assent of the Court the Cause is continued 'till next Court.

```
A. O.    :    JOHN BROWN              )
215      :                            )
L. B.    :         vs                 )        In Case
265      :                            )
         :    ABRAHAM SWAGERTY        )
```

This day came the parties by their Attornies and by their mutual Consent, and with the assent of the Court the trial of the issue is referred 'till next Court.

```
A. R.    :    SAMUEL BOGLE            )
219      :                            )
L. B.    :         vs                 )        In Covenant
J. H.    :                            )
266      :    JOHN BROWN              )
```

This day came the parties by their Attornies and by their Mutual Consent and with the assent of the Court the trial of the issues is referred 'till next Court.

```
L. B. A. O.   :    ISAAC BULLARD          )
    220       :                            )
A. R.  Rhea   :         vs                 )        In Case
    414       :                            )
              :    HUGH BODKIN, Junior     )
```

This day came the parties by their Attornies and by their mutual Consent and with the assent of the Court the trial of the issues is referred 'till next Court. _____

A. R.	:	AMOS BIRD	)	
222	:		)	
A. O.	:	vs	)	In Covenant
293	:		)	
	:	JACOB VANHOOSER	)	

This day came the parties by their Attornies and by their mutual Consent and with the assent of the Court the trial of the issue is referred 'till next Court.

H. L.	:	BENJAMIN BLACKBURN	)	
223	:		)	
Rhea	:	vs	)	Original Attachment
415	:		)	
	:	ROBERT BLACKBURN	)	

This day came the Plaintiff by his Attorney and by his Consent and with the assent of the Court the Cause is continued 'till next Court.

COURT ADJOURNED 'TILL TOMORROW 9 O'CLOCK.

(Pg. 202)

TUESDAY OCTOBER 28th 1794

Tuesday Morning October 28th 1794 Court met according to Adjournment present James White, John Chisolm, David Craig and William Lowry esquires Justices & C.

Rhea	:	NATHANIEL and SAMUEL COWAN	)	
224	:		)	
Reesse	:	vs	)	In Covenant
358	:		)	
	:	PETER McNAMEE	)	

This day came the parties by their Attornies and by their Mutual Consent and with the assent of the Court the trial of the issue is referred 'till next Court. _____

Rhea	:	JOHN COWAN	)	
225	:		)	
L. B.	:	vs	)	Trover and Conversion
239	:		)	
	:	ANDREW MILLER	)	

The Plaintiff not farther prosecuting It is ordered that this
Suit be dismissed and that the Plaintiff pay to the Defendant his Costs.

Rhea :	JOHN CASHALLY	)	
226 :		)	
A. R. :	vs	)	In Case
324 :		)	
:	OBADIAH BOUNDS	)	

This day came the parties by their Attornies and by their Mutual
consent and with the assent of the Court the trial of the issue is
referred 'till next Court._____

W. C. :	WILLIAM DAVIDSON	)	
227 :		)	
Rhea :	vs	)	In Case
267 :		)	
:	JAMES CAREY	)	

This day came the parties by their Attornies and by their mutual
Consent and with the assent of the Court, the Cause is continued 'till
next Court.

A. O. :	JOHN EVANS esquire a	)	
Rhea :	Justice of the Peace	)	
L. B. :		)	
233 :	vs	)	A B
A. R. :		)	
240 :	MICHAEL SWISHER	)	

The Defendant in his proper person appeared and agrees to pay
his own Attorney and his own Witnesses and the Plaintiff not farther
prosecuting It is ordered that this Suit be dismissed.

D. G. :	ROBERT EVANS by his	)	
234 :	next Friend	)	
A. O. :		)	
L. B. :	vs	)	Trover & Conversion
Rhea :		)	
294 :	JOHN EVANS	)	

This day came the parties by their Attornies and by their Mutual
Consent and with the assent of the Court the trial of the issue is
referred 'till next Court._____

(Pg. 203)

A. R. :	JOHN HILL	)	
237 :		)	
Rhea :	vs	)	In Case.
325 :		)	
:	JAMES MILLIKEN and JAMES MILLIKEN, Junior	)	

This day came the parties by their Attornies and by their mutual Consent and with the assent of the Court, the trial of the issue is referred 'till next Court.

A. R.	:	ALEXANDER KELLEY	)	
238	:		)	
L. B.	:	vs	)	In Debt.
J. H.	:		)	
295	:	ABRAHAM SWAGERTY	)	

This day came the parties by their Attorneys and by their mutual Consent and with the assent of the Court the trial of the Issue is referred 'till next Court. _____

Rhea	:	NICHOLAS MANSFIELD	)	
239	:		)	
A. O.	:	vs	)	In Covenant
248	:		)	
	:	JOSEPH SEVIER	)	

This day came the parties by their Attornies and by their mutual Consent and with the assent of the Court the trial of the Issues is referred till next Court.

Rhea	:	JAMES MILLIKIN	)	
A. O.	:		)	
240	:	vs	)	In Covenant
L. B.	:		)	
326	:	ABRAHAM SWAGERTY	)	

This day came the parties by their Attornies and by their Mutual Consent and with the assent of the Court the enquiry of damages is referred till next Court. _____

Rhea	:	JOHN McFARLAND	)	
241	:		)	
296	:	vs	)	In Case
	:		)	
	:	JOHN LINNEY	)	

This day came the Plaintiff by his Attorney and James White Garnashee being first Sworn Saith, that he owes the Defendant nothing but on the Contrary the Defendant owes him Twelve Dollars, that the Defendant lodged in his hands a Note of hand for Twenty Dollars as Security for the payment of the aforesaid twelve dollars that he hath not nor had he at the time he was Summoned Garnashee any other effects of the Defendants in his hands, that he knows of no debts due to or effects belonging to the Defendant in the hands of any other person The Defendant not appearing to replevy the property attached though Solemnly called, It is ordered that a Writ of enquiry of damages be executed at next Court unless the Said Defendant Shall appear replevy the property attached and plead to the Action._____

```
Rhea      :    UNITED STATES                          )
25        :                                           )
560       :         vs                                )        A B
          :                                           )
          :    CHARLES REGAN   Junior                 )
```

The Solicitor not farther prosecuting It is ordered that this prosecution be dismissed.

(Pg. 204)

```
Rhea      :    JAMES MILLER                           )
244       :                                           )
L. B.     :         vs                                )        In Case
A. R.     :                                           )
269       :    ALEXANDER CARMICHAEL and               )
               JOSEPH JANES                           )
```

This day came the parties by their Attornies and by their Mutual consent, and with the assent of the Court the trial of the issue is referred till next Court. _____

```
A. R.     :    NICHOLAS NEAL                          )
246       :                                           )
Rhea      :         vs                                )        In Case
297       :                                           )
          :    WILLIAM TRIMBLE                        )
```

This day came the parties by their Attornies and by their mutual consent and with the assent of the Court the trial of the issues is referred 'till next Court.

```
L. B.     :    JOHN RIDDLE                            )
248       :                                           )
J. H.     :         vs                                )        In Case
A. O.     :                                           )
327       :    JESSE ELDRIDGE                         )
```

This day came the parties by their Attornies and by their mutual Consent and with the assent of the Court the trial of the issue is referred till next Court.

```
Rhea      :    ROBERT RHEA                            )
249       :                                           )
J. H.     :         vs                                )        In Case
328       :                                           )
          :    ROBERT THOMPSON                        )
```

This day came the parties by their Attornies and by their mutual Consent and with the assent of the Court, the trial of the issue is referred 'till next Court.

```
A. R.    :    MICHAEL SWISHER              )
250      :                                 )
A. O.    :           vs                    )        T. A.
L. B.    :                                 )
241      :    JOHN EVANS                   )
Rhea
```

The Defendant in his proper person appeared and agrees to pay his own Attorney and his own Witnesses, and the Plaintiff not farther prosecuting It is ordered that this Suit be dismissed._____

```
W. C.    :    ABRAHAM SWAGERTY             )
251      :                                 )
A. R.    :           vs                    )        In Case
287      :                                 )
         :    JAMES WHITE                  )
```

This day came the parties by their Attornies and by their Mutual Consent and with the assent of the Court, the trial of the issue is referred till next Court. _____

```
W. C.    :    JOSEPH SEVIER               )
A. O.    :                                 )
252      :           vs                    )        In Case   Trover
Rhea     :                                 )
329      :    HUGH DUNLAP                  )
```

This day came the parties by their Attornies and by their mutual consent and with the assent of the Court the trial of the issue is referred till next Court.

```
L. B.    :    JAMES TEMPLETON             )
253      *                                 )
Rhea     :           vs                    )        In Case
270      :                                 )
         :    SAMUEL GIBSON               )
```

This day came the Plaintiff by his Attorney and the Defendant by his next friend and by their mutual consent and with the assent of the Court the trial of the Issue is referred 'till next Court. _____

(Pg. 205)

```
D. G.    :    ARCHIBALD TRIMBLE           )
254      :                                 )
Rhea     :           vs                    )        In Case
298      :                                 )
         :    ROBERT BLACKBURN            )
```

This day came the parties by their Attornies and by their mutual Consent, and with the assent of the Court the trial of the issues is referred 'till next Court. _____

```
A. R.    :    BENJAMIN TIPTON         )
255      :                            )
J. L.    :         vs                 )    A B
242      :                            )
         :    JOHN BRADLEY            )
```

The parties agree each to pay half the Costs and the Plaintiff not farther prosecuting It is ordered that this Suit be dismissed.

```
W. C.    :
C. C.    :
W. C.    :    JACOB VANHOOSER         )
A. O.    :                            )
256      :         vs                 )    In Covenant
A. R.    :                            )
Rhea     :    AMOS BIRD               )
330      :                            )
```

This day came the parties by their Attornies and by their mutual Consent and with the assent of the Court the trial of the issues is referred till next Court. _____

```
J. S.    :
259      :    SAMUEL WEAR             )
Rhea     :                            )
A. O.    :         vs                 )    In Case
W. C.    :                            )
331      :    MATTHEW WALLACE         )
```

This day came the parties by their Attornies and by their mutual consent and with the assent of the Court the trial of the issue is referred 'till next Court.

```
H. L.    :    THOMAS WILLIAMS         )
260      :                            )
299      :         vs                 )    In Case
         :                            )
         :    JOEL MORRISON           )
```

This day came the Plaintiff by his Attorney and by his Consent and with the assent of the Court, the enquiry of damages is referred 'till next Court. ___

```
W. B.    :    DAVID ALLISON           )
264      :                            )
Rhea     :         vs                 )    In Case
416      :                            )
         :    JOHN McDOWELL  Exor. of )
         :    JOSIAH LOVE   deceased. )
```

The Defendant in his proper person appeared and Saving to himself the benefit of retainer confesses Judgment for what may appear due upon Settlement according to assets in his hands and the Cause is Continued 'till next Court. _____

```
W. C.    :    JOHN KEARNS      :
265      :                     :
J. H.    :         vs          :    In Case
359      :                     :
         :    JAMES DALE       :
```

This day came the parties by their Attornies and by their mutual Consent and with the assent of the Court the trial of the issues is referred 'till next Court. _____

```
W. C.    :    JOHN KEARNS      )
266      :                     )
J. H.    :         vs          )    In Case
360      :                     )
         :    JAMES DALE       )
```

This day came the parties by their Attornies and by their mutual Consent and with the assent of the Court the trial of the issues is referred 'till next Court. _____

(Pg. 206)

```
J. L.    :    JAMES CAMRON        )
267      : by his next friend     )
D. G.    :                        )
247      :         vs             )    A B
         :                        )
         :    JOSIAS GAMBLE       )
```

The Defendant Josias Gamble in his proper person appeared and agrees to pay the Costs of this Suit, and upon this the Plaintiff prays that his Costs and charges by him about his Suit in this behalf expended may be adjudged to him. Therefore It is considered by the Court that the Plaintiff recover against the Said Defendant his Costs by him about his Suit in this behalf expended. And the Said Defendant in Mercy & C. And the Plaintiff not farther prosecuting It is ordered that this Suit be dismissed. _____

```
Rhea     :    JAMES GILLESPIE              )
269      :                                 )
W. C.    :         vs                      )    In Case
J. H.    :                                 )
332      :    WILLIAM McBROOM  admr. of    )
              WILLIAM ROSEBERRY  dec'd.    )
```

This day came the parties by their Attornies and by their mutual Consent and with the assent of the Court the trial of the issues is referred till next Court.

```
W. B.    :    JACOB HARMAN                    )
Rhea     :                                    )
270      :         vs                         )    In Debt
A. R.    :                                    )
271      :    ELIZABETH ISH admr. of          )
              JOHN ISH deceased.              )
```

This day came the parties by their Attornies, and Elizabeth Ish having revived this Suit, It is continued till next Court.

```
W. B.    :    ANDREW JACKSON                  )
273      :                                    )
333      :         vs                         )    Origl. Atta.
         :                                    )
         :    ROBERT BELL,                    )
              WILLIAM WALLACE & COMPANY       )
```

James Greenaway and John McDowell Garnashees being first Sworn Say they owe the Defendants nothing, that they have not nor had they at the time they were Summoned Garnashees any effects belonging to the Defendants in their hands, that they know of no debts due to or effects belonging to the Defendants in the hands of any other person.

James Houston Garnashee being first Sworn Saith that there is an unsettled account between him and the Defendants, that the Defendants are Debtors on his account, Sixty three dollars and thirty-eight Cents, that if the Defendants account against him exceeds that Sum he owes them the difference that he hath not nor had he at the time he was Summoned Garnashee any effects belonging to the Defendants in his hands that he knows of no debts due to or effects belonging to the Defendants in the hands of any other person.

John Cochran Garnashee being first Sworn Saith that he owes to a Note of hand given by him to the Defendants, that he has paid Twelve pounds part of Said Note, that he hath not nor had he at the time he was Summoned Garnashee any effects of the Defendants in his hands, that he knows of no other debts due to or effects belonging to the Defendants in the hands of any other person.

James Neeley having been duly Summoned to appear here at this term as Garnashee being Solemnly called came not; Therefore on Motion of the Plaintiff by his Attorney It is considered by the Court that the   (Pg. 207)   Plaintiff recover against the Said James Neely the amount of the Plaintiffs demand against the Said Defendants, and also his Costs unless he appear at the next Court after notice of this Judgment, and Shew Sufficient cause why the Same Should not be confirmed; And it is ordered that a Scire Facias issue against him, And the Cause is continued 'till next Court.

```
Reese    :    NATHANIEL LYONS                 )
J. H.    :                                    )
274      :         vs                         )    In Case
Rhea     :                                    )
300      :    JAMES MITCHELL                  )
```

This day came the parties by their Attornies and by their Mutual Consent and with the assent of the Court the trial of the issues is referred till next Court.

| W. C.
275
449 | : | GERSHAM MOORE

vs

MATTHEW BISHOP |))))) | In Case |

This day came the Plaintiff by his Attorney and the Sheriff having returned too late came to hand On Motion of the Plaintiff by his Attorney a Plurius Capias is awarded him against the Said Defendant returnable here at the next Court.

| Reese
J. H.
277
Rhea
L. B.
450 | : : : : : : | MORDECAI MENDINGHALL

vs

ALEXANDER CARMICHAEL &
JOSEPH JANES |))))) | In Case |

This day came the parties by their Attornies and by their Mutual Consent and with the assent of the Court the Cause is continued till next Court.

| Rhea
278
J. L.
301 | : : : : | JOHN McAMY

vs

JAMES COCHRAN |)))) | In Case |

This day came the parties by their Attornies and by their mutual Consent, and with the assent of the Court, the trial of the issues is referred till next Court.

| Rhea
279
L. B.
248 | : : : : | JOHN MORGAN

vs

MOSES STEGALL |)))) | Trover and Conversion |

The Plaintiff not farther prosecuting It is ordered that this Suit be dismissed and that the Plaintiff pay to the Defendant his Costs.

| Rhea
281
335 | : : : : | JAMES McCOLLOCK

vs

ANDREW LACKY |)))) | In Case |

This day came the Plaintiff by his Attorney and by his Consent and with the assent of the Court the Enquiry of damages is referred 'till next Court.

W. B.	:	BRIAN McCABE admr. of	)	
A. R.	:	TITUS OGDEN dec'd.	)	
282	:		)	
L. B.	:	vs	)	Original Attachment
355	:		)	
	:	ALEXANDER CARMICHAEL	)	

This day came the Plaintiff by his Attorney and by his Consent and with the assent of the Court the Cause is continued 'till next Court.

Court Adjourned 'till tomorrow 9 O'Clock.

(Pg. 208)

WEDNESDAY OCTOBER 29th 1794

Wednesday Morning October 29th 1794 Court met according to Adjournment present John Chisolm, William Lowry John Evans and James Houston esquires Justices & C. & C.

W. B.	:	WILLIAM ROBERSON	)	
283	:		)	
272	:	vs	)	Trover & Conversion
	:		)	
	:	JAMES DERMAND	)	

This day came the Plaintiff by his Attorney and by his Consent and with the assent of the Court the trial of the issue is referred 'till next Court.

Rhea	:	JOHN STONE	)	
285	:		)	
H. L.	:	vs	)	In Debt
451	:		)	
	:	JOSEPH WEST	)	

This day came the parties by their Attornies and by their mutual Consent and with the assent of the Court, the trial of the issue is referred 'till next Court.

Rhea	:	JOHN SOMMERVILLE & COMPANY	)	
286	:		)	
W. C.	:	vs	)	In Case
336	:		)	
	:	WILLIAM McBROOM admr. of	)	
		WILLIAM ROSEBERRY dec'd.	)	

This day came the parties by their Attornies and by their Mutual Consent, and with the assent of the Court the trial of the issues is referred 'till next Court.

J. H. :	JAMES STINSON	)
287 :		)
Rhea :	vs	) In Case
L. B. :		)
338 :	WILLIAM HENRY	)

This day came the parties by their Attornies and by their mutual Consent and with the assent of the Court the trial of the issue is referred 'till next Court. ___

J. L. :	SAMUEL WEAR and WILLIAM LOWRY	)
289 :	Exors. of JAMES WALKER deceased	)
A. R. :	vs	) In Debt.
490 :		)
:	JOHN COWAN and GEORGE TEDFORD	)

This day came the parties by their Attornies and by their mutual consent and with the assent of the Court the trial of the issue is referred till next Court. _____

J. L. :	SAMUEL WEAR and WILLIAM LOWRY	)
290 :	Exors. of JAMES WALKER deceased	)
J. H. :		)
337 :	vs	) In Debt.
:		)
:	JAMES CUNNINGHAM & GEORGE TEDFORD	)

This day came the parties by their Attornies and by their Mutual Consent and with the assent of the Court the trial of the issues is referred 'till next Court. _____

J. L. :	JOHN COWAN	)
291 :		)
302 :	vs	) Original Attachment
:		)
:	ROBERT LIGGET	)

This day came the Plaintiff by his Attorney and by his Consent and with the assent of the Court the enquiry of damages is referred 'till next Court. _____

A. R. :	ROBERT WILSON	)
292 :		)
339 :	vs	) Original Attachment.
:		)
:	SOLOMON MARKS	)

This day came the Plaintiff by his Attorney and by his Consent and with the assent of the Court the enquiry of damages is referred 'till next Court. ___

(Pg. 209)

Reese	:	JOHN ANDERSON	)
294	:		)
Rhea	:	vs	) In Case
H. L.	:		)
361	:	ROBERT McCAMPBELL	)

This day came the plaintiff by his Attorney and having filed his Declaration, the Defendant filed a plea in abatement and the argument thereof is referred 'till next Court. ___

W. C.	:	LUKE BOWYER	)
295	:		)
J. L.	:	vs	) In Debt.
362	:		)
	:	BENJAMIN BLACKBURN	)

This day came the parties by their Attornies and the Plaintiff having filed his Declaration the Defendant filed his plea and the issue being joined the trial thereof is referred till next Court. Whereupon the Defendant is Surrendered by his Bail in discharge of themselves, and William Lowry and Jeremiah Jack of this County comes into Court and undertakes for the Defendant that in case he Shall be cast in this Suit, he Shall Satisfy and pay the condemnation or render his body to prison in execution for the Same or that they the Said William Lowry & Jeremiah Jack will do it for him.

J. H.	:	JOHN BROWN	)
296	:		)
A. R.	:	vs	) IN DEBT.
452	:		)
	:	SAMUEL BOGLE and	)
		GAUIN BLACK	)

This day came the parties by their Attornies and the Plaintiff having filed his Declaration the Defendant filed his plea and the issue being Joined the trial thereof is referred till next Court.

Rhea	:	JAMES BALDRIDGE	)
297	:		)
273	:	vs	) In Debt
	:		)
	:	ROBERT FERGUSON	)

This day came the Plaintiff by his Attorney and having filed his Declaration, the Cause is continued till next Court. ___

Rhea	:	JAMES BALDRIDGE	)	
298	:		)	
274	:	vs	)	In Debt
	:		)	
	:	ROBERT FERGUSON	)	

This day came the Plaintiff by his Attorney and having his Declaration the Cause is continued till next Court. _____

L. B.	:	ALEXANDER CARMICHAEL	/)	
299	:		)	
417	:	vs	)	In Covenant. ____
	:		)	Continued
	:	JAMES DONAHOO	)	

300	:	JAMES CAMPBELL	)	
249	:		)	
	:	vs	)	In Case
	:		)	
	:	GIDEON MORRIS	)	

The Defendant appeared and paid the Costs of this Suit and the Plaintiff not farther prosecuting It is ordered that this Suit be dismissed. _____

A. R.	:	PAUL CUNNINGHAM	)	
301	:		)	
Rhea	:	vs	)	In Case
363	:		)	
	:	JAMES ANDERSON	)	

This day came the parties by their Attornies and the Plaintiff having   (Pg. 210)   filed his declaration the Defendant filed his Pleas and the issues being joined the trial thereof is referred 'till next Court. And on motion of the Plaintiff by his Attorney a Commission is awarded him to take the deposition of his Witnesses giving the Defendant legal notice of the time and place of executing the Same. _____

Rhea	:	GEORGE B. GREER'S lessee	)	
302	:		)	
D. G.	:	vs	)	In Ejectment
A. R.	:		)	
364	:	FEN	)	

Drury Wood Breazeal on his motion is admitted Defendant in this Suit in the Stead of the Said Fen, and thereupon by his Attorney he comes & defends the force and Injury when & C. pleads not Guilty, confesses the lease entry and ouster, in the Declaration Supposed and puts himself upon the Country, And the Plaintiff likewise; And the trial of the issue is referred 'till next Court. _____

Rhea   :   JOHN GOEHEN   )
303   :   )
A. R.   :   vs   )   In Case
303   :   )
        :   JOSEPH COWAN   )

This day came the parties by their Attornies and the Plaintiff having filed his declaration the Defendant filed his Plea and the issue being Joined the trial thereof is referred 'till next Court. ____

L. B.   :   RUTH GIST   )
Reese   :   )
304   :   vs   )   ·   In Case
Rhea   :   )
340   :   STEPHEN DUNCAN   )

This day came the parties by their Attornies and the Plaintiff having filed her declaration, the Defendant filed his Plea and the issue being Joined the trial thereof is referred 'till next Court. ____

Rhea   :   JAMES GEALEY   )
305   :   )
L. B.   :   vs   )   A B
305   :   )
        :   JESSE CLAYWELL   )

This day came the parties by their Attornies and the Plaintiff having filed his declaration, the Defendant filed his Plea and the issue being Joined the trial thereof is referred 'till next Court. ____

Rhea   :   JOHN FINLEY   assignee   )
306   :   )
365   :   vs   )   In Debt.
        :   )
        :   THOMAS MANN   )

This day came the Plaintiff by his Attorney and having filed his declaration, the Cause is continued 'till next Court. ____

307   :   JOSEPH HAMILTON   )
250   :   )
        :   vs   )   In Case
        :   )
        :   WILLIAM McBROOM Admr. of)
        :   WILLIAM ROSEBERRY dec'd.)

The Defendant assumes Costs and the Plaintiff dismisses the Suit. __

(Pg. 211)

308 : WILLIAM HAZLET)
251 :)
    :)
    :   vs)   In Case
    :)
    : WILLIAM TRIMBLE)

     The plaintiff not farther prosecuting It is ordered that this
Suit be dismissed. _____

Reese : CHRISTOPHER HAINS)
309 :)
Rhea :   vs)   In Debt
341 :)
    : NATHANIEL HAYS)

     This day came the parties by their Attornies and the Plaintiff
having filed his Declaration, the Defendant prays Oyer of the writing
obligatory in the Declaration mentioned and to him it is read in these
words to Wit, "On demand I will pay Chris. Hanes Ten pounds virginia
money for value rec'd. Witness my hand this 16th day of March 1794.

                           Nathaniel Hays   "

Test
    Wm. King

     And the Cause is continued 'till next Court. _____

Reesse : CHRISTOPHER HAINS)
310 :)
Rhea :   vs)
342 :)
    : NATHANIEL HAYS)

     This day came the parties by their Attornies and the Plaintiff
having filed his Declaration, the Defendant prays Oyer of the writing
obligatory in the Declaration mentioned and to him it is read in these
words to Wit "On or before the twentyfift day of October next I
promise to pay Chris. Hanes the Sum of One Hundred & Eight Dollars
for value Rec'd. this 11th day Sept'm. 1793

                           Nathl. Hays   "

Test
    Jno. Hanes

     And the Cause is continued 'till next Court.

Rhea : LEVI HINDS)
311 :)
L. B. :   vs)   In Case._____Continued.
275 :)
    : HIRAM GERON)

```
D. G.    :      JAMES JORDAN           )
J. H.    : by his next Friend          )
312      :                             )
Rhea     :         vs                  )    In Case,   Words
366      :                             )
         :      WILLIAM COOPER         )
```

This day came the parties by their Attornies; And the Defendant
prays Oyer of the Declaration; And the Cause is continued 'till
next Court.

```
A. R.    :      ANDREW LUCKEY          )
313      :                             )
L. B.    :         vs                  )    In Covenant
Rhea     :                             )
W. C.    :      EDWARD McFARLAND       )
H. L.    :                             )
367      :                             )
```

· This day came the parties by their Attornies, And the Plaintiff
having   (Pg. 212)   filed his Declaration the Defendant filed
his Pleas and the issues being joined the trial thereof is referred
'till next Court.

```
Rhea     :      DENNIS MURPHY          )
314      :                             )
453      :         vs                  )    Original Attachment.  In Case
         :                             )
         :      THOMAS EVANS           )
```

This day came the Plaintiff by his Attorney and having filed his
Declaration, John Chisolm Garnashee being first Sworn Saith that
he owes the Defendant nothing, that Some time past, a Barrel
Supposed to contain from Twenty to Thirty gallons of Whiskey the property
of the Defendant, was lodged in his hands, that in his absence the
Said Whiskey was made use of by his family; that the Plaintiff Some
time Since Shewed him a note of hand, which he the Plaintiff Said was
the Property of the Defendant that he knows of no debts due to or
other effects belonging to the Defendant in the hands of any other
person. And the Cause is continued 'till next Court. _____

```
Rhea     :      ANNANIAS McCOY         )
315      :                             )
J. L.    :         vs                  )    In Case
418      :                             )
         :      JOHN LUSK              )
```

This day came the Plaintiff by his Attorney and having filed his
declaration; And the Defendant having been arrested and not appearing
though Solemnly called, on motion of the Plaintiff by his Attorney
It is considered by the Court, that the Plaintiff recover against
the Defendant Such damages as he hath Sustained by occasion of the

Defendants Nonperformance of the Assumption in the Declaration
mentioned; which damages are to be inquired of by a Jury at the next
Court. _____

| 316
W. C.
276 | : | JOHN LOWRY assignee

vs

HENRY REGAN, JOHN REGAN, &
AHIMAS REGAN |)))))) | In Cov't.

Continued. |

| L. B.
317
246 | : | GEORGE PRESGROVE

vs

MARTIN FRILEY |))))) | In Case |

The Plaintiff not farther prosecuting It is ordered that this
Suit be dismissed; And that the Plaintiff pay to the Defendant his
Costs.

| L. B.
318
304 | : | WILLIAM TIPTON

vs

JOHN BURDIN |))))) | In Case |

This day came the Plaintiff by his Attorney and having filed his
Declaration; And the Defendant having been arrested and not appearing
though Solemnly called, On motion of the Plaintiff by his Attorney
It is considered by the Court, that the Plaintiff recover against the
(Pg. 213)   Defendant, Such damages as he hath Sustained by occasion
of the Defendants Nonperformance of the assumption in the Declaration
mentioned; which damages are to be enquired of by a Jury at the next
Court.

| 319
246 | : | DAVID WALKER

vs

JAMES McDONOLD |))))) | Sheriff returned,
          compromised;

Costs paid. |

| L. B.
320
Rhea
277 | : | THOMAS WELCH

vs

NATHANIEL LYON |))))) | In Case |

This day came the Plaintiff by his Attorney and having filed his
Declaration the Cause is continued 'till next Court. _____

321	:	JAMES WHITE	)	
244	:		)	
	:	vs	)	In Debt.
	:		)	
	:	JOHN TRIMBLE	)	

The Plaintiff not farther prosecuting, It is ordered that this Suit be dismissed.

L. B.	:	JOSEPH McCULLAH	)	
322	:		)	
243	:	vs	)	In Covenant.
	:		)	
	:	STOCKLEY DONELSON	)	

The Sheriff returned, ordered by Plaintiff not to be executed And the Plaintiff not farther prosecuting It is ordered that this Suit be dismissed.

· James Houston appeared and produced a Commission from Governor Blount, by which it appears that he is appointed a Justice of the peace for this County, who took the Oath to Support the Constitution of the United States, and also the Oath of Office & took his Seat accordingly.

Ordered that the following Justices do take in and return to next Court a List of the Taxables and Taxable property of the respective Companies for which they are appointed. _____

For Captain Stones Company			Joseph Greer
"	"	Singletons "	William Hamilton
"	"	Gillespies "	Jeremiah Jack
"	"	Crawfords "	James White
"	"	Flennikens "	Thomas McCullough
"	"	Henrys "	David Craig
"	"	Samples "	John Evans
"	"	Tedfords "	William Wallace
"	"	Cozbys "	James Cozby
"	"	Menefees "	John Menefee
"	"	Bunches "	John Kearnes
"	"	Campbells "	David Campbell
"	"	Beards "	John Sawyers
"	"	Ewings "	William Lowry
"	"	Blacks and that part of)	

Captn. McGauheys Company that remains)
in this County)

James Houston

(Pg. 214)

Ordered that all Ordinaries in this County be rated as follows to Wit

For Breakfast	20	Cents
Dinner	25	"
Supper	16 2/3	"
Lodging	6	"
Corn or Oats per gallon	8	"
Keeping a horse with a		
Sufficiency of Hay, Fod-)	16 2/3	"
der or Sheaf Oats per night)		
the Same for 24 Hours	33 1/3	"
Pasturage for 24 Hours	8	"
Rum per half pint	16 2/3	"
Brandy per Ditto	8	"
Whiskey per Ditto	8	"
Wine per Quart	1.00	
Beer per Ditto	8	"
Cider per Ditto	8	"
Metheglin	8	"
Meal of Cold Victuals		
half price of other Meals		

Ordered that Benjamin White have liberty to keep an public house where he lives for one Year he having given bond with George Stout and Henry Null his Securities in the Sum of Two thousand five hundred dollars, conditioned as the law directs. _____

COURT ADJOURNED 'TILL COURT IN COURSE.

MONDAY JANUARY 26th 1795

At a Court of Pleas and Quarter Sessions began and held for the County of Knox, at the Court House in Knoxville on the last Monday of January 1795.

Present John Adair, Jeremiah Jack, James Cosby, William Lowry and Abraham Ghormley esquires Justices & C.

Robert Houston esquire Sheriff & C. returned that he had executed our Writ of Venire Facias to him directed upon the following person to Wit   John Kean, Samuel Doak, William Doak, William Reed, William Robeson, Moses Brooks, Hugh Forgey, Nicholas Perkins, Archibald McKillip, Samuel Samples, David Adair, David W. Howell, Thomas Woodward, James Gibson, Alexander Campbell, Joseph Taylor Alexander Kelley, Matthew Neal, Nicholas Gibbs, George Hays, Thomas Ritchey, Patrick Sharkey, James McElwee, David Walker, George Martin, Garret Hendrix, Christian Pickle, Robert McTier, Hugh Beard, Nathaniel Hays, William Richey, Archibald Lackey, David Scott, and James Brook.___

Out of which Venire the following persons were elected a Grand
Inquest for the Body of this County to Wit, Alexander Kelley, Foreman,
Samuel Doak, Garret Hendrix, Samuel Samples, William Doak, Hugh Forgey,
Nicholas Gibbs, David Scott, Christian Pickle, William Richey, George
Martin, William Robeson, James Brock, Moses Brooks, and Thomas Ritchey
who have been Sworn received their Charge and withdrew to enquire
of their presentments. _____

(Pg. 215)

James Moore appeared and produced a Commission from Governor
Blount, by which it appears that he is appointed a Justice of the
Peace for this County who took the Oath to Support the Constitution
of the United States, And also the Oath of Office and took his
Seat accordingly. _____

```
W. B.    :    ANDREW JACKSON                              )
273      :                                                )   Original
333      :              vs                                )   Attachment.
         :                                                )
         :    ROBERT BELL, WILLIAM WALLACE & COMPANY      )
```

This day came the Plaintiff by his Attorney; And James Scott
Garnashee being first Sworn Saith that he is indebted to the Defendants
One pound fourteen Shillings, and that he hath nor had he at the time
he was Summoned Garnashee any effects belonging to the Defendants
in his hands, that he knows of no other debts due to or effects belonging to the Defendants in the hands of any other person.

Samuel Henry Garnashee being first Sworn Saith he oweth
the Defendants nothing that he hath not, nor had he at the time he
was Summoned Garnashee any effects of the Defendants in his hands
that he knows of no debts due to or effects belonging to the Defendants in the hands of any other person. _____

James Neeley Garnashee being first Sworn Saith he executed
the Note of hand now produced to him, payable to the Defendants for
Five pounds Sixteen Shillings and Nine pence, that he was Summoned
Garnashee at the Suit of David Stewart against the Said Defendants
and as Garnashee paid the amount of the Said Note, that he hath not
nor had he at the time he was Summoned Garnashee any effects belonging
to the Defendants in his hands, that he knows of no debts to or
effects belonging to the Defendants in the hands of any other person.___
And the Cause is continued 'till next Court. _____ Whereupon on Motion
of the Said James Neeley It is ordered that the Judgment obtained
against him at the last Court be Set aside. _____

Court Adjourned 'Till Tomorrow 9 O'Clock.

TUESDAY JANUARY 27th 1795

Tuesday Morning January 27th 1795 Court met according to Adjournment Present John Adair, Jeremiah Jack and William Lowry esquires Justices & C. & C. & C.

J. H.	:	SOLOMON MARKS	)
36	:		)
Rhea	:	vs	) In Case
252	:		)
	:	ROBERT KING	)

This day came the parties by their Attornies and thereupon (Pg. 216) came a Jury to Wit, Thomas Woodward, Robert McTier, John Kean, David Adair, James Gibson, Nathaniel Hays, Jacob Tarwater, Matthew Neal, William Lea, James Blair, Charles Collins and Benjamin Blackburn, who being elected tried and Sworn the truth to Speak upon the issues Joined upon their Oath do Say the Defendant did not assume upon himself in manner and form as the Plaintiff against him hath complained as in pleading he hath alledged. Therefore It is considered by the Court that the Plaintiff take nothing by his bill and for his false clamour be in Mercy and the Defendant go hence without day and recover against the Plaintiff his Costs by him about his defence in this behalf expended. ___

Samuel Acklin who was Summoned to appear here this day as a Witness for the Plaintiff in this Suit, was Solemnly called but came not, therefore on Motion of the Plaintiff by his Attorney It is considered by the Court that the Plaintiff Solomon Marks recover against the Said Samuel Acklin One hundred and twenty five dollars unless he appear at the next Court after notice of this Judgment and Shew Sufficient cause why the Same Should not be confirmed. And it is ordered that a Scire Facias issue against him.

Rhea	:	JOHN CHISOLM	)
49	:		)
662	:	vs	) In Case
	:		)
	:	RICHARD HAMILTON	)

This day came the Plaintiff by his Attorney and by his Consent and with the assent of the Court, the enquiry of damages is referred till next Court.

A. O.	:	MARY STEPHENSON and	)
88	:	EDWARD STEPHENSON	)
J. H.	:	Executors of	)
288	:	ROBERT STEPHENSON deceased	) In Case
	:		)
	:	vs	)
	:		)
	:	BENJAMIN BLACKBURN	)

This day came the parties by their Attornies and by their mutual Consent and with the assent of the Court, the trial of the issues is referred 'till next Court. _____

A. R.	:	ROBERT THOMPSON	)	
115	:		)	
Rhea	:	vs	)	In Case
253	:		)	
	:	JOHN McALLISTER	)	

It appearing to the Court, that the parties have mutually agreed to Submit all matters in dispute between them in this Suit to the final determination of William Lowry, David Craig, Thomas McCullough, David Caldwell, and William Hamilton or any three of them, whose award thereupon, they have mutually agreed Shall be made the Judgment of this Court, which Arbitrators now return their Award in the following   (Pg. 217)   Words to Wit, " We the arbitrators viz William Lowry, David Craig, Thomas McColloh, David Caldwell, and Wm. Hamilton have agreed that John McAllister Shall pay to Robert Thompson One hundred and twenty bushels of Corn or an equal quantity of other property on or before the first day of January next ensuing the date hereof and all Costs to Said Thompson except McAllisters Attorney.

Given under our hands and Seals Septr. ye. 18th 1794 N B   the property to be paid at Captain John Singletons. _____

	Wm. Lowry	(Seal)
Therefore It is considered)	David Craig	(Seal)
by the Court that the Said award)		
be Confirmed....................)	Thos. McColloh	(Seal)
	David Caldwell	(Seal)
	Wm. Hamilton	(Seal)

A. O.	:	JOHN HUTCHINSON	)	
133	:		)	
J. H.	:	vs	)	In Case
567	:		)	
	:	ANDREW PAUL admr. of	)	
	:	JAMES PAUL deceased	)	

This day came the parties by their Attornies and by their mutual Consent and with the assent of the Court the trial of the issues is referred 'till next Court. _____

S. M.	:	JAMES ALLISON	)	
135	:		)	
J. H.	:	vs	)	In Covenant
L. B.	:		)	
356	:	ABRAHAM SWAGERTY	)	

This day came the parties by their Attornies and the Death of the Plaintiff is suggested in Abatement: And on Motion It is ordered that a notice issue to the Executors or Administrators of the Said James Allison to appear at next Court and prosecute this Suit. ____

A. R.	:	JOHN WALLACE	)	
141	:		)	
255	:	vs .	)	Original Attachment, In Case
	:		)	
	:	JAMES BRIANT	)	

This day came the plaintiff by his Attorney, and John Franklin Garnashee being first Sworn Saith that he is indebted to the Defendant Twenty bushels Corn, that he hath not, nor had he at the time he was Summoned Garnashee any other effects of the Defendants in his hands that he knows of no debts due to or effects belonging to the Defendant in the hands of any other person. And thereupon came a Jury to Wit, Benjamin Pride, Benjamin White, James Campbell, Samuel Bogle, William Cowan, Paul Cunningham, William Tipton, William Ewing, Lewis Brim, William Burden, George McEwen, and John Caldwell, who being elected tried and (Pg. 218) Sworn diligently to enquire of damages in this Suit upon their Oath do Say that the Plaintiff hath Sustained damages by occasion of the Defendants Nonperformance of the Assumption in the declaration mentioned to Thirty eight dollars and fifty Cents besides his Costs Therefore it is considered by the Court that the Plaintiff recover against the Defendant his damages aforesaid in form aforesaid assessed and his Costs by him about his Suit in this behalf expended. And the Said Defendant in Mercy & C._____

Rhea	:	SAMUEL FLANNAGAN	)	
149	:		)	
Reese	:	vs	)	In Covenant
256	:		)	
	:	JOHN SEVIER and	)	
	.	ADAM MEEK Excrs. of	)	
		ISAAC TAYLOR deceased	)	

This day came the parties by their Attornies and thereupon came a Jury to Wit, Thomas Woodward, Robert McTier, John Kean, David Adair, James Gibson, Nathaniel Hays, Jacob Tarwater, Matthew Neal, William Hazlet, James Blair, Charles Collins and Benjamin Blackburn who being elected tried and Sworn diligently to enquire of damages in this Suit upon their Oath do Say that the Plaintiff hath Sustained damages by occasion of the Defendants Nonperformance of the Covenant in the declaration mentioned to One hundred dollars besides his Costs. Therefore It is considered by the Court that the Plaintiff recover against the Said Defendants his damages aforesaid in form aforesaid assessed and his costs by him about his Suit in this behalf expended, to be levied of the goods and chattels of the decedent, in the hands of the Said Defendants to be administered if So much thereof they have, but if not then the Costs to be levied of their proper goods and chattels, lands and tenements And the Said Defendants in Mercy & C.

```
A. R.    :    THOMAS EMBREE        )
152      :                         )
S. M.    :         vs             )    In Case
Rhea     :                         )
257      :    JOHN CHISOLM         )
```

This day came the parties by their Attornies and thereupon came a Jury   to Wit, James Kerr, Charles Regan, Junior, Amos Bird, James Martin, John Cowan, James Scott, William Sharp, James King, William Lea, Samuel Bogle, William Snoddy and Alexander Campbell who being elected tried and Sworn the truth to Speak upon the issue Joined. The Attorney for the Plaintiff having examined his Witnesses to Support the issue aforesaid the Defendants Attorney moved that the Plaintiff Should be Non, Suit, alledging that the evidence offered to the Said Jury was not Sufficient to maintain the Said Action, to which the Plaintiff by his Attorney did object, but the Justices of the Said Court to Wit   (Pg. 219)   John Adair, William Wallace, James Moore, and James Cozby ordered that a Non Suit Should be entered and that the Jurors aforesaid from rendering their Verdict be discharged. Whereupon the Defendant was put under a rule to Shew cause why the Said Non Suit, Should not be Set aside and a new trial granted, which was argued and discharged. Therefore It is considered by the Court that the Plaintiff take nothing by his Bill but for his false clamour be in Mercy and C. and that the Said Defendant go hence without day and recover against the Plaintiff his Costs by him about his defense in this behalf expended.

```
Rhea     :    SAMUEL FINLEY        )
158      :                         )
J. Love  :         vs             )    A. B.
258      :                         )
         :    JOHN BIRD            )
```

It appearing to the Court, that the arbitrators to whom the determination of the matters in difference between the parties were Submitted by a rule of this Court; did agree that the Defendant Should pay all Costs, until February 1794 and the continuance of that Court, and that the Plaintiff Should pay all other Costs of this Suit. Therefore it is considered by the Court that the Said Award be Confirmed.

```
Reesse   :    WILLIAM DAVIDSON     )
171      :                         )
J. L.    :         vs             )    In Covenant
321      :                         )
         :    WILLIAM LOWRY        )
```

By consent of the parties the matters in difference between them in this Suit, are referred to the final determination of Samuel Wear, Joseph Nance, Joshua Gist, Hugh Henry, and Josias Gamble, whose award thereupon, or the award of a Majority of them, is to be made the Judgment of the Court, and the Same is ordered accordingly._____

Rhea	:	BRIAN McCABE admr. of	)	
172	:	TITUS OGDEN deceased	)	
357	:		)	
	:	vs	)	In Case
	:		)	
	:	EZEKIEL HENRY and	)	
	:	WILLIAM HENRY	)	

This day came the Plaintiff by his Attorney, and by his Consent, and with the assent of the Court, the enquiry of damages is referred 'till next Court. _____

J. L.	:	JOHN DUNCAN	)	
179	:		)	
A. R.	:	vs	)	In Covenant
412	:		)	
	:	JOHN McNUTT &	)	
		JAMES CALLISON	)	

This day came the parties by their Attornies and by their mutual Consent, and with the assent of the Court the Argument of the Demurrer is referred 'till next Court. _____

Court Adjourned 'Till Tomorrow 9 O'Clock.

(Pg. 220)

WEDNESDAY JANUARY 28th 1795

Wednesday Morning January 28th 1795 Court met according to adjournment Present   James White, George McNutt, John Adair, David Craig, John Menefee, William Wallace, James Moor, John Evans, Abraham Ghormly, and William Lowry esquires Justices & C. & C.

558	11.	:	Ordered that Process issue against Zapher Tannery
559	16.	:	and James Bunch to cause them to appear at the next
		:	Court to answer the Indictments found against them
		:	by the Grand Jury.

Rhea	:	UNITED STATES	)	
26	:		)	
283	:	vs	)	A B
	:		)	
	:	DAVID MOOR	)	

Be it remembered that heretofore to Wit, At a Court held for this County, on the last Monday of October last past, the Grand Jurors for the Said County presented an Indictment against David Moor for an Assault and Battery a true Bill and the Sheriff having returned the Capias on Indictment executed. And now at this day

came as well the Solicitor for the County as the Defendant in his
proper person and the Said Defendant because he will not contend
Saith that he is guilty in manner and form as in the Indictment
against him is alledged and putteth himself upon the Grace and
Mercy of the Court; Therefore It is considered by the Court,
that for Such his offense he be fined five dollars and pay the
Costs of this prosecution.

Rhea	:	UNITED STATES	)	
27	:		)	
350	:	vs	)	PETIT LARCENY
	:		)	
	:	JOSEPH LAIRD	)	

Be it remembered that heretofore to Wit At a Court held for
this County, on the last Monday of October last past, the Grand
Jurors for the Said County presented an Indictment against Joseph
Laird for Petit Larceny a true Bill, and that the Said Joseph Laird
Stood bound in recognizance bearing date the 21st day of August
1794 in the Sum of One hundred Dollars, for his appearance at the
Said Court, and to abide & perform the Judgment thereof and David
Laird & Martin Armstrong Junior also Stood bound in recognizance
bearing date the 21st day of August 1794 in the Sum of Fifty dollars
each for the appearance of the Said Joseph Laird Nevertheless the
Said Joseph Laird when Solemnly called upon came not, therefore for-
feited his recognizance and the Said David Laird and Martin Armstrong
Junior being Solemnly called to Surrender the Said Joseph Laird
failed So to do, therefore forfeited their Said Recognizance and it
was ordered that a Scire Facias issue (Pg. 221) against them.
And now at this day came the Solicitor for the County And the Sheriff
having returned the Scire Facias made known to David Laird Martin
Armstrong Junior not found and the Said Joseph Laird being again ·
Solemnly called came not, And the Said David Laird being Solemnly
called to Shew cause if any he had why final Judgment Should not be
rendered against him came not: Therefore on Motion of the Said
Solicitor It is considered by the Court, that Judgment final be
entered against the Said David Laird for the aforesaid Fifty Dollars
in the Said recognizance mentioned, and Costs; And that Alias Scire
Facias's issue against the Said Joseph Laird and Martin Armstrong
Junior returnable here at the next Court. _____

Rhea	:	UNITED STATES	)	
28	:		)	
351	:	vs	)	Petit Larceny
	:		)	
	:	WILLIAM KENNEDY	)	

Be it remembered that heretofore to Wit, at a Court held for
this County on the last Monday of October last past the Grand Jurors
for the Said County presented an Indictment against William Kennedy
for Petit Larceny a true Bill, and that the Said William Kennedy
Stood bound in Recognizance bearing date the 21st day of August

1794 in the Sum of One hundred Dollars for his appearance at the
Said Court and to abide and perform the Judgment of Said Court;
and Alexander Carmichael his Security also Stood bound in Re-
cognizance bearing date the 21st day of August 1794 in the Sum
of Fifty dollars for the appearance of the Said William Kennedy;
Nevertheless the Said William Kennedy when Solemnly called upon
came not, Therefore forfeited his Recognizance And the Said
Alexander Carmichael being Solemnly called to Surrender the
Body of the Said William Kennedy failed So So to do; therefore
Forfeited his Said Recognizance and it is ordered that a Scire
Facias issue against them, And now at this day came the Solicitor
for the County and the Sheriff having returned the Scire Facias
made known to Alexander Carmichael, and the Said William Kennedy
being again Solemnly called came not And the Said Alexander
Carmichael being Solemnly called appeared and prays time until the
next Court; to Surrender the principal which is granted him.

Rhea	:	UNITED STATES	)
29	:		)
L. B.	:	vs	) T.V.A.
A. O.	:		)
284	:	SAMUEL HINDMAN Junior	)

This day came as well the Solicitor for the County as the
Defendant by his Attorney and the Said Defendant being charged
pleads not   (Pg. 222)   Guilty and thereupon came a Jury
to Wit   Thomas Woodward, Robert McTier, John Kean, James Gibson,
Nathaniel Hays, Alexander Campbell, Matthew Neal, Charles Collins,
Jacob Vanhooser, William Rogan, Robert Black, and Andrew Paul who
being elected tried and Sworn the truth of and upon the premises
to Speak upon their Oath do Say that the Said Samuel Hindman Junior
is Guilty of the trespass in manner and form as charged in the Bill
of Indictment: And the Jurors aforesaid upon their Oath aforesaid
further Say that the Said Samuel Hindman Junior is not Guilty
of the taking and carrying away as in pleading he hath alledged.
Therefore it is considered by the Court that for Such his offence
he be fined Fifty Cents and that he pay the costs of this prosecution.

Rhea	:	UNITED STATES	)
30	:		)
285	:	vs	) A B
	:		)
	:	JAMES COCHRAN	)

This day came as well the Solicitor for the County as the
Defendant in his proper person and the Said Defendant because he
will not contend Saith that he is Guilty in'manner and form as in
the Indictment against him is alledged and putteth himself upon
the Grace and Mercy of the Court; Therefore It is considered by
the Court that for Such his offence he be fined One Dollar and pay
the Costs of this prosecution. _____

Rhea	:	UNITED STATES	)	
31	:		)	
286	:	vs	)	A B
	:		)	
	:	JAMES COCHRAN	)	

This day came as well the Solicitor for the County as the Defendant in his proper person and the Said Defendant because he will not contend Saith that he is guilty in manner and form as in the Indictment against him is alledged and putteth himself upon the Grace and Mercy of the Court. Thereofre It is considered by the Court that for Such his offence he be fined One Dollar and that he pay the costs of this prosecution. _____

RHEA	:	UNITED STATES	)	
32	:		)	
319	:	vs	)	A B
	:		)	
	:	CHARLES REGAN Junior	)	

This day came as well the Solicitor for the County as the Defendant by his Attorney, and the Said Defendant being charged pleads not Guilty and by their Mutual Consent and with the assent of the Court, the trial of the issue is referred 'till next Court. _____

(Pg. 223)

The Grand Jury appeared and for reasons appearing to the Court Nicholas Gibbs and Hugh Forgey are discharged from further attendance, and James Blair and Joseph Cowan Sworn in their place.

H. L.	:	JOHN DAVIS	)	
181	:		)	
Rhea	:	vs	)	In Case
322	:		)	
	:	JOSEPH JANES	)	

This day came the parties by their Attornies and thereupon came a Jury to Wit, Thomas Woodward, Robert McTier, John Kean, James Gibson, Nathaniel Hays, Alexander Campbell, Charles Collins, Jacob Vanhooser, William Regan, Andrew Paul, Robert Willson, and Andrew Jackson, who being elected tried and Sworn the truth to Speak upon the issues joined went out of Court to consult of their Verdict and after Some time returned into Court and declared they could not agree in their Verdict by consent of the parties and with the assent of the Court one of the Jurors aforesaid was withdrawn and the rest of the Said Jurors from rendering their verdict discharged. And the Cause is continued 'till next Court for a New trial to be had thereon._____

Court Adjourned 'till tomorrow 9 O'Clock

THURSDAY JANUARY 29th 1795.

Thursday Morning January 29th 1795 Court met according to
adjournment, Present   David Craig, William Wallace, John Evans,
and Abraham Ghormly esquires Justices & C.

Rhea	:	ALEXANDER CARMICHAEL	)	
118	:		)	
A. O.	:	vs	)	In Case
254	:		)	
	:	JOSEPH SEVIER	)	

This day came the parties by their Attornies and thereupon
came a Jury to Wit, Thomas Woodward, Robert McTier, James Gibson,
Nathaniel Hays, Amos Bird, Andrew Jackson, James Kerr, Jacob
Vanhooser, Hugh Bodkin, John Kean, Benjamin Pride and Charles .
Collins who being elected tried and Sworn the truth to Speak upon
the issue Joined upon their Oath do Say, that the Defendant did
assume upon himself in manner and form as the Plaintiff against him
hath complained and they do assess the Plaintiffs damages by occasion
of the Defendants Nonperformance of that assumption to Thirty four
Dollars and Sixty Cents besides his his Costs; Therefore it is con-
sidered by the Court that the Plaintiff recover against the Said
Defendant his Damages aforesaid in form aforesaid assessed and his
Costs by him about his Suit in this behalf expended and the Said
Defendant in Mercy & C. _____

(Pg. 224)

W. C.	:	JAMES BRIGGAM	)	
C. C.	:		)	
H. L.	:	vs	)	In Covenant
D. G.	:		)	
186	:	JOHN CHISOLM	)	
A. R.	:			
A. O.	:			
323	:			

This day came the parties by their Attornies and
by their mutual consent and with the assent of the
Court the trial of the issue is referred 'till next
Court. _____

A. R.	:	FRANCIS BIRD	)	
188	:		)	
Rhea	:	vs	)	In Case
A. O.	:		)	
259	:	JOHN CHISOLM and JOHN MILLER	)	

This day came as well the Plaintiff by his Attorney as the
Defendants in their proper persons; And the parties agree that the
Plaintiff hath Sustained Fifty nine dollars and Sixty Cents damages
by occasion of the Defendants Nonperformance of the Assumption in the

Declaration mentioned. Therefore it is considered by the Court,
that the Plaintiff recover against the Defendants the damages agreed
as aforesaid and his Costs by him about his Suit in this behalf expended. And the Said Defendants in Mercy & C. _____

A. R.	:	PEARSON BROCK	)	
189	:		)	
Rhea	:	vs	)	In Case, Words
260	:		)	
	:	JAMES THOMPSON	)	

The Arbitrators to whom the determination of matters in
difference between the parties, were Submitted, returned their
Award in these words. " November 14 1794, We the Arbitrators
after being duly Sworn to decide and agree a matter of controversy
now Subsisting in Knox Court, wherein Pearson Brook is Plaintiff
and James Thompson is Defendant; the parties appeared with their
Witnesses and being Sworn and heard; We the Said Arbrs. award
for the Defendant. _____ James White, James Davis, Robert Black
Andw. McCampbell, John Patterson, Deveroux Gilliam, F. A. Ramsey,_____
The Defendant having Summoned Agnes Reed and Mary Walker, as witnesses;
And the Arbitrators concieving them as unnecessary witnesses; There-
fore it is considered by the Court that the Said Award be confirmed.
And that the Defendant pay the Costs of the attendance of Agnus
Reed and Mary Walker._____

H. L.	:	DAVID WRIGHT	)	
192	:		)	
Rhea	:	vs	)	In Case
289	:		)	
	:	JAMES SPENCE	)	

This day came the parties by their Attornies and by their mutual
Consent and with the assent of the Court the trial of the issues is
referred 'till next Court. _____

S. M.	:	THOMAS KING	)	
Rhea	:		)	
193	:	vs	)	In Case
J. H.	:		)	
290	:	JOSEPH BEARD	)	

This day came the parties by their Attornies and by their
Mutual Consent and with the assent of the Court the trial of the
issues is referred until next Court._____

(Pg. 225)

Rhea	:	AQUILLA JOHNSTON	)	
194	:		)	
J. H.	:	vs	)	In Case
261	:		)	
	:	MAJOR LEA	)	

This day came the parties by their Attornies and thereupon
came a Jury to Wit, Michael Swisher, Andrew McCosland, James
Montgomery, George McEwn, James Campbell, Henry White, Taylor
Townsend, Samuel Bogle, John Regan, William Regan, William Cooper
and William McBroom who being elected tried and Sworn the truth
to Speak upon the issue joined upon their Oath do Say that the Defendant is not guilty in manner and form set forth in the Plaintiffs
declaration as in pleading he hath alledged; Therefore it is considered by the Court, that the Plaintiff take nothing by his Writ, but
for his false clamour he be in Mercy & C. and that the Defendant
go hence without day and recover against the Said Plaintiff his
costs by him about his defence in this behalf expended___ From which
Judgment the aforesaid Aquilla Johnston by John Chisolm his Attorney
in fact hath prayed for and obtained an Appeal to the Honorable the
Superior Court of law for Hamilton District to be held at the Court
House in Knoxville on the Second Tuesday of April 1795, and hath
filed bond and Security together with the reasons for appeal as the
law directs._____ Note a Bill of exeeptions was Tendered and
refused to be Signed and Sealed._____

J. L.	:	JAMES WEAR	)	
196	:		)	
Rhea	:	vs	)	In Case
262	:		)	
	:	DANIEL WILLSON	)	

The Defendant by his Attorney appeared and agrees to pay the Costs
of this Suit, and upon this the Plaintiff prays that his Costs and
charges by him about his Suit in this behalf expended may be adjudged
to him. Therefore it is considered by the Court that the Plaintiff
recover against the Said Defendant his costs by him about his Suit
in this behalf expended. And the Said Defendant in Mercy & C. and the
Plaintiff not farther prosecuting It is ordered that this Suit be
dismissed._____

Rhea	:	BRIAN McCABE admr. of	)	
201	:	TITUS OGDEN deceased	)	
703	:		)	
	:	vs	)	In Case
	:		)	
	:	WILLIAM TATHAM	)	

This day came the Plaintiff by his Attorney and by his consent
and with the assent of the Court the Cause is continued 'till next
Court._____

H. L.	:	JOSEPH WEST	)	
202	:		)	
413	:	vs	)	In Debt.
	:		)	
	:	RICHARD FINDLESTON	)	

This day came the Plaintiff by his Attorney and the Defendant in his proper person and by their Mutual Consent and with the assent of the Court the argument of the Demurrer is referred 'till next Court.

(Pg. 226)

Rhea	:	ANNANIAS McCOY	)	
203	:		)	
263	:	vs	)	Original Attachment In Case
	:		)	
	:	JOHN LUSK	)	

This day came the Plaintiff by his Attorney and thereupon came a Jury to Wit, Thomas Woodward, Robert McTeir, James Gibson, Nathaniel Hays, Amos Bird, Andrew Jackson, Hugh Bodkin, John Kean, Charles Collins, Major Lea, Joseph Wear and William Lea, who being elected tried and Sworn diligently to enquire of damages in this Suit upon their Oath do Say the Plaintiff hath Sustained damages by occasion of the Defendants nonperformance of the assumption in the declaration mentioned to One Cent besides his Costs, Therefore   it is considered by the Court that the Plaintiff recover against the Said Defendant his damages aforesaid in form aforesaid assessed and his Costs by him about his Suit in this behalf expended. And the Said Defendant in Mercy & C.

John McKee appeared and produced a license from Governor Blount authorizing him to practice as an Attorney in the Several Courts of Pleas and Quarter Sessions within this territory who took the Oath to Support the Constitution of the United States, and also took the Oath prescribed by law for Attornies he is therefore admitted.

Rhea	:	STEPHEN DUNCAN & COMPANY	)	
204	:		)	
739	:	vs	)	Original Attachment
	:		)	
	:	JOSEPH WEST	)	In Case.

This day came the Plaintiff by his Attorney and by his Consent and with the assent of the Court the inquiry of damages is referred 'till next Court.____ On Motion of the Plaintiff by his Attorney An Alias Scire Facias is awarded him against James Anderson Garnashee returnable here at the next Court.____

Rhea	:	ROBERT FERGUSON	)	
205	:		)	
264	:	vs	)	Original Attachment,
	:		)	In Case
	:	WILLIAM TATHOM	)	

This day came the Plaintiff by his Attorney and thereupon came a Jury to Wit, John McIntire, Robert Reed, James Cochran, Henry Pickle, Lewis Brim, George McEwn, Hugh Bodkin, Abner Wit, John Cowan, Henry Swisher, Alexander Caldwell and William Reed, who being elected tried and Sworn diligently to inquire of damages in this Suit upon their Oath do Say the Plaintiff hath Sustained damages by

occasion of the Defendants Nonperformance of the assumption in the
Declaration mentioned to Twenty Six dollars eighty Seven and one
half Cents besides his Costs, Therefore It is considered by the Court
that the Plaintiff recover against the Said Defendant his Damages
aforesaid in form aforesaid assessed and his Costs by him about his
Suit in this behalf expended. And the Said Defendant in Mercy & Co. ___

(Pg. 227)

Rhea	:	GEORGE PRESTON	)	
206	:		)	
448	:	vs	)	Original Attachment,
	:		)	
	:	JOSEPH ROBINSON	)	In Case

Samuel McBee Garnashee being first Sworn Saith he owes the
Defendant Eight pounds in trade, that he hath not, nor had he at the
time he was Summoned Garnashee any effects belonging to the Defendant in his hands, that he knows of no other debts due to or
effects belonging to the Defendant in the hands of any other person.____

The Defendant not appearing to replevy the property attached
though Solemnly called; On motion of the Plaintiff by his Attorney
It is considered by the Court that the Plaintiff recover against the
Said Defendant Such damages as he hath Sustained by occasion of the
Defendants nonperformance of the assumption in the Declaration men-
tioned which damages are to be enquired of by a Jury unless the
Said Defendant Shall appear replevy the property attached and plead
to the Action & A Judicial attachment is awarded the Plaintiff to
Jefferson County against the estate of the Said Defendant returnable
here at the next Court. _____

On motion of Samuel McBee It is ordered that the Judgment
obtained against him for failing to appear as Garnashee in this Suit
at last August Court, be Set aside._____

A. R.	:	DAVID CALDWELL	)	
207	:		)	
J. L.	:	vs	)	Appeal
291	:		)	
	:	WILLIAM LOWRY	)	

This day came the parties by their Attornies and thereupon came
a Jury to Wit, Thomas Woodward, Robert McTier, James Gibson, Nathaniel
Hays, Andrew Jackson, Hugh Bodkin, John Kean, Charles Collins, Major
Lea, Joseph Wear, William Lea, and Thomas Gillespie who being elected
tried and Sworn, well and truly to try the matters of controversy
between the parties The Plaintiff was Solemnly called but came not;
Therefore on motion of the Defendant, It is considered by the Court,
that the Jurors aforesaid from rendering their verdict be discharged,
and that the Plaintiff be nonsuited. Whereupon on Motion of the Plaintiff by his Attorney, and for reasons appearing to the Court the Said
Non Suit is Set aside and the cause is continued 'till next Court. _____

```
L. B.   :   WILLIAM HENRY        )
210     :                        )
292     :          vs           )      Original Attachment
        :                        )
        :   JAMES DAVIS          )
```

This day came the Plaintiff by his Attorney and on Motion of a Judicial attachment is awarded him against the estate of the Said Defendant returnable here at the next Court. _____

Court Adjourned 'Till Tomorrow 9 O'Clock.

(Pg. 228)

FRIDAY JANUARY 30th 1795

Friday Morning January 30th 1795 Court met according to Adjournment Present James White, George McNutt, David Craig James Cozby and William Lowry esquires Justices & C. & C.

```
A. O.   :   JOHN BROWN            )
215     :                         )
L. B.   :          vs            )      In Case
265     :                         )
        :   ABRAHAM SWAGERTY       )
```

This day came the parties by their Attornies and thereupon came a Jury to Wit, Benjamin Pride, Hugh Bodkin, William Regan, William McMurry, James Cunningham, Samuel Bogle, Alexander Montgomery, John Sommerville, Charles Gilliam, William Cooper, Druary Wood, Breazeale and James Gibson who being elected tried and Sworn the truth to Speak upon the issue joined. The Plaintiff was Solemnly called but came not Therefore on Motion of the Defendant It is considered by the Court that the Jurors aforesaid from rendering their verdict be discharged and that the Plaintiff be Non Suited. Whereupon the Defendant was put under a rule to Shew cause why the Said Non Suit Should not be Set aside and a New trial Granted, which being argued for reasons appearing to the Court, the Said Non Suit is Set aside and it is ordered that the Plaintiff pay the Costs that have accrued in this Suit, and that a New trial be had at the next Court. From which Judgment an Appeal is prayed to the next Superior Court of law to be holden for the district of Hamilton at the Court house in Knoxville, reasons filed and bond and Security entered into with condition for the prosecution of the Said appeal with effect which appeal is allowed. _____

```
A. R.   :   SAMUEL BOGLE          :
219     :                         :
L. B.   :          vs            :      In Covenant
J. H.   :                         :
266     :   JOHN BROWN            :
```

This day came the parties by their Attornies and thereupon came
a Jury to Wit, Benjamin Pride, William Regan, William McMurry,
James Cunningham, Alexander Montgomery, John Sommerville, Charles
Gilliam, William Cooper, Drury Wood Breazeale, James Gibson, Michael
Swisher and James Scott who being elected tried and Sworn, the truth
to Speak upon the issues Joined   (Pg. 229)   upon their Oath do
Say, the writing obligatory declared on is the deed of the Defendant
in Manner and form as the Plaintiff against him hath complained, and
that the Said Defendant hath not performed the Same and they do assess
the Plaintiffs damages by occasion of the Nonperformance thereof to
Fifty six dollars besides his Costs. Therefore It is considered by
the Court that the Plaintiff recover against the Said Defendant his
damages aforesaid in form aforesaid assessed and his costs by him about
his Suit in this behalf expended. And the Said Defendant in Mercy & C.

Note, In this Cause the Plaintiff was put under a rule to Shew
cause why the Verdict Should not be Set aside and a new trial Granted
which was argued and overruled._____

L. B.	:	ISAAC BULLARD	)	
A. O.	:		)	
220	:	vs	)	In Case.
R	:		)	
Rhea	:	HUGH BODKIN Jr.	)	
414				

This day came the parties by their Attornies and thereupon came a
Jury to Wit, John McAmy, Benjamin Pride, William Regan, William McMurry,
James Cunningham, Alexander Montgomery, John Sommerville, Charles
Gilliam, William Cooper, Drury W. Breazeale, Michael Swisher, &
James Scott who being elected tried and Sworn the truth to Speak upon
the issues joined went out of Court to consult of their verdict,
and after Sometime returned into Court and declared they could not
agree in their verdict, by consent of the parties and with the assent
of the Court one of the Jurors aforesaid was withdrawn and the rest
of the Said Jurors from rendering their verdict discharged. And the
Cause is continued 'till next Court for a New trial to be had thereon.

A. R.			:			
222			:			
A. O.		256	:	AMOS BIRD	)	
293		A.R.	:		)	
W.G.		Rhea	:	vs	)	In Covenant
G.G.		330	:		)	
W.G.	A.O.		:	JACOB VANHOOSER	)	

W. C.	:		)	
C. C.	:		)	
W. C.	:	JACOB VANHOOSER	)	
A. O.	:		)	
256	:	vs	)	In Covenant
A. R.	:		)	
Rhea	:	AMOS BIRD	)	
330	:		)	

By Consent of the parties the matters in difference between them in these Suits are referred to the final determination of James White George McNutt, Nicholas Perkins, Nicholas T. Perkins, James Lea, Isaac McBee, John Adair, Alexander Kelly, David Campbell, Nathaniel Hays, John Kean and John Hackett, whose award thereupon or the Award of a Majority of them is to be made the Judgment of the Court and the Same is ordered accordingly. _____

(Pg. 230)

H. L.	:	BENJAMIN BLACKBURN	)	
223	:		)	
Rhea	:	vs	)	Original Attachment
415	:		)	
	:	ROBERT BLACKBURN	)	

This day came the Plaintiff by his Attorney and by his consent and with the assent of the Court the Cause is continued 'till next Court. ____

Rhea	:	NATHANIEL & SAMUEL COWAN	)	
224	:		)	
Reesse	:	vs	)	In Covenant
358	:		)	
	:	PETER McNAMEE	)	

This day came the parties by their Attornies and by their mutual Consent and with the assent of the Court the trial of the issue is referred 'till next Court. ____

Rhea	:	JOHN CASHALLY	)	
226	:		)	
A. R.	:	vs	)	In Case
324	:		)	
	:	OBADIAH BOUNDS	)	

This day came the parties by their Attornies and on Affidavit of the Plaintiff the trial of the issue is referred 'till next Court. ____

W. C.	:	WILLIAM DAVIDSON	)	
227	:		)	
Rhea	:	vs	)	In Case
267	:		)	
	:	JAMES CAREY	)	

This day came the Defendant by his Attorney and the Plaintiff though Solemnly called came not, but made default nor is his Suit further prosecuted, Therefore on the prayer of the Said Defendant It is considered by the Court that he recover against the Plaintiff his costs by him about his defence in this behalf expended.

```
D. G.    :    ROBERT EVANS           )
234      :    by his next Friend     )
A. O.    :                           )
L. B.    :          vs               )    Trover & Conversion
Rhea     :                           )
294      :    JOHN EVANS             )
```

This day came the parties by their Attornies and by their Mutual Consent and with the assent of the Court the trial of the issue is referred 'till next Court. _____

```
A. R.    :    JOHN HILL              )
237      :                           )
Rhea     :          vs               )    In Case
325      :                           )
         :    JAMES MILLIKIN and     )
              JAMES MILLIKIN Junior  )
```

This day came the parties by their Attornies and by their Mutual Consent and with the assent of the Court the trial of the Issue is referred 'till next Court. _____

```
A. R.    :    ALEXANDER KELLY        )
238      :                           )
L. B.    :          vs               )    In Debt
J. H.    :                           )
295      :    ABRAHAM SWAGERTY       )
```

This day came the parties by their Attornies and by their Mutual Consent and with the assent of the Court the trial of the Issue is referred 'till next Court. _____

(Pg. 231)

```
Rhea     :    NICHOLAS MANSFIELD     )
239      :                           )
A. O.    :          vs               )    In Covenant
268      :                           )
         :    JOSEPH SEVIER          )
```

This day came the parties by their Attornies and thereupon came a Jury to Wit, Robert Reed, Henry Pickle, Lewis Brim, George McEwn, Hugh Bodkin, Abner Witt, John Cowan, Henry Swisher, Alexander Caldwell, William Reed, Alexander Carmichael and John Sherrell who being elected tried and Sworn the truth to Speak upon the issue Joined upon their Oath do Say, the Defendant hath not performed the Covenant in the Declaration mentioned but hath broken the Same in manner and form as the Plaintiff against him hath complained and they do assess the Plaintiffs damages by occasion thereof to Twenty eight dollars and four Cents besides his costs. Therefore it is considered by the Court that the Plaintiff recover against the Defendant his damages aforesaid in form aforesaid assessed and his costs by him about his Suit in this behalf expended. And the Said Defendant in Mercy & C.

Rhea : JAMES MILLIKIN
A. O. :
240 :   vs   In Covenant
L. B. :
326 : ABRAHAM SWAGERTY

  This day came the parties by their Attornies and by their mutual
consent and with the assent of the Court, the enquiry of damages is
referred 'till next Court. ____

Rhea : JOHN McFARLAND
241 :
296 :   vs   In Case
  :
  : JOHN LINNEY

  This day came the Plaintiff by his Attorney and by his Consent
and with the assent of the Court, the inquiry of damages are referred
'till next Court. _____

Rhea : JAMES MILLER
244 :
L. B. :   vs   IN CASE
A. R. :
Rhea : ALEXANDER CARMICHAEL &
269 : JOSEPH JANES

  The Plaintiff not farther prosecuting It is ordered that this Suit
be dismissed and the Plaintiff pay to the Defendant their Costs. ____

A. R. : NICHOLAS NEAL
246 :
Rhea :   vs   In Case
297 :
  : WILLIAM TRIMBLE

  This day came the parties by their Attornies and by their mutual
Consent and with the assent of the Court, the trial of the issues is
referred 'till next Court. _____

L. B. : JOHN RIDDLE
248 :
J. H. :   vs   In Case
A. O. :
327 : JESSE ELDRIDGE

  This day came the parties by their Attornies and by their mutual
Consent and with the assent of the Court the trial of the issue is
referred 'till next Court. _____

(Pg. 232)

```
Rhea      :    ROBERT RHEA              )
249       :                             )
J. H.     :         vs                  )       In Case
328       :·                            )
          :    ROBERT THOMPSON          )
```

This day came the parties by their Attornies and by their mutual Consent and with the assent of the Court the trial of the issue is referred 'till next Court. _____

```
W. C.     :    ABRAHAM SWAGERTY         )
251       :                             )
A. R.     :         vs                  )       In Case
287       :                             )
          :    JAMES WHITE              )
```

The Plaintiff not farther prosecuting It is ordered that this Suit be dismissed._____Note Martha White assumes payment of Costs.

```
W. C.     :    JOSEPH SEVIER            )
A. O.     :                             )
252       :         vs                  )       Trover and Conversion
Rhea      :                             )
329       :    HUGH DUNLAP              )
```

This day came the parties by their Attornies and by their mutual Consent and with the assent of the Court, the trial of the issue is referred 'till next Court._____

```
L. B.     :    JAMES TEMPLETON          )
253       :                             )
Rhea      :         vs                  )       In Case
270       :                             )
          :    SAMUEL GIBSON            )
```

This day came the Defendant by his next friend, and the Plaintiff tho' Solemnly called came not, but made default, nor is his Suit further prosecuted therefore on the prayer of the Said Defendant by his next friend, It is considered by the Court that he recover against the Said Plaintiff his costs by him about his defence in this behalf expended.

```
D. G.     :    ARCHIBALD TRIMBLE        )
254       :                             )
Rhea      :         vs                  )       In Case
298       :                             )
          :    ROBERT BLACKBURN         )
```

This day came the parties by their Attornies and thereupon came a Jury to Wit   John Sommerville, Michael Swisher, Major Lea, Benjamin Pride, George Hays, Alexander Carmichael, Henry Swisher, John McFarland, Hugh Dunlap, Joseph Kearns, Joseph Shadden, and John McIntire, who being elected tried and Sworn the truth to Speak upon the issue Joined. The Plaintiff was Solemnly called but came not. Therefore on Motion of the Defendant It is considered by the Court that the Jurors aforesaid from rendering their Verdict be discharged, and the Plaintiff be Nonsuited. Whereupon the Defendant was put under a rule to Shew cause why the Said Nonsuit Should not be Set aside, and a New trial Granted, Which being argued; for reasons appearing to the Court, the Said Nonsuit is Set aside; and it is ordered that the Plaintiff pay the costs that have accrued in this Suit, and that a new trial be had at the next Court; to which time the Cause is continued.

J. L.	:	SAMUEL WEAR	)	
259	:		)	
A. O.	:	vs	)	In Case
W. C.	:		)	
Rhea	:	MATTHEW WALLACE	)	
331				

This day came the parties by their Attornies, and by their Mutual consent and with the assent of the Court, the trial of the issue is referred 'till next Court. _____

(Pg. 233)

H. L.	:	THOMAS WILLIAMS	)	
260	:		)	
	:	vs	)	In Case
299	:		)	
	:	JOEL MORRISON	)	

This day came the Plaintiff by his attorney and by his consent and with the assent of the Court the enquiry of damages is referred 'till next Court. _____

W. B.	:	DAVID ALLISON	)	
264	:		)	
Rhea	:	vs	)	In Case.
416	:		)	Continued.
	:	JOHN McDOWELL Exr. of	)	
		JOSIAH LOVE deceased	)	

W. C.	:	JOHN KEARNS	)	
265	:		)	
J. H.	:	vs	)	In Case
359	:		)	
	:	JAMES DALE	)	

This day came the parties by their attornies and by their mutual Consent and with the assent of the Court the trial of the Issues is referred 'till next Court. _____

```
W. C.    :   JOHN KEARNS          )
266      :                        )
.J. H.   :        vs              )      In Case
360      :                        )
         :   JAMES DALE           )
```

This day came the parties by their Attornies and by their
mutual Consent and with the assent of the Court, the trial of the
Issues is referred 'till next Court. _____

```
Rhea     :   JAMES GILLESPIE      )
269      :                        )
W. C.    :        vs              )      In Case
J. H.    :                        )
332      :   WILLIAM McBROOM  admr. of )
             WILLIAM ROSEBERRY  dec'd. )
```

This day came the parties by their Attornies and by their Mutual
Consent and with the assent of the Court, the trial of the issues is
referred 'till next Court. _____

```
W. B.    :   JACOB HARMAR         )
Rhea     :                        )
270      :        vs              )      In Debt
A. R.    :                        )
271      :   ELIZABETH ISH  admr. of   )
             JOHN ISH      deceased    )
```

This day came the parties by their Attornies and by their mutual
Consent and with the assent of the Court the Cause is continued 'till
next Court. _____

```
Reesse   :   NATHANIEL LYON       )
J. H.    :                        )
274      :        vs              )      In Case
Rhea     :                        )
300      :   JAMES MITCHELL       )
```

This day came the parties by their Attornies and by their mutual
consent and with the assent of the Court the trial of the issues is
referred till next Court. _____

```
W. C.    :   GERSHAM MOORE        )
275      :                        )
449      :        vs              )      In Case
         :                        )
         :   MATTHEW BISHOP       )
```

This day came the Plaintiff by his Attorney And on Motion a
Plurus Capias is awarded him against the Defendant returnable here
at next Court.

```
Reesse      :   MORDECAI MENDINGHALL          )
J. H.       :                                 )
277         :           vs                    )   In Case
Rhea        :                                 )
L. B.       :   ALEXANDER CARMICHAEL and      )
450         :   JOSEPH JANES                  )
```

This day came the parties by their Attornies and by their mutual
Consent, and with the assent of the Court, the trial of the Causes
is referred 'till next Court. _____

(Pg. 234)

```
Rhea        :   JOHN McAMY                    )
278         :                                 )
J. L.       :           vs                    )   In Case
301         :                                 )
            :   JAMES COCHRAN                 )
```

This day came as well the Plaintiff by his Attorney as the
Defendant in his proper person; and the parties agree that the Plaintiff
hath Sustained Twenty one dollars damages, by occasion of the Defendants Nonperformance of the assumption in the Declaration mentioned,
Therefore it is considered by the Court that the Plaintiff recover
against the Defendant the damages agreed as aforesaid and his Costs
by him about his Suit in this behalf expended. And the Said Defendant
in Mercy & C. And the Plaintiff agrees to Stay the Execution, of this
Judgment three Months.

```
Rhea        :   JAMES McCOLLOCK               )
281         :                                 )
335         :           vs                    )   In Case
            :                                 )
            :   ANDREW LUCKY                  )
```

This day came the Plaintiff by his Attorney and by his consent
and with the assent of the Court, the enquiry of damages is referred
untill next Court. _____

```
W. B.       :   BRIAN McCABE   admr. of       )
A. R.       :   TITUS OGDEN  deceased          )
282         :                                 )
L. B.       :           vs                    )   Original
355         :                                 )   Attachment
            :   ALEXANDER CARMICHAEL          )
```

This day came the Plaintiff by his Attorney and by his consent
and with the assent of the Court, the Cause is continued 'till next
Court. _____

W. B. : WILLIAM ROBINSON)
283 :)
272 ; vs) Trover and Conversion.
:)
: JAMES DERMOND)

The Plaintiff not farther prosecuting It is ordered that this
Suit be dismissed; and that the Plaintiff pay to the Defendant his
Costs._____

Rhea : JOHN STONE)
285 :)
H. L. : vs) In Debt.
451 :)
: JOSEPH WEST)

This day came the parties by their Attornies and by their mutual
Consent and with the assent of the Court, the trial of the issues is
referred 'till next Court. _____

Rhea : JOHN SOMMERVILLE & COMPANY)
286 :)
W. C. : vs) In Case
336 :)
: WILLIAM McBROOM admr. of)
WILLIAM ROSEBERRY   deceased)

This day came the parties by their Attornies and by their mutual
Consent and with the assent of the Court, the trial of the issues is
referred 'till next Court.

J. H. : JAMES STINSON)
287 :)
Rhea : vs) In Case
L. B. :)
338 : WILLIAM HENRY)

This day came the parties by their Attornies and by their mutual
Consent and with the assent of the Court the trial of the issues is
referred 'till next Court. _____

(Pg. 235)

J. L. : SAMUEL WEAR)
289 : and)
A. R. : WILLIAM LOWRY, Exors. of)
490 : JAMES WALKER deceased)
:)
: vs) In Debt.
:)
: JOHN COWAN and GEORGE TEDFORD)

This day came the parties by their Attornies and by their mutual consent and with the assent of the Court the trial of the issue is referred till next Court. _____

J. L.	:	SAMUEL WEAR, and WILLIAM LOWRY	)	
290	:	Excrs. of JAMES WALKER deceased	)	
J. H.	:	vs	)	In Debt
337	:		)	
	:	JAMES CUNNINGHAM & GEORGE TEDFORD	)	

This day came the parties by their Attornies and by their mutual Consent and with the assent of the Court the trial of the issues is referred 'till next Court._____

J. L.	:	JOHN COWAN	)	
291	:		)	
302	:	vs	)	Original Attachment
	:		)	
	:	ROBERT LIGGITT	)	

This day came the Plaintiff by his Attorney and by his Consent and with the assent of the Court the enquiry of damages is referred until next Court._____

A. R.	:	ROBERT WILLSON	)	
292	:		)	
339	:	vs	)	Original Attachment.
	:		)	
	:	SOLOMON MARKS	)	

This day came the Plaintiff by his Attorney and by his consent and with the assent of the Court, the enquiry of damages is referred until next Court. _____

Reese	:	JOHN ANDERSON	)	
294	:		)	
Rhea	:	vs	)	In Case
H. L.	:		)	
361	:	ROBERT McCAMPBELL	)	

This day came the parties by their Attornies and by their Mutual Consent and with the assent of the Court the argument of the Plea in abatement is referred 'till next Court.

W. C.	:	LUKE BOWYER	)	
295	:		)	
J. L.	:	vs	)	In Debt
362	:		)	
	:	BENJAMIN BLACKBURN	)	

This day came the parties by their Attornies and by their mutual consent and with the assent of the Court the trial of the issue is referred 'till next Court._____

J. H.	:	JOHN BROWN	)
296	:		)
A. R.	:	vs	) In Debt
452	:		)
	:	SAMUEL BOGLE AND GAWIN BLACK	)

This day came the parties by their Attornies and by their Mutual consent, and with the assent of the Court the trial of the issue is referred until the next Court. _____

Court Adjourned 'till Tomorrow 9 O'Clock.

(Pg. 236)

SATURDAY JANUARY 31st 1795.

Saturday Morning January 31st 1795 Court met according to adjournment present James White, George McNutt, John Adair, Jeremiah Jack, James Cozby, John Evans, Abraham Ghermly, and William Lowry esquires Justices & C. & C. & C.

12	:	DAVID CRAIG	)
179	:		)
	:	vs	) Scire Facias
	:		)
	:	SAMUEL ACKLIN, and	)
		SAMUEL NEWELL	)

This day came the Plaintiff by his Attorney and the Sheriff having returned the Defendants not to be found in his County on Motion of the Plaintiff by his Attorney an Alias Scire Facias is awarded him against the Said Defendants returnable here at the next Court.

A. R.	:	JOHN REYNOLDS	)
350	:		)
282	:	vs	) Trover and Conversion
	:		)
	:	ROBERT REYNOLDS	)

This day came the Plaintiff by his Attorney and the Defendant in his proper person, and the Said Defendant acknowledges Service of the Writ in due time, Whereupon the Plaintiff filed his Declaration and the Defendant filed his plea, and the issue being joined by consent of the parties & with the assent of the Court, thereupon came a Jury to Wit, John Bradley, James Kerr, Charles Regan, Amos Bird, Andrew Paul, James Ray, James Martin, John Cowan, Andrew Miller, James Scott,

William Sharp, and James King who being elected tried and Sworn
the truth to Speak upon the issue joined upon their Oath do Say the
Defendant is Guilty of the Trover and Conversion, in manner and form
as the Plaintiff against him hath complained, and they do assess the
Plaintiffs damages by occasion thereof to Fifty five dollars besides
his Costs. Therefore it is considered by the Court that the Plaintiff
recover against the Said Defendant his damages aforesaid in form aforesaid assessed, and his Costs by him about his Suit in this behalf
expended. And the Said Defendant in Mercy & C.

Rhea	:	JAMES BALDRIDGE	)	
297	:		)	
273	:	vs	)	In Debt
	:		)	
	:	ROBERT FERGUSON	)	

This day came as well the Plaintiff by his attorney as the Defendant in his proper person, and the Defendant Saith he cannot gainsay the
Plaintiffs action for One hundred One Dollars and fifty cents, Therefore by consent of the parties, It is considered by the Court that the
Plaintiff recover against the Defendant the Said One hundred One Dollars
fifty Cents, and also his Costs by him about his Suit in this behalf
expended. And the Said Defendant in Mercy & C. _____

(Pg. 237)

Rhea	:	JAMES BALDRIDGE	)	
298	:		)	
274	:	vs	)	In Debt
	:		)	
	:	ROBERT FERGUSON	)	

This day came as well the Plaintiff by his Attorney as the De-
fendant in his proper person and the Defendant Saith he cannot gain-
say the Plaintiffs action for Forty three Dollars and Ninety Six
Cents. Therefore by consent of the parties, It is considered by the
Court that the Plaintiff recover against the Defendant, the Said
Forty three Dollars and Ninety Six Cents and also his Costs by him
about his Suit in this behalf expended. And the Said Defendant in
Mercy & C. _____

L. B.	:	ALEXANDER CARMICHAEL	)	
299	:		)	
417	:	vs	)	In Covenant
	:		)	
	:	JAMES DONAHOE	)	

This day came the Plaintiff by his Attorney and having filed his
declaration and the Defendant having been arrested and not appearing
though Solemnly called, on motion of the Plaintiff by his Attorney
It is considered by the Court that the Plaintiff recover against the
Defendant Such damages as he hath Sustained by occasion of the Defendants Nonperformance of the Covenant in the declaration mentioned;

which damages are to be enquired of by a Jury at the next Court. _____

A. R.	:	PAUL CUNNINGHAM	)	
301	:		)	
Rhea	:	vs	)	In Case
363	:		)	
	:	JAMES ANDERSON	)	

This day came the parties by their Attornies and by their mutual Consent and with the assent of the Court the trial of the issues is referred 'till next Court.

Rhea	:	GEORGE B. GREER lessee	)	
302	:		)	
D. G.	:	vs	)	In Ejectment.
A. R.	:		)	
364	:	DRURY W. BREAZEALE	)	

This day came the parties by their Attornies and by their Mutual consent and with the assent of the Court the trial of the Issue is referred till next Court.

Rhea	:	JOHN GOEHEN	)	
303	:		)	
A. R.	:	vs	)	In Case
303	:		)	
	:	JOSEPH COWAN	)	

By consent of the parties the matters in difference between them in this Suit is referred to the final determination of James White, Charles McClung, Paul Cunningham, Joseph Greer, Samuel Givens, and Samuel Flannagan whose award thereupon or the award of a Majority of them is to be made the Judgment of the Court and the Same is ordered accordingly. _____

(Pg. 238)

L. B.	:	RUTH GIST	)	
Reesse	:		)	
304	:	vs	)	In Case
Rhea	:		)	
340	:	STEPHEN DUNCAN	)	

This day came the parties by their Attornies and by their mutual Consent and with the assent of the Court, the trial of the issues is referred till next Court._____

Rhea	:	JAMES GEALEY	)	
305	:		)	
L. B.	:	vs	)	A B
305	:		)	
	:	JESSE CLAYWELL	)	

This day came the parties by their Attornies and by their mutual Consent and with the assent of the Court, the trial of the issue is referred 'till next Court.

Rhea	:	JOHN FINLEY assignee	)	
306	:		)	
365	:	vs	)	In Debt
	:		)	
	:	THOMAS MANN	)	

This day came the Plaintiff by his Attorney and by his Consent and with the assent of the Court, the Cause is continued 'till next Court.

Reesse	:	CHRISTOPHER HAINS	)	
309	:		)	
Rhea	:	vs	)	In Debt
341	:		)	
	:	NATHANIEL HAYS	)	

This day came the parties by their Attornies and by their mutual consent and with the assent of the Court the Cause is continued 'till next Court.

Reese	:	CHRISTOPHER HAINS	·)	
310	:		)	
Rhea	:	vs	)	In Debt.
342	:		)	
	:	NATHANIEL HAYS	)	

This day came the parties by their Attornies and by their mutual consent and with the assent of the Court the Cause is continued 'till next Court.

Rhea	:	LEVI HINDS	)	
311	:		)	
L. B.	:	vs	)	In Case
275	:		)	
	:	HIRAM GERAN	)	

The parties appeared and each agree to pay half the Costs and the Plaintiff not farther prosecuting; It is ordered that this Suit be dismissed. _____

D. G.	:	JAMES JORDAN by his next friend	)	
J. H.	:		)	
312	:	vs	)	In Case Words
366	:		)	Continued
Rhea	:	WILLIAM COOPER	)	

A. R.   :   ANDREW LUCKY   )
313   :   )
L. B.   :   vs   )   In Covenant.
Rhea   :   )
W. C.   :   EDWARD McFARLAND   )
H. L.
367

    This day came the parties by their Attornies and by their mutual
Consent and with the assent of the Court, the trial of the issues is
referred 'till next Court. _____

(Pg. 239)

Rhea   :   DENNIS MURPHY   )
314   :   )
453   :   vs   )   Original Attachment
         :   )   In Case
         :   THOMAS EVANS   )

    This day came the Plaintiff by his Attorney and the Defendant
not appearing to replevy the property attached though Solemnly called;
On motion of the Plaintiff by his Attorney It is considered by the
Court that the Plaintiff recover against the Said Defendant Such damages
as he hath Sustained by occasion of the Defendants nonperformance of the
assumption in the Declaration mentioned which damages are to be enquired of by a Jury unless the Said Defendant Shall appear replevy
the property attached and plead to the action.

Rhea   :   ANNANIAS McCOY   )
315   :   )
J. L.   :   vs   )   In Case.
418   :   )
         :   JOHN LUSK   )

    This day came the Plaintiff by his Attorney and by his consent
and with the assent of the Court, the enquiry of damages is referred
till next Court. _____

316   :   JOHN LOWRY assignee   )
W. C.   :   )
276   :   vs   )   In Covenant
         :   )
         :   HENRY REGAN, JOHN REGAN &)
         :   AHEMAS REGAN   )

    The Plaintiff not farther prosecuting It is ordered that this
Suit be dismissed and that the Plaintiff pay to the Defendants their
Costs.

L. B. : WILLIAM TIPTON)
318 :)
: vs) In Case
:)
: JOHN BURDIN)

This day came the Plaintiff by his Attorney and by his consent and with the assent of the Court, the enquiry of damages is referred 'till next Court. _____

L. B. : THOMAS WELSH)
320 :)
Rhea : vs) In Case.
277 :)
: NATHANIEL LYON)

This day came the parties by their Attornies and the Defendant filed a plea in abatement which was argued and because it Seems to the Court that the Said Plea and the matters therein contained are Sufficient in law to abate the Plaintiffs Writ, Therefore It is considered by the Court that this Suit abate and that the Plaintiff pay to the Defendant his Costs.

(Pg. 240)

A. R. : OBADIAH BOUNDS)
323 :)
Rhea : vs) In Covenant.
W. C. :)
368 : STOCKLEY DONELSON and)
ANNANIAS McCOY)

This day came the parties by their Attornies and the Defendant prays Over of the Declaration and the Cause is continued till next Court.

J. C. : JACOB BRADBERRY)
324 :)
S. M. : vs) In Case
343 :)
: JOHN McNEILL)

This day came the parties by their Attornies and with the consent of the Defendant time is given the Plaintiff till next Court to file his declaration. _____

325 : JAMES BLAIR)
306 :)
: vs) In Case
:)
: ALEXANDER CARMICHAEL)

This day came the parties and with the Consent of the Defendant time is given the Plaintiff till next Court to file his Declaration,_____

Rhea	:	NATHANIEL AND SAMUEL COWAN	)	
326	:		)	
A. R.	:	vs	)	In Case
W. C.	:		)	
C. C.	:	HUGH DUNLAP	)	
445	:			

This day came the parties by their Attornies and the Plaintiffs having filed their declaration, the Defendant filed his plea and the issue being Joined the trial thereof is referred until next Court. _____

Rhea	:	NATHANIEL AND SAMUEL COWAN	)	
327	:		)	
A. R.	:	vs	)	In Case
W. C.	:		)	
C. C.	:	HUGH DUNLAP	)	
446	:			

This day came the parties by their Attornies and the Plaintiffs having filed their declaration the Defendant filed his Plea and issue being joined the trial thereof is referred till next Court. _____

Rhea	:	ISAAC CONLEY	)	
328	:		)	
W. C.	:	vs	)	In Case
C. C.	:		)	
L. B.	:	ALEXANDER SWAINEY	)	
419	:			

This day came the parties by their Attornies and the Plaintiff having filed his Declaration the Defendant filed his plea and the issue being Joined the trial thereof is referred 'till next Court. _____

Rhea	:	DUNLAP and GREER	)	
329	:		)	
W. C.	:	vs	)	In Case
A. R.	:		)	
369	:	CHARLES REGAN Junior.	)	

This day came the parties by their Attornies and the Plaintiff having filed their declaration the Defendant filed his pleas and the issues being Joined the trial thereof is referred till next Court.

(Pg. 241)

L. B.	:	JOHN FRAZIER	)	
330	:		)	
278	:	vs	)	In Covenant
	:		)	
	:	DAVID WILLSON and	)	
	:	ISAAC McBEE	)	

The Plaintiff not farther prosecuting It is ordered that this
Suit be dismissed, and that the Plaintiff pay to the Defendants their
Costs. _____

| Rhea
331
370 | : : : : : | JOHN FINLEY assignee

vs

DAVID MOOR and JOHN CHISOLM |)
)
)
)
) | In Debt |

This day came the Plaintiff by his Attorney and the Sheriff
having returned Ordered by Plaintiff not to execute 'till further
orders; On motion the Cause is continued 'till next Court._____

| Rhea
332
W. C.
454 | : : : : | JOHN FINLEY   assignee

vs

JOHN HUNT |)
)
)
)
) | In Case |

This day came the Plaintiff by his Attorney and having filed
his declaration the Defendant prays and hath leave to imparle,
till the next Court and there to plead.

| Rhea
333
A. R.
371 | : : : : | JOHN FINLEY assignee

vs

GEORGE ROULSTONE |)
)
)
)
) | In Case |

This day came the Plaintiff by his Attorney and having filed
his declaration, the Defendant prays and hath leave to Imparle till
next Court and then to plead._____

| Rhea
334
A. R.
420 | : : : : | GEORGE B. GREER and HUGH DUNLAP

vs

ANNANIAS McCOY |)
)
)
)
) | In Case |

This day came the parties by their Attornies and the Plaintiff
having filed his declaration, the Defendant prays and hath leave to
Imparle till next Court and then to plead._____

| Rhea
335
307 | : : : : | GEORGE HAVARD

vs

JOHN SHIRKY |)
)
)
) | In Case |

This day came the Plaintiff by his Attorney and the Sheriff having
returned Ordered by Plaintiff not to Execute, On motion the Cause is
continued till next Court. _____

W. B.	:	JOHN HILLSMAN	)	
Rhea	:		)	
336	:	vs	)	In Debt
W. C.	:		)	
372	:	GERSHAM MOORE and JOHN McDOWELL	)	

This day came the parties by their Attornies and the Plaintiff having filed his declaration, the Defendants filed their pleas and the Issues being Joined the trial thereof is referred 'till next Court._____

(Pg. 242)

Rhea	:	ELIZABETH ISH admr. of	)	
A. R.	:	JOHN ISH Deceased	)	
377	:		)	
W. C.	:	· vs ·	)	In Case
421	:		)	
	:	JOHN McDOWELL	)	

This day came the parties by their Attornies and the Plaintiff having filed his Declaration the Defendant filed his pleas and the issues being Joined the trial thereof is referred till next Court. _____

A. R.	:	THOMAS DENTON	)	
338	:	·	)	
W. C.	:	vs	)	In Case
Rhea	:		)	
422	:	JAMES McDOWELL	)	

This day came the Parties by their Attornies and the Plaintiff having filed his declaration the Defendant filed his plea and the issue being Joined the trial thereof is referred till next Court. _____

W. B.	:	GERSHAM MOORE	)	
Rhea	:		)	
339	:	vs	)	In Case
W. C.	:		)	
C. C.	:	ALEXANDER SWAINEY	)	
L. B.	:		)	
455	:			

This day came the parties by their Attornies and the Plaintiff having filed his declaration the Defendant filed his pleas and the issues being Joined the trial thereof is referred till next Court._____

A. R.	:	SAMUEL PAXTON	)	
340	:		)	
Rhea	:	vs	)	In Case
279	:		)	
	:	ROBERT BELL and DAVID CRAIG	)	

The Defendants Robert Bell and David Craig, in their proper persons appeared and agrees to pay the Costs of this Suit, and upon this the Plaintiff prays that his costs and charges by him about his Suit in this behalf expended may be adjudged to him. Therefore it is considered by the Court that the Plaintiff recover against the Said Defendants his costs by him about his Suit in this behalf expended. And the Said Defendants in Mercy & C. And the Plaintiff not farther prosecuting It is ordered that this Suit be dismissed.

W. B.	:	JOHN REGAN	)
341	:		)
J. L.	:	vs	) In Case
Rhea	:		)
280	:	WILLIAM LOWRY	)

The Plaintiff not farther prosecuting It is ordered that this Suit be dismissed and that the Plaintiff pay to the Defendant his Costs._____

W. C.	:	ALEXANDER SWAINEY	)
C. C.	:		)
D. G.	:	vs	) In Case
L. B.	:		)
342	:	GERSHAM MOORE and DAVID MOORE	)
Rhea	:		
373	:		

This day came the parties by their Attornies and the Plaintiff having filed his declaration the Defendants filed their pleas and the issues being Joined the trial thereof is referred 'till next Court._____

(Pg. 243)

W. C.	:	MESHECK TIPTON	)
C. C.	:		)
L. B.	:	vs	) In Case
343	:		)
J. H.	:	JAMES KERR	)
J. L.	:		
456			

This day came the parties by their Attornies and the Plaintiff having filed his declaration the Defendant filed his plea . and the issue being Joined the trial thereof is referred 'till next Court.‗

Rhea	:	JOHN WOOD	)
344	:		)
A. R.	:	vs	) In Case
568	:		)
	:	WILLIAM HENRY	)

This day came the Plaintiff by his Attorney and having filed his declaration and the Defendant having been arrested and not appearing though Solemnly called, on motion of the Plaintiff by his Attorney,

It is considered by the Court that the Plaintiff recover against the
Defendant Such damages as he hath Sustained by occasion of the Defendants
Nonperformance of the Assumption in the declaration mentioned which
damages are to be inquired of by a Jury at the next Court._____

Rhea	:	JOHN STONE	)	
345	:		)	
281	:	vs	)	In Case
	:		)	
	:	GEORGE ROULSTONE	)	

The Defendant George Roulstone appeared and agrees to pay the
Clerks fees, and one half the Attorney's fee; The Plaintiff not farther
prosecuting It is ordered that this Suit be dismissed.

Rhea	:	JAMES McCULLOCK	)	
346	:		)	
374	:	vs	)	Original Attachment, In Case
	:		)	
	:	CHARLES ONEAL	)	

· This day came the Plaintiff by his Attorney and having filed his
declaration; and the Defendant not appearing to replevy the property
attached though Solemnly called, On motion of the Plaintiff by his
Attorney It is considered by the Court, that the Plaintiff recover
against the Defendant Such damages as he hath Sustained by occasion of
the Defendants Nonperformance of the Assumption in the Declaration
mentioned, which damages are to be inquired of by a Jury unless the
Said Defendant Shall appear and replevy the property attached & plead
to the Action._____

H. L.	MOSES CAVETT admr. of	)	
347	ALEXANDER CAVETT dec'd.	)	
Rhea		)	
375	vs	)	In Debt
		)	
	PETER McNAMEE & GEORGE HAYS	)	

This day came the parties by their Attornies and the Plaintiff
having filed his declaration the Defendant filed his plea and the
issue being Joined the trial thereof is referred till next Court._____

(Pg. 244)

Rhea	:	JAMES MILLER	)	
348	:		)	
457	:	vs	)	In Case
	:		)	
	:	EDWARD FREEL	)	

This day came the Plaintiff by his Attorney and having filed his
declaration and the Defendant having been arrested and not appearing
though Solemnly called, on Motion of the Plaintiff by his Attorney It

is considered by the Court that the Plaintiff recover against the Defendant Such damages as he hath Sustained by occasion of the Defendants Nonperformance of the assumption in the Declaration mentioned which damages are to be enquired of by a Jury at the next Court.

Rhea	:	STEPHEN DUNCAN	)	
349	:		)	
Reese	:	vs	)	In Case
423	:		)	
	:	PETER MCNAMEE	)	

This day came the parties by their Attornies and with the Consent of the Defendant time is given the Plaintiff till next Court to file his Declaration.

Ordered that the Sheriff Summon the following persons to attend at the next Superior Court as Jurors to Wit, James White, George McNutt, William Lowry, Thomas McCullough, John Adair, Jeremiah Jack, Abraham Ghormly, William Hamilton, James Cozby, William Wallace, David Craig, David Campbell, John Menefee, and James Houston.

. Ordered that the Sheriff do notify the Ranger of this County to meet Joseph Greer, James White and John Adair esquires on the third Monday of March next, at the Court House in Knoxville and that the Said Joseph Greer, James White and John Adair do examine into and make report to next Court of the Sums of Money that are due from the different persons who have taken up Strays in this County.

Drury Wood Breazeale is by the Court appointed Standard keeper, for this County and it is ordered that the Weights, Stamps, brands and measures, be kept in Knoxville and that the expence of procuring the Same be paid out of the County Tax.

Ordered that John Chisolm, William Lowry and John Adair, esquires be Commissioners to Settle with the Sheriff and make report of the Collection and expenditures of the County Tax for the Years of 1793 and 1794 to next Court.

(Pg. 245)

The Court proceeded to lay the County Tax for the present Year which is laid as follows to Wit.

On each hundred acres of land	$12\frac{1}{2}$ Cents
On each free poll	$12\frac{1}{2}$ "
On each taxable Slave	25 "

The following Instrument of Writing was acknowledged by Thomas McCollock, and admitted to record, to Wit.

June 2nd 1794   This is to Certify that about three Weeks ago
I received a Due Bill from William Lowry dated November 1793
of the amount of Eighteen dollars and Some Cents, which bill I have
lost and no probability of it ever being found; Given under my hand
and Seal this day and date above written.

                                        Thomas McCollock   (Seal)

Attest
    Chas. McClung

    On motion of Charles Collins and for reasons appearing to the
Court: It is ordered that he be released from the payment of Tax
on fifty acres of land which he Stands charged with, for the Year
1794.

                COURT ADJOURNED 'TILL COURT IN COURSE.

                MONDAY APRIL 27th 1795

    At a Court of Pleas and Quarter Sessions began and held for the
County of Knox at the Court House in Knoxville on the last Monday
of April 1795.

    Present, James White, George McNutt, William Wallace and James
Moor esquires Justices & C. & C. & C.

    Robert Houston esquire Sheriff & C. returned that he hath
executed our Writ of Venire Facias to him directed upon the following
persons to Wit James W. Lackey, John Bird, Devereux Gilliam, Thomas
Gillespie, William Kerr, Junior, James Anderson, James Adair, John
Dermand, David Dermand, Samuel Flenikin, James Boyles, James Cunningham,
James Greenaway, Edward Higgins, Simeon Adamson, Samuel Bowman, Felix
Brown, John Alexander, Junior, James Bolds, John Craig, Thomas
Anderson, John Cowan, Robert Cozby, Robert Armstrong, Charles Coates,
John Braden, Jacob Arnett, Dolin Assher, Joseph Beaird, James Campbell,
William Ewing, and John Fryar.

(Pg. 246)   Out of which Venire the following persons were elected a
Grand Inquest for the body of this County to Wit, Samuel Flennekin,
Foreman, William Ewing, Joseph Beaird, John Cowan, James Anderson,
Thomas Gillespie, John Alexander, Junior, Devereux Gilliam, Robert
Cozby, John Craig, Charles Coats, John Braden and Simeon Adamson,
who have been Sworn received their charge and withdrew to inquire of
their presentments.

    Ordered that Anderson Ashburn have liberty to keep a public House,
where he lives for one Year, he having given Bond with Assahel Rawlings
and Lewis Brim his Securities in the Sum of Two thousand five hundred
dollars, conditioned as the law directs.

Court adjourned till tomorrow 9 O'Clock.

TUESDAY APRIL 28th 1795

Tuesday Morning April 28th 1795 Court met according to adjournment present David Campbell, William Lowry and John Adair esquires Justices & C. & C. & C.

Rhea : JOHN CHISOLM)
49 :)
662 : vs) In Case
 :)
 : RICHARD HAMILTON)

This day came the Plaintiff by his Attorney and by his consent and with the assent of the Court, the enquiry of damages is referred 'till next Court.

A. O. : MARY STEPHENSON and EDWARD STEPHENSON))
88 : Executors of ROBERT STEPHENSON deceased))
J. H. :)
288 : vs) In Case
 :)
 : BENJAMIN BLACKBURN)

The parties appeared and each agree to pay their own Costs and the Plaintiff not farther prosecuting It is ordered that this Suit be dismissed.

A. O. : JOHN HUTCHINSON)
133 :)
J. H. : vs) In Case
 :)
 : ANDREW PAUL admr. of JAMES PAUL dec'd.)

This day came the parties by their Attornies and by their Mutual consent and with the assent of the Court the trial of the issues is referred 'till next Court. _____

(Pg. 247)

S. M. : JAMES ALLISON)
135 :)
J. H. : vs) In Covenant
L. B. :)
356 : ABRAHAM SWAGERTY)

This day came the parties by their Attornies, And on motion It is ordered that a Notice issue to Washington County to the Executors or Administrators of the Said James Allison to appear at next Court & prosecute this Suit. _____

```
Reesse   :   WILLIAM DAVIDSON        )
171      :                           )
J. L.    :        vs                 )    In Covenant
321      :                           )
         :   WILLIAM LOWRY           )
```

This day came the parties by their Attornies and the Cause is continued for the award of the Arbitrators till next Court.

```
Rhea     :   BRIAN McCABE  admr. of TITUS OGDEN dec'd.   )
172      :                                               )
357      :                  vs                           )   In Case
         :                                               )
         :   EZEKIEL HENRY and  WILLIAM HENRY            )
```

This day came the Plaintiff by his Attorney and by his Consent and with the assent of the Court, the inquiry of damages is referred till next Court.

```
J. L.    :   JOHN DUNCAN                       )
179      :                                     )
A. R.    :        vs                           )   In Covenant
412      :                                     )
         :   JOHN McNUTT and  JAMES CALLISON   )
```

This day came the parties by their Attornies and by their mutual Consent and with the assent of the Court, the Argument of the Demurrer is referred untill next Court.

```
H. L.    :   DAVID WRIGHT       )
192      :                      )
Rhea     :        vs           )   In Case
289      :                      )
         :   JAMES SPENCE       )
```

This day came the parties by their Attornies and thereupon came a Jury to Wit, James Campbell, William Hutton, John Sherrell, Andrew Evans, Andrew Paul, James Ewing, Andrew Thompson, Lewis Brim, Enos Johnston, Charles Collins, William Cooper, and Samuel Doak who being elected tried and Sworn the truth to Speak upon the issues joined upon their Oath do Say that the Defendant did not assume upon himself in manner and form as the Plaintiff against him hath complained as in pleading he hath alledged. Therefore It is considered by the Court that the Plaintiff take nothing by his bill but for his false clamor be in Mercy & C. and the Defendant go hence without day and recover against the Plaintiff his Costs by him about his defence in this behalf expended.

(Pg. 248)

```
S. M.    :   THOMAS KING       )
Rhea     :                     )
193      :        vs           )   In Case
J. H.    :                     )
290      :   JOSEPH BEAIRD     )
```

The Plaintiff not farther prosecuting It is ordered that this
Suit be dismissed And that the Plaintiff pay to the Defendant his Costs.

Rhea	:	BRIAN McCABE admr. of TITUS OGDEN dec'd.	)	
201	:		)	
703	:	vs	)	In Case
	:		)	
	:	WILLIAM TATHEM	)	

This day came the Plaintiff by his Attorney and by his consent
and with the assent of the Court the Cause is continued 'till next
Court.

H. L.	:	JOSEPH WEST	)	
202	:		)	
413	:	vs	)	In Debt
	:		)	
	:	RICHARD FINDLESTON	)	

This day came the Plaintiff by his Attorney and the Defendant
in his proper person and by their mutual consent and with the assent of
the Court, the argument of the Demurrer is referred till next Court.

Rhea	:	STEPHEN DUNCAN.& COMPANY	)	
204	:		)	
739	:	vs	)	Original Atta.
	:		)	In Case
	:	JOSEPH WEST	)	

This day came the Plaintiff by his Attorney and James Anderson
Garnashee   being first Sworn Saith he owes the Defendant Nineteen
Shillings Virginia Currency that he hath not nor had he at the time
he was Summoned Garnashee any effects belonging to the Defendants in his
hands, that he knows of no other debts due to or effects belonging to
the Defendant in the hands of any other person. And on motion of a Commission is awarded the Plaintiff de bene esse to examine and take the Deposition of his Witnesses and a Judicial attachment is awarded him against the
estate of the Said Defendant returnable here at the next Court; to which
time the inquiry of damages is referred.

Rhea	:	GEORGE PRESTON	)	
206	:		)	
448	:	vs	)	Original Attachment,
	:		)	In Case
	:	JOSEPH ROBINSON	)	

This day came the Plaintiff by his Attorney And on Motion a Judicial
attachment is awarded him against the estate of the Said Defendant
returnable here at the next Court to which time the enquiry of damages
is referred.

(Pg. 249)

```
A. R.    :    DAVID CALDWELL        )
207      :                          )
J. L.    :         vs              )    APPEAL
291      :                          )
         :    WILLIAM LOWRY         )
```

This day came as well the Plaintiff by his Attorney as the Defendant in his proper person, and the Said Defendant Saith he cannot gainsay the Plaintiffs action for Seven dollars, forty three and one third Cents, therefore by consent of the parties It is considered by the Court that the Plaintiff recover against the Defendant the Said Seven dollars forty three and one third Cents, and also his costs by Him about his Suit in this behalf expended. And the Said Defendant in Mercy & C. ____

```
L. B.    :    WILLIAM HENRY         )
210      :                          )
292      :         vs              )    Original Attachment
         :                          )
         :    JAMES DAVIS           )
```

The Plaintiff not farther prosecuting It is ordered that this Suit be dismissed.

```
H. L.    :    BENJAMIN BLACKBURN    )
223      :                          )
Rhea     :         vs              )    Original Attachment
415      :                          )
         :    ROBERT BLACKBURN      )
```

This day came the Plaintiff by his Attorney and On Motion a Judicial Attachment is awarded him against the Estate of the Said Defendant returnable here at the next Court. _____

```
Rhea     :    NATHANIEL & SAMUEL COWAN    )
224      :                                )
Reesse   :         vs                    )    In Covenant
358      :                                )
         :    PETER McNAMEE               )
```

This day came the parties by their Attornies and by their mutual consent and with the assent of the Court, the trial of the Issue is referred till next Court. _____

```
Rhea     :    JOHN CASHALLY         )
226      :                          )
A. R.    :         vs              )    In Case
324      :                          )
         :    OBADIAH BOUNDS        )
```

This day came the parties by their Attornies and by their Mutual consent and with the assent of the Court the trial of the Issue is referred 'till next Court. _____

D. G.   :   ROBERT EVANS   by his next Friend   )
234   :   )
A. O.   :   vs   )   Trover & Conversion
L. B.   :   )
Rhea   :   JOHN EVANS   )
294   :

     This day came the parties by their Attornies and thereupon came a
Jury to Wit   James Boyles, Benjamin Blackburn, Samuel Bowman, Henry Regan,
Jacob Vanhooser, William Hazlet, Junior, William Snoddy, James Ray,
Richard Gooden, John Rhea, Caleb Carter, and Acquilla Low who being elected
tried and Sworn, the truth to Speak upon the issue joined upon their Oath
do Say the Defendant is not Guilty of the Trover and Conversion in
(Pg. 250)   manner and form as the Plaintiff against him hath complained
as in pleading he hath alledged. Therefore It is considered by the
Court that the Plaintiff take nothing by his Bill, but for his false
clamour be in Mercy & C. And that the defendant go hence without day
and recover against the Plaintiff his costs by him about his defence in
this behalf expended.

A. R.   :   JOHN HILL   )
237   :   )
Rhea   :   vs   )   In Case
325   :   )
         :   JAMES MILLIKIN and   )
              JAMES MILLIKIN Junior   )

     This day came the Parties by their Attornies and by their Mutual
consent and with the assent of the Court the trial of the issue is
referred till next Court as if on affidavit of the Plaintiff.

A. R.   :   ALEXANDER KELLEY   )
238   :   )
J. H.   :   vs   )   In Debt
L. B.   :   )
295   :   ABRAHAM SWAGERTY   )

     This day came the parties by their Attornies and thereupon came a
Jury to Wit,   James Campbell, William Hutton, John Sherrell, Andrew
Evans, Andrew Paul, David Adair, Andrew Thompson, Lewis Brim, Enos
Johnston, Charles Collins, William Cooper and Samuel Doake, who being
elected tried and Sworn, the truth to Speak upon the issue joined,
upon their Oath do Say the Defendant doth owe to the Plaintiff One
thousand dollars the debt in the declaration mentioned. Therefore
it is considered by the Court, that the Plaintiff recover against the
Defendant his Debt aforesaid and his Costs by him about his Suit in
this behalf expended. And the Said Defendant in Mercy & C. but this
Judgment is to be discharged by the payment of Two hundred and Ninety
Six Dollars and Eighty Cents and the Costs of this Suit. _____

```
Rhea     :    JAMES MILLIKIN           )
A. O.    :                             )
240      :         vs                  )    In Covenant
L. B.    :                             )
326      :    ABRAHAM SWAGERTY         )
```

This day came the Plaintiff by his Attorney and by his Consent and with the assent of the Court, the enquiry of damages is referred 'till next Court. _____

```
Rhea     :    JOHN McFARLAND           )
241      :                             )
296      :         vs                  )    In Case
         :                             )
         :    JOHN LINNEY              )
```

The Plaintiff not farther prosecuting It is ordered that this Suit be dismissed. ___

```
A. R.    :    NICHOLAS NEAL            )
246      :                             )
Rhea     :         vs                  )    In Case
297      :                             )
         :    WILLIAM TRIMBLE          )
```

The Plaintiff not farther prosecuting It is ordered that this Suit be dismissed. _____ Note, Stockley Donelson assumes payment of Costs. _____

(Pg. 251)

```
L. B.      :    JOHN RIDDLE            )
248        :                          )
J. H. A. O.:         vs               )    In Case
327        :                          )
           :    JESSE ELDRIDGE        )
```

This day came the parties by their Attornies and by their mutual consent and with the assent of the Court, the trial of the Issue is referred 'till next Court. _____

```
Rhea     :    ROBERT RHEA              )
249      :                             )
J. H.    :         vs                  )    In Case
328      :                             )
         :    ROBERT THOMPSON          )
```

This day came the parties by their Attornies and by their mutual consent and with the assent of the Court, the trial of the issue is referred 'till next Court. _____

```
W. C.   :   JOSEPH SEVIER          )
A. O.   :                          )
252     :        vs                )      Trover and Conversion
Rhea    :                          )
329     :   HUGH DUNLAP            )
```

This day came the parties by their Attornies and by their mutual Consent and with the assent of the Court the trial of the issue is referred 'till next Court. _____

Court Adjourned 'Till Tomorrow 9 O'Clock.

WEDNESDAY APRIL 29th 1795

Wednesday Morning April 29th 1795   Court met according to Adjournment present James White, John Adair and David Campbell esquires Justices & C. & C. & C. _____

```
558  11  )     Ordered that Process issue against Zapher Tannery
559  16  )     and James Bunch to cause them to appear at the next
               Court to answer the Indictments found against them
               by the Grand Jury.
```

```
Rhea    :   UNITED STATES          )
24      :                          )
318     :        vs                )      A B
        :                          )
        :   JESSE CLAYWELL         )
```

Be it remembered that heretofore to Wit at a Court held for this County on the first Monday of August last past the Grand Jurors for the Said County presented an Indictment against Jesse Claywell for a Trespass Assault and Battery a true Bill; and the Sheriff having returned the Capias on Indictment executed. Now at this day came as well the Solicitor for the County as the Said Jesse Claywell in his proper person, and the Said Jesse Claywell because he will not contend Saith that he is guilty in manner and form as in the Indictment against him is alledged and putteth himself upon the Grace and mercy of the Court; Therefore it is considered by the Court, that for Such his offence he be fined five Dollars, and pay the Costs of this prosecution. _____

(Pg. 252)

```
Rhea    :   THE UNITED STATES      )
27      :                          )
350     :        vs                )      Petit Larceny
        :                          )
        :   JOSEPH LAIRD           )
```

This day came the Solicitor for the County, and the Sheriff having returned the Second Writ of Scire Facias against Joseph Laird and Martin Armstrong Junior not found: Therefore on Motion of the Said Solicitor, It is considered by the Court, that Judgment be final be entered against the Said Joseph Leaird for One hundred Dollars, and Costs, and that Judgment final be entered against Martin Armstrong Junior for Fifty dollars and Costs: the Sums in their Said Recognizance mentioned.

Rhea	:	THE UNITED STATES	)	
28	:		)	
351	:	vs	)	Petit Larceny
	:		)	
	:	WILLIAM KENNEDY	)	

This day came the Solicitor for the County; And on Motion of Alexander Carmichael, Security of William Kennedy, time is given him until next Court, to Surrender the principal in discharge of himself.

Rhea	:	THE UNITED STATES	)	
32	:		)	
319	:	vs	)	A B
	:		)	
	:	CHARLES REGAN Junior	)	

This day came as well the Solicitor for the County as the Defendant by his Attorney and thereupon came a Jury to Wit, John Bird, James Boyle, Jacob Arnett, James Campbell, Samuel Bowman, Jacob Vanhooser, Archibald McKillip, Andrew Jackson, Joseph Evans, Charles Bradley, Samuel Sterling and Benjamin Tipton who being elected tried and Sworn the truth of and upon the premises to Speak upon their Oath do Say that the Defendant is not Guilty as in pleading he hath alledged. Therefore it is considered by the Court that he be acquitted of the Assault and Battery aforesaid, but that he pay the Costs of this prosecution.

The Grand Jury returned and presented An Indictments against William Thompson, for an Assault and Battery a true Bill, against Peter Dosier for an Assault and Battery, a true Bill, against Jacob Welker for an Assault and Battery a true Bill, and having nothing further to present were discharged. Whereupon it is ordered that Process issue against the Said William Thompson, Peter Dosier, and Jacob Welker to cause them to appear Instanter to answer the Indictments this day found against them by the Grand Jury.

353	33	
352	34	
320	35.	

Rhea	:	THE UNITED STATES	)	
33	:		)	
353	:	vs	)	A B
	:		)	
	:	WILLIAM THOMPSON	)	

This day came the Solicitor for the County and the Defendant having been arrested appeared, and being charged pleads not Guilty and the trial of the issue is referred 'till next Court.

(Pg. 253)

Rhea : UNITED STATES)
34 :)
352 : vs) A B
    :)
    : PETER DOSIER)

This day came the Solicitor for the County and the Defendant having been arrested appeared, and being charged pleads not Guilty, and the trial of the issue is referred 'till next Court.

Rhea : UNITED STATES)
35 :)
320 : vs) A B
    :)
    : JACOB WELKER)

This day came the Solicitor for the County, and the Defendant having been arrested appeared, and being charged pleads not Guilty, and by consent of the parties and with the Assent of the Court, thereupon came a Jury to Wit, Andrew Paul, Amos Bird, Samuel Doak, Jeremiah Matthews, David Laird, Benjamin Blackburn, Peter Stout, Daniel Hasting, Watson Reed, Hugh Bodkin, William Miller, and John Hill, who being elected tried and Sworn the truth of and upon the premises to Speak upon their Oath do Say the Defendant is not Guilty as in pleading he hath alledged. Therefore it is considered by the Court that he be acquitted of the Assault and Battery aforesaid; Whereupon the Defendant by his Attorney moved the Court to order the prosecutor to pay the costs of this prosecution, which was argued and the motion discharged.

H. L. : JOHN DAVIS)
181 :)
Rhea : vs) In Case
322 :)
    : JOSEPH JANES)

This day came the parties by their Attornies and thereupon came a Jury to Wit, William Cooper, Andrew Thompson, Richard Gooden, Archibald McKillip, Hugh Bodkin, Paul Cunningham, Benjamin Blackburn, William Hutton, Amos Bird, Annanias McCoy, James Cunningham and Samuel Bowman who being elected tried and Sworn the truth to Speak upon the issues joined upon their Oath do Say that the Defendant did assume upon himself in manner and form as the Plaintiff against him hath complained, within three Years next before the Suing out the Writ of Capias in this Suit and they do assess the Plaintiffs damages by occasion of the Defendants Nonperformance of that assumption to Seventy three dollars, Eighty

Seven and one half Cents besides his Costs. Whereupon on Motion of the Defendant, and for reasons appearing to the Court, the Said Verdict is Set aside, and It is ordered that a new trial be had at the next Court, 'till which term the Cause is continued.

Jacob Koose appeared and made Oath, that John Goldman in a fight bit off the Ear of John Aldridge. _____

COURT ADJOURNED 'TILL TOMORROW 9 O'CLOCK.

Gibson,James (Cont'd) - 174,175,176,178,
        179,181,186,229,231,233,237,
        238,239,242,243,244,245
Gibson,Samuel - 166,192,215,249
Gillespie, ----- (Capt.) - 37,136,228
Gillespie,Allen - 95,96,98,100
Gillespie,James - 17,87,196,203,217,251
Gillespie,Thomas - 23,25,27,64,78,93,98,
        137,138,139,144,177,186,202,
        243,267
Gillespie,William - 7,108
Gillespie,William Junior - 137
Gilliam (Gillam),Charles - 203,244,245
Gilliam (Gillam),Devereaux - 172,207,
        240,267
Gist,Joshua - 234
Gist,Ruth - 224,257
Given,Robert - 27,73
Givens,Samuel - 257
Glassgow,James - 136,138
Goehen,John - 224,257
Goldman,John - 277
Gooden,Richard - 272,276
Gray,Robert - 59,90
Gray,William - 3
Grayson,Benjamin - 23,25,40,44,45,46
Green,Jesse - 44,45,170
Greenaway,James - 218,267
Greer, ----- - 261
Greer,David - 17
Greer,George - 88,94,95,96,98,100,104,
        148,153
Greer,George B. - 223,257,262
Greer,Joseph - 13,21,24,37,228,257,266
Grills,Elliott (Elliot) - 28,69,89,102,
        120,146,203
Grills,Richard - 157

Hackett, John - 7,16,31,38,49,55,67,88,
        98,99,127,136,202,246
Hail, James - 133
Hail, Richard - 73,74
Hailey, David - 64
Haines (Hanes), Christopher - 56,225,258
Hainey (Haney), Barney - 82,98,99
Hale, Nicholas - 58,125
Hale, Sarah - 58,125
Hall, William Q. - 105
Hamilton, James - 121
Hamilton, Joseph - 2,4,224
Hamilton, Richard - 31,49,67,88,109,140,
        171,204,231,268
Hamilton, Thomas - 176,178,179
Hamilton, William - 2,3,17,37,78,85,86,
        89,121,136,137,148,156,169,177,
        202,203,228,232,266

Hanes, Jno. - 225
Hanley, Alexander - 127
Hannah, Samuel - 20
Hannah, William - 23,25,38
Hardin, Sarah - 196
Hardin, Thomas - 108,175,196,203
Harlin, Rezin - 129
Harman, Jacob - 218
Harmer (Harmar), Jacob - 196,251
Harralson (Harrelson), James - 17,108,
        109,138,144,145,148,168
Harralson, William - 203
Harrell, James - 87
Harrison, Solomon - 87,92,93
Hart, John - 3
Hart, Joseph - 3,144
Harvard, George - 262
Hastings, Daniel - 276
Hauk, Adam - 7
Hauk, Elizabeth - 7
Haven, James - 25
Hays, George - 64,108,138,203,229,248,
        265
Hays,Nathaniel - 225,229,231,233,237,
        238,239,242,243,246,258
Hays,William - 157
Hazlet (Haislet), William - 20,64,176,
        178,179,180,225,233
Hazlet, William Junior - 176,272
Hazlet, William Senior - 203
Henderson, James - 29
Henderson, Samuel - 8,19,68,87,110,111
Hendrix, Garret - 229,230
Henry, ----- (Capt.) - 37,136,228
Henry, Ezekiel - 107,123,149,178,206,
        235,269
Henry, John - 45,50
Henry, Hugh - 234
Henry, Samuel - 15,17,230
Henry, William - 32,33,51,62,67,77,92,
        107,123,135,149,155,167,176,
        186,193,197,206,210,221,235,
        244,253,264,269,271
Herron (Herran,Heron), John - 16,39,41,
        114,115,117,118,132,156
Hicklin (Hicklan), John - 15,19,25
Hickman, Jacob - 21
Higgins, Edward - 29,47,66,86,267
Hill, John - 163,189,212,247,272,276
Hillsman, John - 263
Hindman, Samuel - 44,47,48,73,74,75,81,
        93,96,98,100,130,142,151,178,
        182
Hindman, Samuel Junior - 237
Hinds, Joseph - 137
Hinds, Levi - 170,225,258

Lea, John - 73
Lea, Joseph - 18,19,40,41,43,60,71,85
Lea, Luke - 16,17,19,38,50,98,99,136,
     137,179,202
Lea, Major - 8,12,18,19,23,25,26,32,
     40,43,44,45,50,54,59,65,69,
     73,74,78,87,91,94,95,118,131,
     138,148,153,170,183,202,203,
     208,240,242,243,248
Lea, William - 7,18,21,23,24,41,45,71,
     74,85,93,138,139,141,176,180,
     202,203,231,234,242,243
Leaky, William - 38
Lee, William - 46,114
Liddy, Flora - 58
Liddey (Liddy), John - 3,13,14,58,114,
     115,117,118,175,176
Liggett (Liggitt), Robert - 31,49,67,
     88,201,221,254
Lindsey (Linsey), David - 6,8,9,18,19,
     36,54,69
Linney, John - 84,91,100,110,114,115,
     117,163,190,213,248,273
Looney, David - 26
Looney, Joseph - 41,110,138,179
Looney, Joseph Senior - 64
Looney, Moses - 25,26,43,64,138,170
Love, Joiah - 195,216,250
Love, Robert - 137,179,197
Love, Samuel - 44,85
Love, William - 37,54
Low, Aquilla - 48,49,50,88,144,272
Lowe (Low), John - 65,68
Low, Richard - 73
Lowry, John - 10,23,27,38,43,58,73,129,
     151,180,201,227,259
Lowry, William - 2,3,7,12,13,17,21,23,
     29,37,40,42,46,47,57,69,78,84,
     86,89,100,104,107,117,122,123,
     135,136,145,147,149,155,169,
     170,172,175,178,179,185,186,
     200,201,202,203,206,210,211,
     220,221,222,228,229,231,232,
     234,235,243,244,254,255,264,
     266,267,268,269,271
Luckey, Andrew - 191,199,226,252,259
Lusk, John - 133,154,184,209,226,242,
     259
Lyle, John - 62
Lyon (Lyons), Nathaniel - 103,104,121,
     197,218,227,251,260

Mabry, James - 2
Mansfield, Nicholas - 11,163,190,213,247
Mann, Thomas - 224,258
Marks, Solomon - 6,9,15,19,28,32,46,50,
     Cont'd

Marks, Solomon (Cont'd) - 66,81,85,88,
     97,101,109,116,118,140,145,
     170,201,204,221,231,254
Martin, Andrew - 137
Martin, George - 229,230
Martin, James - 234,255
Martin, Warner - 64,137,170,172,174,175
Mason, James - 44,45,48,54
Matthews, Jeremiah - 2,276
McAllister (McAlister), John - 23,25,27,
     79,92,93,95,114,140,141,142,
     143,171,204,232
McAmey (McAmy), John - 29,56,69,70,85,
     87,110,141,198,219,250,252
McAmey, Robert - 85
McBee, Isaac - 261
McBee, Samuel - 185,210,243
McBee, William - 138, 168
McBroom, William - 25,26,74,170,172,174,
     196,200,217,220,224,241,251,253
McCabe, Brian - 123,133,149,154,178,184,
     199,206,208,220,235,241,252,269
     270
McCallister, John - 118,119
McCampbell, Andrew - 64,65,66,88,145,176,
     207
McCampbell, Robert - 222,254
McCampbell, Solomon - 5,20
McCampbell, William - 64,65,66,69
McCarter, Jeremiah - 100
McCauley, John - 105,122,147,175
McClain, Jeremiah - 88
McCleary, Abraham - 138,139,141,142,143,
     157
McCloud, Charles - 56,70
McClain, James - 81,98
McClung, Charles - 2,3,55,169
McCormack, William - 60,75,90
McCosland, Andrew - 241
McCoy, Annanias (Ananias) - 5,9,17,21,23,
     24,26,37,38,39,73,74,93,96,110,
     111,125,133,154,184,209,226,
     242,259,260,262,276
McCullah, Joseph - 228
McCullah, Samuel - 175
McCullock (McCollock), James - 199,219,
     252,265
McCullock, Thomas - 137,139,203,266,267
McCullough, Thomas - 2,17,19,37,78,93,
     108,112,136,169,202,228,232,266
McCullough, James - 89,98,100
McCullough, Samuel - 38,42,43,139
McDonald, Daniel - 5,85,174,175,176
McDonold, James - 227
McDowell, James - 263
McDowell, John - 148,195,216,218,263

285

288